MAN'S MANY VOICES
Language in Its Cultural Context

ROBBINS BURLING
University of Michigan

HOLT, RINEHART AND WINSTON, INC.
New York/Chicago/San Francisco/Atlanta/Dallas
Montreal/Toronto/London/Sydney

Library of Congress Catalog Card Number: 78–111258
ISBN 0-03-081001-9
Printed in the United States of America
56   038   9876

PREFACE

This book has grown out of a good many years of wandering back and forth across the border between anthropology and linguistics and fiddling with one or another of that miscellaneous grab bag of topics embraced by the rubric "language and culture." Among other things I have struggled with a course by that title, a course that all nonlinguistic anthropologists seem to feel must be included within the curriculum of a progressive anthropology department. After some nearly disastrous experiments, I concluded that to touch upon all the topics which everyone expected in a language and culture course could result only in chaos. I then began to slough off many of the traditional topics and gradually concentrate upon the few that seemed to offer some hope of unity. The contents of this book reflect the narrowing of my concern, and I want to emphasize that this book is not intended to be a survey of what I regard as the hopelessly disparate field of language and culture.

My topic is much narrower. I like to think of it as an investigation into the nonlinguistic factors that affect our use of language. As I try to explain in the first chapter, I think it fair to say that linguists have largely dealt with linguistic variables that depend upon other linguistic phenomena. Their rules are internal to language. But man's use of language is also dependent upon the context in which he speaks and upon his varied personalities. It is these extralinguistic variables and the way in which they affect the patterns of our language that concern me.

Unlike many anthropologists who have written on language and culture, I am not concerned with the way in which the rest of culture is dependent upon or similar to language, but I am concerned instead with the way language is affected by the rest of culture. On the other hand, unlike most linguists, I am not primarily concerned with the internal structure of language, but only with the way that structure is affected by and dependent upon things other than language. I am convinced that not even the structure of language can be decently understood without some understanding of the animal that uses language and of the setting within which he speaks.

Writing on the border between disciplines, I have difficulty avoiding examples and terminology that will seem unfamiliar to one side or the other. Linguists may be appalled by the heavy dose of kinship terminology, but since kinship terminology has been studied so much more thoroughly than the terminology of any other semantic domain, reliance upon it is almost inevitable for one who wants to deal with semantics from the viewpoint that interests me. I find it equally impossible to write about language without using a good deal of the special terminology of linguistics. I presume that most of those who turn to this book will have had at least some background in linguistics, and even a limited knowledge should make the viewpoint and terminology clear enough. Since my topics may be of interest to non-linguists, I have tried to define as many terms as possible, but it would be annoying to stop and define every phonetic term and every phonetic symbol. The glossary beginning on page 201 may help with a few terms, but for the most part I have written with the assumption that readers will already have some background in linguistics.

My examples come from many sources, but one particular parochial bias will be seen in my heavy reliance upon examples from south and southeast Asia. Equally valid and interesting examples could surely be gathered from any other part of the world, but my own anthropological and linguistic research has been confined to southern Asia, and even when I am not reporting my own work, I am most familiar with the literature of these areas. I can only hope that my geographical bias will be compensated for by the greater confidence with which I can present the examples. My own trips to south and southeast Asia were made possible by generous fellowships. The Ford Foundation supported more than two years of field work between 1954 and 1956 in the Garo Hills of Assam, India, and the Fulbright Foundation sent me to Burma in 1959–1960. As always, it is a pleasure to thank these institutions for their help.

Most of the examples and ideas reported, however, have come from the work of others. In the bibliographic notes, assembled at the end of the volume, I have tried to indicate my debt to these scholars and suggest my dependence upon their work. My debt to them is enormous. If there is any originality in the organization which I have given to these topics, it is in large part the outgrowth of my several attempts to teach the course called Language and Culture. The course has not always been successful, but I have learned much from my students. They deserve my thanks for bearing with me as I tried out various unsuccessful ideas upon them and groped my way toward the viewpoint presented here.

My attitude toward these topics has also been shaped by close association with many outstanding scholars. I have drawn upon their work for some of my examples, but more important has been the subtle help derived from my many long conversations with them. In particular I want to acknowledge my debt to A. L. Becker, John L. Fischer, Paul Friedrich, Ward H. Goodenough, John J. Gumperz, and Floyd G. Lounsbury. I hardly dare to guess whether these men would recognize their own points of view coming through in my formulation. I hope they will. I know that I could not have written this book without the benefit of my association with them.

Ann Arbor, Michigan   R. B.
February 1970

CONTENTS

MAN'S MANY VOICES
Language in Its Cultural Context

1 Language and Its Setting

Language and Culture

Language has always held a central place in the affairs of man—in his education, his art, and his science. Language is among the very first forms of behavior that we learn as children. When we later learn other skills and acquire other knowledge, much of our learning can reach us only through the medium of language. Other animals learn. Only men can receive explanations. Whether in oratory, in singing, or in written form, language has been an important medium of artistic expression for all peoples. Science too is conducted in language. Whether we are casual observers of the world around us or taxonomic biologists, we feel compelled to give names to the objects we examine. Even when science is expressed in mathematical form, language is not really absent, for the language of mathematics is, to a large degree, an abstract and idealized version of the natural language that all men use. Quite possibly our ability to reason, to argue logically, and even in some sense our very ability to think rest upon qualities first evolved as part of our use of language. Certainly it is language as much or more than any other human trait that sets us off as unique within the animal kingdom.

Since language is so important in our lives, it is hardly surprising that when men have turned to examine their own behavior, language has always figured among their most lively interests. To travelers, historians, and anthropologists, language has always seemed a convenient way to classify nations and tribes. Philosophers of many persuasions have been concerned with language, and it has been central to the work of many psychologists. Students of literature have carefully examined the medium through which literature is expressed. All these disciplines, however, have examined language within a larger context—as language serves to classify tribes, as it bears upon questions of truth, existence, or knowledge, as it is related to memory

1

and learning, or as it is used artistically. Their interest in language has, to some degree, been instrumental, for through the instrument of language they have sought to gain an understanding of other phenomena—of history, logic, art, or the mind.

The scholar who calls himself a linguist differs from his colleagues in other disciplines in examining language for its own sake rather than as an instrument by which to seek an understanding of other matters. The results of linguistic investigation may be of interest to its sister disciplines, but solving their problems has not been the linguist's major goal. In fact, it is reasonable to suggest that real progress in learning about the structure and organization of language only came when a few men began to narrow their interest down to language itself and to set aside any concern for the uses to which language is put. They could then see language as a system with its own internal logic and its own internal rules, for it turned out that many striking features of language could be described with little or no reference to the natural or human context within which language is used. By temporarily ignoring the place of language within the broad range of human behavior, linguists have been able to concentrate upon the internal organization of language, the patterning of its sounds and its syntax, and the ways in which the various aspects of a linguistic system are interdependent. By minimizing their concern for the relationship of these purely linguistic phenomena to other aspects of our behavior, linguists have vastly simplified their task. I believe it has been this narrowing of focus that has allowed a rather rapid development of the specialized field of linguistics.

The major subdivisions of linguistics illustrate the tendency toward autonomy. In syntax, for instance, an attempt is made to formulate rules which can account for the arrangements of words and their major parts such as prefixes, bases, suffixes (the units that linguists refer to as morphemes) and to distinguish the permissible sequences of words and morphemes from the many conceivable sequences that cannot be used. One might suppose that linguists would search for an explanation for their rules, perhaps in the organization of the human mind or in the influence of human history, but they have rarely done so. Instead, they have usually been content when they could successfully show what speakers accept as normal and what they reject as aberrant.

Phonology, the study of the sound patterns of language, is, to be sure, tied to something outside of language—anatomy. Sounds are most conveniently described in terms of the mechanics of the vocal organs, the lips, tongue, teeth, and larynx. Nevertheless, as developed by linguists, much of phonology has been abstracted far away from the mechanics of sound production. Even in phonology abstract rules that show the mutual influence of sounds upon one another and the way in which sounds join together into syllables or larger units have sometimes taken precedence over the anatomical aspects of their production. To some linguists it has seemed plausible to suggest that just as phonology is grounded in anatomy, and in a sense anchored at that point to the nonlinguistic world, so syntax or at least lexicography, the study of words, is anchored to the world through meaning. Many difficult problems have beset the linguistic study of meaning, however, and it is by no means as well developed as phonology. Syntax has actually developed a far greater autonomy from meaning than phonology from anatomy.

Phonology, syntax, and lexicon can all be studied historically as well as descriptively (or synchronically), and, here again, many linguists have been content to describe changes without searching for the forces that have encouraged or caused them. It is true that in studying the history of a lexicon cultural factors are inescapable. One can hardly examine the coming and going of words without at the same time considering the pressures of cultural changes. But the heart of historical linguistics has been in phonology, and here, as in the study of historical grammar, linguists have been extremely wary of attributing any sort of cultural explanation to the changes they have observed. They have worked out remarkably subtle descriptions of linguistic change, but the factors that have fostered the changes have been poorly understood and sometimes have even been dismissed as irrelevant or unknowable.

In making these observations, I do not mean to imply that linguists should be blamed for neglecting the context within which language is used. On the contrary, they can hardly have been expected to do everything at once. It has probably been excellent strategy to limit attention to the internal organization of language and to set aside for a time any serious concern for its context. Nevertheless, anyone who has a broad interest in the role of language must sooner or later be drawn to see language in a much wider perspective and to try to understand how language and its setting interact.

In a rough way, three factors can be seen to influence our use of language. One is meaning, for we certainly choose our words and our sentences so as to communicate meaning of some sort. A second is social organization, for sociological variables, such as the class and status of the speaker or the formality of the situation in which he speaks, deeply influence the use of language. A third is individual variability among speakers. An understanding of the variability within a language, whether that variability is patterned by social class or is an expression of individual skill, helps to give us an understanding of the factors encouraging linguistic change. Beginning with meaning, the chapters of this book consider these topics. They try to suggest how meaning, social structure, and individual variability affect the use of language, and how these bear upon linguistic change.

Grammar and Meaning

Nothing in the long history of man's examination of language has evoked more controversy than the relation between grammar and meaning. Linguists have hardly been able to deny what the layman has always taken for granted, that something called meaning plays an important part in language, but linguists have never been able to agree upon exactly what they *mean* when they use words like meaning or semantics. Linguists have been far clearer when dealing with grammar, but I wish to deal with topics for which, in a broad sense, I feel the label "meaning" to be appropriate, and I want to consider these topics within the context of all our use of language. I must therefore, indicate, as clearly as I can, how I feel terms such as meaning and semantics can be usefully understood and how I would like to keep those distinct terms from grammar.

When linguists present grammatical analyses they almost always attempt to account for some features of a language by reference to other features of the language. They may state how a word or a morpheme varies from one linguistically definable situation to another. They may write a transformation that can show the relationship among sentences, but they rarely ask what is it that induces a speaker to choose a sentence requiring a transformation. Their rules practically never include terms that stand for variables outside of language. But linguistic events also depend, in some way, upon nonlinguistic phenomena, and terms like semantics or meaning can be reasonably applied to studies that seek to relate linguistic forms to something outside of language. More specifically, to give the meaning of some linguistic event can be understood as stating rules for its use in terms of nonlinguistic events.

To formulate semantic rules of this sort requires some way of measuring or pointing out the events to which the linguistic form is related. When studying color terms, for instance, we may specify colors by a chart or by wave length. Or perhaps we can manage less formally, by pointing at objects or by recalling things in the world whose color we have all experienced: the sky, a lump of coal, a buttercup. Similarly, when anthropologists study kinship terms, they need a way of specifying the objects in the world (the particular referents of the expression) to which the terms refer. For this purpose they have worked out elaborate ways of distinguishing all imaginable kinsmen from one another. When we say *kitty* over and over again to a small child in the presence of a cat, we are teaching him to relate a linguistic event to a different sort of event, which he can see and feel. When we introduce a man as *Mr. Brown*, we are doing the same thing more efficiently for the benefit of an adult who has learned the trick of relating linguistic labels to such extralinguistic phenomena as Mr. Brown. When we notice that a certain tone of voice indicates anger, we are relating one aspect of language, its phonology, to an emotion that is not itself a part of language. When we realize that on formal occasions many speakers of English say *going* but on informal occasions are likely to say *goin'*, we are relating a linguistic variable, (*-ing* versus *-in*) to a nonlinguistic variable, the degree of formality of the situation. To the extent that we must refer to nonlinguistic events when we describe these linguistics events, our descriptions can be reasonably labeled semantic.

In understanding the way in which nonlinguistic variables affect our language, it may be helpful to look upon speech as being subject to different levels of constraint. First, and least avoidably, a speaker is constrained in his choice of morphemes, words, and constructions by the surrounding morphemes, words, and constructions. These are the constraints that we can call grammatical. But any speaker can produce a limitless number of grammatically acceptable sentences, and out of this number he is forced to make a further choice. He must select only those sentences that make sense—those which correspond to the events he wishes to discuss and those which are suitable to the situation in which he speaks. These choices go beyond the linguist's usual concern, but they are just as essential to clear conversation as those that can be described entirely by means of internal linguistic variables.

If we imagine that a speaker's first requirement is to produce sentences which fit the code of his language—which are well formed or grammatical—then we might also say that the linguist's first task is to look for patterns and specify grammatical rules that characterize well-formed sentences. However, any set of grammatical rules has to contain options—points of freedom where a more open choice is possible. Indeed, a set of rules that provided no options would be capable of generating only a single sentence. A linguist who wants only to formulate grammatical rules can afford to dismiss these varied features of the language as optional and then forget them. Nothing in the linguistic context dictates which alternative is to be chosen. But any full attempt to characterize a language ought to look beyond the purely grammatical constraints and examine the determinants of meaningful choices as well.

When we think of meaningful options, we think most often of the syntactical and particularly, the lexical, components of language. A linguist may show an adverb to be optional (perhaps by enclosing it in parentheses), when he describes the permitted sentence patterns; its optionality implies that decision about whether or not to include an adverb in the sentence is dependent not upon the internal grammatical constraints of the language, but rather upon the meaning that is to be expressed. The choice between active and passive constructions has sometimes been said to be optional, and this would make it a choice that potentially could carry meaning. Similarly, the choice among particular lexical items (*left*, or *right*, *gradually* or *slowly*, *dog* or *cat*) is a choice of meaning rather than of grammar. A wide choice among lexical items is usually allowed at each location in a sentence, and this choice is left open by grammar and depends largely upon extralinguistic factors. Even some of our choices among certain features of segmental phonology (the choice between a whisper and a shout, for instance) are not contrained by rules that could be called grammatical but instead by the situation of the speaker.

To say certain choices are not amenable to grammatical description does not imply that an explicit and careful description is not possible. We should be able to formalize semantic rules just as we can formalize grammatical rules, but the semantic rules would reflect quite different variables. They would have to reflect the same sort of extralinguistic variables that a speaker uses when he decides what to say.

Reference, Situation, and Personality

I have written as if a speaker faced only two types of choices and con-straints, but the extralinguistic variables that bear upon our language use are not all of the same type. By sorting out the different types of variables the notion of semantic can be somewhat refined. First of all, of course, we have rules of reference, definitions of the referents of terms. Such rules of reference should provide explicit criteria for deciding between such terms as *dog* and *cat, left* and *right, hot* and *warm*. Rules of reference greatly reduce the degree of optionality left by the grammatical rules, but rules of reference still leave some choices open. Synonyms refer to the same phenomena and partial synonyms overlap in their reference, so reference rules can be said to leave the choice among synonyms as optional. Rules of reference should distin-guish between *mother* and *father*, but (in most conventional analyses of kinship terminology at least) *father, daddy, papa,* and *pop* are left as syn-onyms—the choice among them is referentially optional.

Clearly *father, daddy* and *pop* are not identical even though they all refer to the male parent. The choice among these forms is governed not by the referent to which they all refer, but by such factors as the speaker's person-ality, his father's presence or absence, his feelings toward his father, and the formality of the situation. Perhaps all languages make some distinction between formal and informal styles. In English we often use the passive in relatively formal situations, so if the passive is produced by a grammatically optional transformation, the transformation does not really leave the mean-ing unchanged. Javanese has an elaborate series of speech levels, character-ized primarily by many alternative lexical choices, but the choice among these levels depends not upon literal reference but upon such factors as the formality of the situation, and the relative status of speaker and hearer (see Chapter 7). Some English speakers probably switch between *he doesn't* and *he don't*, depending upon the situation.

We express something about the context of the situation not only by syntactic and lexical choices but even by phonological choices. A number of studies have shown that phonological variables such as the presence or absence of the post vocalic /–r/ (*r* when following a vowel) or the precise articulatory position of /θ/ (the sound we spell *th* as in *th*ink) in New York English depend upon both the social class of the speaker and the situation in which he speaks (see Chapter 7). All of us can modify our phonology by whining, shouting, or whispering. Here we have examples where aspects of the extralinguistic environment seem to penetrate language not at the syntactical or lexical level but clear down at the phonological level.

Even beyond the situational factors, some linguistic choices are governed by the idiosyncrasies of our individual personalities. From a strictly individual point of view, of course, these are hardly *choices* except perhaps when we deliberately imitate someone else or try to hide our own personality. But from the broader viewpoint of the linguistic community, people certainly vary in their personal styles, and the variations are no doubt correlated with other aspects of personal behavior. Some people are consistently more formal than others in speech, and this may well reflect other aspects of their personality. Individuals have favorite words. A few lisp so badly that they lose a phonemic contrast, and we all have our individual voice qualities.

So the constraints that bear upon our use of language can be sorted roughly into at least four major types which we can label as grammatical, referential, situational, and personal. By the definitions which I have given, all but the strictly grammatical choices are meaningful, and if we are to understand how these choices are made, we will have to consider features of the world outside of language.

Perhaps the very success that linguists have had in discovering patterns within language and in formulating theories to account for these patterns, has occasionally blinded us to the place that language must occupy in any broader view of human behavior. Sooner or later one would hope that the findings of the linguists could be brought to bear upon these larger problems. When cornered, even linguists know that language is used to communicate ideas. We talk about *things*. In one way or another, language is involved in everything that we do. Yet linguists are surely correct in recognizing that language has some sort of internal organization and many subtle aspects of this internal organization can be expressed with no reference to things or ideas outside of language. Any full view of language must embrace both the linguists' insight into the internal organization of language and the broader view of the part language plays in all of human life.

Beginning with reference, I will consider a number of these extralinguistic factors and give a few examples that suggest what bearing they have upon our linguistic choices. Table 1–1 suggests a way of conceptualizing the kinds of choices given to speakers. The rows represent various levels of linguistic

Table 1-1 Examples of Linguistic Choices

	Grammar (= syntax + phonology)	Meaning		
		Referential	Situational	Personal
Syntax-Phrase Structure	Most of conventional grammar	Introduction of optional categories such as (adverb)		Individual style of sentence structure
Lexicon	Obligatory lexemes such as do	Most ordinary lexical chocies	Javanese "levels"	Favorite words
Transformation	Obligatory transformations	Negation transformation	Passive transformation	
Intonation	Question intonation when required by the syntax	Varying intonation as in "He's here" and "He's here?"		
Phonological Opposition	Conventional phonology		-ing/-in'	A lisp which overrides a contrast
Phonetic Detail	Conventional phonetics		Phonetic effects of shouting	Individual voice quality

organization, but they are not intended to form a definitive set or to conform to any particular linguistic theory. Indeed every linguistic theory would suggest a somewhat different set of rows. The columns represent the various factors that bear upon our choices at all these levels, and the cells suggest examples. The variables in the column headed grammar have been extensively studied by linguists and generally will be taken for granted in the remainder of this book. The other variables will be considered in more detail.

Lexical Reference

If we can agree to use the term "meaning" for ways in which features of language are related to things outside of language and if we can agree that meaning is important to language, then we must ask how this relationship between language and the world can be most naturally and accurately characterized. How can we best describe the meaning of words or of sentences? It seems best to begin with reference, the most insistent influence upon our language use, and with the lexicon, the level of language most characteristically used for reference.

The most naïve view of reference is to imagine that for each object or idea in the world a language provides a label. If this were all there was to semantics, our job would be merely to list the world's objects and then to specify their label. Such an easy equivalence between words and things would make it far simpler than it actually is to learn the meanings of words in a foreign language. If each language could be expected to have labels for the same objects, one would only have to learn the foreign equivalent for the words already known. When foreign language students memorize long lists of equivalent terms and suppose that they can, in this way, learn what words really mean, they seem to imagine that languages do have this simple kind of equivalence, but they quickly face impossible problems. It always turns out that some native words require two, three, or even more equivalents in the foreign language. These alternative translations are used under somewhat different conditions, but the student is apt to find it difficult to remember which term to use on which occasion. On the other hand, the native language will also have sets of two or three words, all of which seem to be translated by the same word in the foreign language. This can also be disturbing to the new language student, for he cannot help feeling that this new language is vague and ambiguous. What he feels to be two separate things must be crudely called by the same term.

Of course the situation is really far more complex than these naïve reactions of the foreign language student might suggest. It is too simple just to say that a single word in one language covers an area of meaning requiring two or more words in another. Rather, the whole flux of events in our perceptible world is apportioned differently to the terms of each language. We can learn to recognize an unlimited range of objects, events, and distinctions in the observable world, but even if very large, the size of our vocabulary is still finite. We cannot possibly have a different word for every single item that we recognize as unique. Inevitably, the words of our language refer to a range of events and perceptions. Some events are always assigned to different terms, while others are classed together. Each language has its unique way of grouping some events at the same time that it distinguishes others. Having learned one language, we may have to fight the all too easy notion that its particular way of grouping events is somehow correct. Only an examination of the variation among languages can really disabuse us of such a notion.

An example in which events are grouped under lexical labels in a quite different way from English can be provided by certain verbs of motion in Garo, a Tibeto-Burman language spoken by a tribal people in northeastern India. In English we recognize a rather sharp distinction between *go* and *come*, a distinction that depends upon the direction of motion with respect to the position of the speaker or occasionally with respect to some other reference point. Garo has a single verb, *re-*, which covers approximately the area of meaning of both *go* and *come*. *Re-* indicates movement on somebody's part, but it does not indicate anything about the direction of movement. English has no close equivalent to *re-*. Our verb *move* is in some ways similar, but it is used not only intransitively to describe actions for which we might also use *go* or *come*, but also, much more broadly as when we *move a finger* or *move our household belongings*. In none of these transitive senses could *re-* serve as an equivalent.

If a Garo speaker wants to specify the direction of motion, *re-* alone is not enough, but he can easily add an affix to the end of the word base, making his meaning more precise. *reang-* means something quite close to 'go' and *reba-* indicates something quite close to 'come,' but the equivalence between the two languages is still not precise. Even leaving aside all sorts of special and idiomatic uses of the English terms (*come on, go on*, and so forth) Garos do not use quite the same point of reference for analyzing motion as do English speakers. In saying, "you go now, and I will come tomorrow," the English tendency is to shift the reference point from the momentary position of the speaker and hearer to the location that will later become the object of the motion. Garos tend to cling much more closely to the position of the speaker at the particular time he is speaking, so that the natural Garo translation of this sentence would use the same form of the verb in both of its clauses: "you *reang-* today and I will *reang-* tomorrow." Beyond this, where English speakers commonly use compounds such as *come in, go out*, and so on, Garo has unique terms not constructed from the verb *re-* at all. *Nap-* for instance means 'enter,' 'go in' or 'come in.' *Nap-* can also take the affixes *-ang-* and *-ba-*, so that *napang-* means roughly 'go in' while *napba-* can often be translated as 'come in' although the same caution about the shifting reference point applies here as it does for the forms built upon *re-*.

If we now consider various situations where we would use words like *bring, take, carry*, and so forth, several further complications arise. As with *going* and *coming*, a single Garo term, *ra-*, covers roughly the areas of both *bring* and *take*. *Ra-* can often be translated by the English *carry* although it can be used for a broader range of behavior than *carry*. Even if the object is not held off the ground (if it is dragged, for instance) or if it is brought (or taken) in a separate package, perhaps tied to the roof of the bus in which a man travels, *ra-* would be an appropriate term in Garo, though, of course, *carry* would not do in English. So *ra-* has a broader meaning than 'carry,' and in one way it is also more general than either *take* or *bring* since *ra-* does not specify the direction of the motion. In another respect, however, the meaning of *ra-* is more limited than any of these English words, for *ra-* can only be used with inanimate objects. For 'bringing' or 'taking' a person, an entirely separate word, *rim*, must be used. Both *rim* and *ra-* can take the affixes *-ang-* and *-ba-* if it should be necessary to specify the direction of motion.

A speaker who is used to English and who wants to say something like *carry* in Garo may feel that *ra-* is far too general for his purposes, but in looking for a slightly more specific word he will meet with frustration. Garo has no general word that is at all close to the English word *carry* but instead has a series of terms each referring to a different technique of carrying. *ol-* means specifically 'to carry something in a basket that is held in a strap over the forehead'; *itchil-* means 'to carry on the head'; *ripe-* means 'to carry on the shoulder,' as one might carry a log; *ke-* means 'to carry in a bag that hangs from a strap over the shoulder'; *detom-* means 'to carry in the arms' and is most often used for 'carrying' a baby. The English speaker who is beginning to learn Garo is apt to feel some annoyance when he comes to a situation in which the English word *carry* seems appropriate. Either he must be very general and use a word like *ra-*, which strikes him as vague and inexact, or he must get absurdly specific and indicate precisely how the object is carried.

Yet in one way these terms that can translate *carry* have a broader meaning than our term, for they can also be used in situations where we might use *hold*. That is, unlike *carry*, they do not necessarily imply motion. *Ol-* can mean 'to hold in a basket suspended from a strap from the forehead' and one can *detom-* a baby while standing still. Each of these terms, which describe how something is carried or held, is as capable as *re-*, *ra-* or *rim-* of taking the affixes *-ba-* and *-ang-*. These affixes show that the carrier is moving and they indicate the direction of motion, a distinction which we can make in English only with a rather more elaborate construction: *to carry away* or *to carry in that direction*.

Inherently, neither English nor Garo appears to be superior to the other in describing these various actions. Either language can be used to describe any situation and one can always use longer and more detailed phrases so as to reach any desired degree of precision. The English word *carry* might seem imprecise to a Garo, but we can say *carry from a strap hung over the shoulder* if we need to, and Garos can use comparably elaborate phrases too. Over all, neither language is more precise or accurate than the other, but the range of observable action is apportioned differently among the various verbs of the two languages. None of the Garo verbs covers exactly the same range of events as the English verbs. No two verbs seem to mean quite the same thing.

The various words for *carry* cover but one of a number of domains in which Garo has several words where English seems to get along with one. In some cases, there are obvious cultural factors encouraging an elaborate vocabulary. Garo has dozens of words for different types of baskets, and it has entirely separate words for 'rice plant,' 'unhusked rice,' 'husked rice,' 'cooked rice,' various subspecies of rice, and preparations made with rice. Baskets and rice are far more important for the Garos than for us, and so they need a more refined terminology. Garos also have at least a dozen words for different varieties of ants—black ants, red ants, big ants, small ants—but they have no single generic term that corresponds at all closely to our word. Ants play no overwhelmingly important role in Garo culture, but they are plentiful in their country and a good deal more varied than in ours.

Examples like these have led some observers to imagine that people like the Garos are deficient in their ability to generalize. It has been said that they have only specific terms, no general or class terms. This is surely nonsense, for it is easy to give counterexamples. Where English has three words, *speak*, *say*, and *talk*, Garo gets along nicely with one, *agan-*, though Garo does have terms corresponding to our more specialized words such as *whisper* or *shout*. Garo also has only four basic color terms, meaning roughly 'black,' 'white,' 'red' and 'yellow' and the many colors of the spectrum can all be called by one or another of these terms. The same term, *gisim* can be used for the color of soot, of leaves or of the sky. If one is determined to pin the label "primitive" to a language like Garo, he can cite its single word *agan-* or its rather limited color vocabulary to suggest that Garo is vague, imprecise, and impoverished in its vocabulary, but this characterization would be no fairer than to accuse it of lacking generalizing capacity. Indeed the two accusations are diametrically opposed, for, to the extent that a large and descriptive vocabulary avoids the charge of impoverished imprecision, it risks the charge of deficiency in generalizing capacity. The fairer way to describe the situation is simply to point out that Garo and English vary in the domains to which they choose to give lexical elaboration. Both languages seem equally capable of generalization or precision. At least, the techniques by which we might hope to measure the precision of a language, its potentiality for abstraction, or its vocabulary size are not yet subtle enough to demonstrate differences among languages.

English speakers who study only western languages may fail to realize how diverse the assignment of phenomena to terms can be. European languages, like European cultures, share a long common tradition. Constant translation among these languages has brought some congruence to the semantic ranges of their words. A word in English may have a rather close translation in French, German or Swedish. It is less likely to have a close equivalent in Garo, Chinese or Zulu, for these languages have not shared as long a period of mutual adjustment with English. It is hardly an exaggeration to say that few words in Garo can stand as precise semantic equivalents to any word in English. Scarcely a Garo term, in other words, is used under precisely the same extralinguistic conditions as a term in English.

Formal Analysis of Meaning

To characterize the meaning of terms as I have done for a few Garo verbs is at best informal and impressionistic. We are a long way from a precise characterization of the meaning of any words. For one thing, it is misleading to suppose that we can define the terms of one language simply by a list of terms in another language or even by a fairly elaborate description in another language. Inevitably, the terms of one language carry a burden of irrelevant connotations that interfere with our grasp of the terms of the other. Our real goal should be to specify how the terms in a language relate to situations in the world, and for this a second language with all its additional complexities is likely to be more misleading than helpful.

There is another problem. In an informal characterization of terms, it is difficult not to point to certain specific phenomena to which each term applies. Logically, however, any term (*tree, blue, go,* and so on) can apply to an infinite, and therefore unlistable, variety of events. We may hope for more precision in characterizing the range of a term's application if we consider how it *differs* from the range of other terms. If we could carefully specify the criteria which serve to distinguish the ranges of similar terms from one another, we would in that way delimit the range of meaning of any particular term.

Can we aim at a formal account of semantic distinctions?[1] That is, can we

---

[1] It is important to realize that my use of formal here does not correspond at all to the old distinction made by many linguists between form and meaning. This was a way of characterizing a distinction somewhat parallel to my distinction of grammar and semantics. My use of formal refers instead to a type of explicit description, one done in an explicit and systematic manner. There is thus no contradiction in writing of a "formal analysis of meaning" and there would be no redundancy in writing of a "formal analysis of form" so long as different meanings of form are intended.

try to be as explicit about the semantically appropriate conditions for a term as linguists hope to be for grammatical conditions? We can phrase the problem in this way: what do we have to know (about conditions outside of the language) in order to specify which term or which terms are appropriate for any specific occasion? In one sense, every fluent speaker of a language has such rules at his command, since he is quite capable of using terms in recognizable and coherent ways. In analyzing meaning, our task should be to construct explicit rules that will account for, or duplicate, the native speaker's almost effortless skills. If we can characterize a set of terms in this way, we will have what can be called a formal description of the meaning of the set.

The rationale of such a formal semantic analysis is precisely the same as the rationale of grammatical analysis. A linguist who studies a language's grammar also tries to construct explicit and formal rules. His rules should provide for those (grammatical) sentences that a native speaker might use but reject the same (nongrammatical) sentences that the native speaker would reject. Formal semantic rules differ only in their incorporation of features of the nonlinguistic environment and in some way specify those features *outside* of language that account for a speaker's choice of terms. To characterize a speaker's total competence, both types of rules are necessary.

Componential Analysis: Palaung Pronouns

Pronouns are usually simple enough to be rather easily described but not quite so simple as to be uninteresting. Almost any set of pronouns could serve as a simple example of a formal semantic analysis. A system quite different from our own may be most interesting, and such a system is found in Palaung, a language of the Mon-Khmer family, spoken by a small tribe in the northern Shan States in Burma. Like other languages, Palaung has a small and distinctive set of terms that act as personal pronouns. But just as verbs of motion in Garo and English categorize aspects of our behavior somewhat differently, so pronouns are far from uniform in the way they categorize people. Palaung has eleven pronouns and the approximate meaning of each of these eleven is given in the following list. I will temporarily designate the pronouns by numbers rather than by their phonological shape, so as to make it clear that my analysis depends only upon their meaning.

1.   'I'
2.   'thou,'   (that is, you, singular, without the archaic or ecclesiastical connotations of English *thou*)
3.   'he, she' (that is, third person singular with no distinction of sex)

4.   'he or she, and I'   (that is, one other person and I)
5.   'thou and I'
6.   'they and I'   (that is, two or more other people and I)
7.   'thou, I, and he, she, or they'   (that is, the person spoken to, the speaker, and one or more additional persons)
8.   'he or she, and thou'
9.   'they and thou'
10.   'they two'   (that is, third person dual)
11.   'they, three or more'

To an English speaker, 1, 2, and 3 look familiar, and they can easily be viewed as first, second, and third person singular. Their differences from English are quite trivial: 2 is a natural and colloquial singular with neither the special archaic connotations of English *thou* nor the connotations of familiarity characteristic of French *tu* or German *du*. Palaung does not blur the contrast between singular and plural as does English *you;* no sex distinction is made in the third person singular.

The Palaung plurals appear to be far more complex, for instead of the three simple plural pronouns that seem adequate for English, Palaung has no fewer than eight. In English, 4, 5, 6, and 7 would all have to be translated as 'we.' To a Palaung speaker, the English *we* must seem confusingly ambiguous for it covers a range of meaning that he carefully apportions among four distinct terms. An English speaker who tries to learn Palaung, however, would surely find it difficult to remember which particular term was needed for a situation where he is accustomed so casually to use *we*. Seven and 8 would both be translated by *you* while 10 and 11 correspond to *they*. Again Palaungs make finer distinctions than English speakers find necessary.

Considered in this way, as seen from the perspective of English, the Palaung terms seem almost illogical. They certainly do not conform to the common patterns of European pronouns, and they appear to be a good deal more complex than the simpler first, second, and third person singular and plural to which we are accustomed. We must ask, however, whether it is not possible to arrange these terms in a more orderly way. Can we not find reasonably simple dimensions of contrast that apportion the pronouns into semantically differing sets, which, even if unknown in European languages, illuminate the Palaung system more clearly than the familiar European contrasts.

First, it should be apparent that several of the pronouns are duals, for they refer to no more nor less than two people. Therefore it seems reasonable to separate the duals from the plurals, giving us singular, dual, and plural numbers. Four, 5, 8, and 10 are duals; 6, 7, 9, and 11, plurals; while 1, 2, and 3 remain as singulars. One significant dimension of contrast, then, seems to be number (as is English) but the components of meaning that are recognized along this dimension are singular, dual, and plural, rather than the simpler singular-plural contrast of English and most modern European languages.

Second, certain terms include the speaker, while others do not. This corresponds to our own distinction between first person pronouns and all others, but here the first person category has five separate pronouns—1, 4, 5, 6 and 7, instead of the paltry pair of English.

A third dimension of contrast can be recognized that is less familiar. Just as the inclusion or exclusion of the speaker divides the terms into semantically contrasting sets, so does the inclusion or exclusion of the person spoken to. As in the case of the speaker, five terms include the hearer (2, 5, 7, 8, 9), while six exclude him (1, 3, 4, 6, 10, 11).

Taken together, the three dimensions of contrast are enough to distinguish each of the eleven Palaung pronouns from every other. Any two pronouns differ from one another along at least one of these three dimensions. The pronouns can easily be displayed in a chart that incorporates the three dimensions, and they then appear far more symmetrically arranged than when forced into a European mold.

Table 1-2   Palaung Prounouns

	Speaker Included		*Speaker Not Included*	
Hearer Included			2.	(singular)
	5.	(dual)	8.	(dual)
	7.	(plural)	9.	(plural)
Hearer Not Included	1.	(singular)	3.	(singular)
	4.	(dual)	10.	(dual)
	6.	(plural)	11.	(plural)

The four cells of Table 1-2 apportion the terms by inclusion of the speaker and the hearer and three of the four cells contain three terms—singular, dual, and plural. The cell, for terms which include both speaker and hearer, however, has only two pronouns. It would appear to be a contradiction in terms to have a singular in a cell which includes a minimum of two people.

The chart provides the same information about the meaning of these terms as the list given first, though the chart seems a bit more orderly and symmetrical and might seem to reflect the native categories that the Palaung use a bit more closely than the original descriptions. Possibly too, a foreigner who wished to learn to use the terms correctly would find the symmetrical organization of the chart more helpful than the less organized definitions.

Finally, the phonological form of the pronouns can be given in a similar chart.

		2.	mi
5.	ar	8.	par
7.	ε	9.	pε
1.	ɔ	3.	ʌn
4.	yar	10.	gar
6.	yε	11.	gε

A simple inspection of the forms of the Palaung pronouns will show that they parallel, in part at least, the semantic analysis that has already been given. Singulars assume varied forms, but the ending *-ar* is consistently used for dual pronouns, and *-ε,* for plural, while *y-*, *p-*, *g-* and the absence of any initial, correspond to the various sets defined by inclusion and exclusion of the speaker and hearer. It might seem that we could have arrived at the same analysis more easily by operating directly upon the forms instead of upon their meanings. Had we done so, we might have emerged with similar results, though, of course, the forms alone would not have told us how to associate the singulars with the appropriate duals and plurals. The point to emphasize, however, is that it is possible to arrange these pronouns in a symmetrically satisfying manner *without* knowing anything of their phonological form. An analysis done in ignorance of phonological form can only have been based upon the meanings of the pronouns, and it deserves to be called a purely semantic analysis. It should be no cause for surprise that the semantic analysis and a grammatical analysis (that is, one based upon form) are in considerable degree parallel, but this should not obscure the sharp distinction between the two types of analysis.

The treatment of Palaung pronouns is a simple example of what anthropologists have called a componential analysis. Several dimensions of semantic contrast were recognized (number, inclusion of the speaker, inclusion of the hearer) and each of these dimensions included two or three contrasting components. Each pronoun can be defined by the intersection of one component from each dimension. Semantic components are similar to what linguists have sometimes called semantic features except that anthropologists have quite consistently referred the variables of componential analysis to the extralinguistic setting of language rather than to linguistic criteria. Indeed, componential analysis has been used most specifically to relate the linguistic phenomena of terms to the nonlinguistic phenomena to which terms refer and to show how nonlinguistic variables bear upon the choice of terms.

Pronouns, of course, form a rather simple terminological set. Certainly it is easier to give a semantic analysis of pronouns than of almost any other semantic domain, but the techniques that prove revealing for pronouns may be applicable to more complex sets, and it is to this possibility that we will now turn.

2 *Kinship Terminology*

The Study of Kinship

To the outsider, anthropologists must at times have seemed strangely obsessed with kinship and in particular with kinship terminology. Hundreds of pages of learned journals have been filled with accounts of how Australians and Africans address their uncles and cousins. This concern with such a seemingly recondite subject has not, however, been without considerable justification. Kinship after all plays a uniquely important part in the lives of many of the people whom anthropologists have studied. Among these people, specialized governmental and economic institutions are often so rudimentary that men are left to rely upon their kinsmen and upon a complex kinship system for the kinds of assistance and cooperation that more specialized institutions would provide in a society such as our own. All societies, moreover, have a rather clearly delimited set of kinship terms, a set that segments the universe of all possible kinsmen into a limited number of named categories. It is not too difficult to elicit a reasonably complete list of kinship terms used by members of a community. The universal nature of the human family and of geneological reckoning make it relatively easy to assign meanings according to the genealogical ties between the speaker and the people to whom the various terms refer. The meanings of kinship terms moreover tend to be patterned in ways that are simple enough to be comprehensible and yet varied enough to be interesting. As a result, kinship terms occupy a peculiarly strategic position among the various sets of lexical items that one can try to extract from a language, and many of the possibilities and the problems of semantic analysis can be seen with a special clarity in kinship terms.

As with other sets of terms, various approaches have been taken by those who have wished to characterize the meaning of kinship terms. The most

18

naïve approach is simply to ask for the equivalent in some other language of each of one's own terms. No anthropologist today would ask this question quite so crudely but some such notion must have been held by earlier observers who noted with surprise that some people "address their mother's sister as 'mother,'" and imagined that such people were unable to distinguish their own mother from the other women whom they called by the same term.

It has been many years since anthropologists described kinship terms in quite so simple-minded a fashion. The more common means of description has been to list the terms of a language and with each term to give a series of genealogical categories to which it can apply. For instance, a term might be said to designate father, father's brother, father's father's brother's son, mother's sister's husband, etc., or in rather transparent abbreviations: Fa, FaBr, FaFaBrSo, MoSiHu, etc. The meaning of each term is shown by a list of positions on a genealogical tree, and since anthropologists call these positions kin-types, this method of definition uses what can be called a kin-type notation. The trouble with a kin-type notation is that the definition of each term almost always trails off with an "etc." at the end, and this "etc." obscures a number of implicit assumptions about the manner in which the term is applied. Anyone who is familiar with the varieties of kinship terminology used around the world can make intelligent guesses about the additional kin-types hidden under the "etc.," but he can do so only by an appeal to hidden assumptions about how kinsmen are likely to be categorized. The major goal of a formal semantic analysis is to make such assumptions explicit, and the dangling "etc." must be accepted as an admission of an incomplete analysis. In many societies, kinship terms are applied to an unbounded set of kin-types; no genealogical limit is recognized beyond which a man no longer rates a kinship term. In some societies people can even assign a kinship term to anyone they meet, whether or not they are able to trace any real genealogical relationship. If a single term can be used for an unlimited set of kin-types, then no kin-type notation could fully characterize the meaning of kinship terms, any more than a finite list of sentences could fully characterize the infinite potentials of a language.

To escape a simple list of kin-types, one promising approach is to look for general dimensions of semantic contrast that can serve to distinguish classes of kinsmen and sets of kinship terms. Since kinship terms are applied in an area that reflects rather obvious genealogical and biological phenomena, such as parenthood and marriage, it is reasonable to look for semantic contrasts that reflect our biological nature. An obvious example is that of sex. Perhaps all kinship terminologies reflect in some degree the contrast between male and female, though some systems are a good deal less consistent in their use of this criterion than is English. Except for cover terms like *ancestor* or *parent*, our only sexually ambiguous term is *cousin*, while some other languages have many terms that are used equally for both men and women. Another widely recognized distinction is that of generation. Parents, uncles, and aunts are likely to be distinguished from siblings, and the latter distinguished from sons and daughters.

Many other criteria can be recognized that also depend in some way upon the genealogical nature of kinship, and a few anthropologists have hoped that it might be possible to construct a list of all the ways in which terms could conceivably be distinguished. The task of analyzing any particular terminological system would amount simply to finding out which of the universal set of criteria are needed in that system and which other criteria are ignored. This technique should avoid some of the difficulties of kin-type analysis, since the various criteria should block out whole categories of kin-types to which terms could apply, and the implicit principles hidden by the "etc.'s" of a kin-type notation should be unnecessary.

There is a pitfall to this approach however: the assumption that distinctions among kinship terms are made only on the basis of biological or genealogical variables—masculine versus feminine, one generation versus another, blood versus marriage, and so on. Perhaps it is also possible for sociological distinctions to be made by some sets of kinship terms and if sociological distinctions are admitted, we are unlikely to be able to limit ourselves to any finite set of semantic contrasts. Whenever a new system is examined it is possible that new criteria will emerge that no anthropological observer had ever noticed or thought of before. The reasonable approach then would seem to be to look for whatever dimensions of contrast (genealogical or not) serve to divide the set of kinship terms into reasonable subsets, adding more dimensions until every kinship term is distinct from every other. These dimensions of contrast would be defined by means of nonlinguistic criteria (sex, generation, membership in a kinship group, and so on) and hence would be semantic rather than grammatical, but collectively they should permit a speaker to decide which term would be appropriate for any particular kinsman just as the dimensions of contrast worked out for Palaung pronouns would allow a choice of a pronoun. Nothing less than this, of course, could serve as an explicit formal analysis, or as an adequate guide for a speaker who must choose terms as he speaks.[1]

[1]It should be obvious that the logic of such an analysis is virtually identical to the logic of familiar types of phonological analyses. In phonology we divide the universe of possible vocal noises by certain distinctive features which cross each other in various complex ways and in doing so serve to segregate the noises of any particular language into mutually contrasting sounds. In kinship analysis, we divide the universe of possible kin-types by a different kind of distinctive feature, and these too cross each other in various complex ways and so serve to segregate the kin-types used by any particular society into mutually contrasting sets. Both phonology and this type of semantic analysis refer the linguistic phenomena (contrasting words or contrasting sounds) to extralinguistic criteria—generally to articulatory features in the case of phonology and to differences among kinsmen in the case of kinship analysis.

Njamal

I will illustrate these principles by means of the kinship terminology of the Njamal, a tribe of Australian aborigines. Like most Australian tribes, the Njamal have always been few in number. They may have reached 500 at one time, but, by the early 1950s when P. J. Epling collected these data, they were reduced to no more than a hundred. Originally they lived in northwest Australia, where they hunted animals and gathered whatever wild plants could be scraped from their desolate territory. As if to make up for their small numbers and meager technology, the Njamal like other Australians had a wonderfully complex family and kinship organization. It was through their intricately defined ties of kinship that they guided most of their activities.

The list below gives the Njamal kinship terms together with some of the kin-types to which each term refers. These kin-types indicate kinsmen who fill genealogical positions in the set of all kinsmen as reckoned out from some particular individual as a point of reference. The abbreviations used for the kin-types are: Mo, mother, (or mother's); Fa, father; Br, brother; Si, sister; Hu, husband; Wi, wife; So, son; Da, daughter; E, elder; Y, younger; ♂, male speaker; ♀, female speaker. Thus MoFa indicates mother's father, and EBr indicates elder brother. The male symbol, ♂, preceding a kin-type indicates that only male speakers use the term for kinsmen of this type, while ♀ stands for a female speaker. When neither ♂ nor ♀ is present the term can be used equally by both men and women.

Maili	FaFa, FaFaBr, MoMoBr, MoFaWiBr, FaMoHu, FaMoSiHu, FaMoBrWiBr, ♂SoSo, ♂SoDa, ♂BrSoSo, ♂BrSoDa, ♂DaDaHu, ♂DaSoWi, ♂DaSoWiSi, etc.
Mabidi	MoFa, MoFaBr, MoMoHu, FaFaSiHu, FaMoBr, ♂DaSo, ♂DaDa, ♂SoSoWi, ♂SoDaHu, etc.
Kandari	MoMo, MoMoSi, MoFaWi, FaFaSi, FaMoBrWi, ♀DaSo, ♀DaDa, ♀SoDaHu, etc.
Kabali	FaMo, FaMoSi, FaFaBrWi, MoFaSi, MoMoBrWi, ♀SoSo, ♀SoDa, ♀DaSoWi, ♀DaDaHu, etc.
Mama	Fa, FaBr, MoSiHu, FaFaBrSo, FaMoSiSo, MoMoBrSo, etc.
Karna	MoBr, FaSiHu, MoFaBrSo, FaFaSiSo, ♂WiFa, SiHuFa, ♀HuFa, BrWiFa, etc.

Midari	FaSi, MoBrWi, FaFaDa, MoMoBrDa, ♂WiMo, ♂WiMoSi, SiHuMo, ♀HuMo, ♀HuMoSi, BrWiMo, etc.
Kurda	EBr, FaBrESo, MoSiESo, etc.
Turda	ESi, FaBrEDa, MoSiEDa, etc.
Maraga	YSi, YBr, FaBrYSo, FaBrYDa, MoSiYSo, MoSi-YDa, etc.
Njuba	♂Wi, ♂MoBrDa, ♂FaSiDa, ♂MoMoSoDa, ♂FaFaSiSoDa, ♂MoMoBrDaDa, ♂BrWi, ♂FaBrSoWi, ♂SiHuSi; ♀Hu, ♀MoBrSo, ♀FaSiSo, ♀MoMoBrDaSo, ♀FaFaSiSoSo, ♀SiHu, ♀BrWiBr, ♀FaBrDaHu, etc.
Ngarbari	♂WiBr, ♂SiHu, ♂MoBrSo, ♂FaSiSo, ♂MoMoSiSoSo, ♂FaFaSiSoSo, etc.
Julburu	♀HuSi, ♀BrWi, ♀MoBrDa, ♀FaSiDa, ♀MoMoSiSoDa, ♀FaFaSiSoDa, etc.
Ngaraija	♂SiDa, ♂WiBrDa, ♂SoWi, ♂DaHuSi, ♀BrDa, ♀HuSiDa, ♀SoWi, ♀DaHuSi, etc.
Tjilja	So, Da, DaHu, BrSo, SiSo, ♂BrDa, ♀SiDa, ♂WiBrSo, ♀BrDaHu, SoWiBr, HuSiSo, DaHu, etc.

A simple inspection of this list permits a few conclusions. For one thing every term except for the first four, is confined to kin-types of a single generation, either to that of ego's parents', to his own, or to his children's. ("Ego" is simply the name anthropologists give to the individual who occupies the center or reference point of the calculation, the person from whom the relationship is reckoned.) The kin-types of the first four terms, include both those in ego's grandparents (second ascending) and his grandchildren's (second descending) generation. Generation then seems to be one important criteria by which the Njamal categorize their kinsmen. The sex of the referent (the person to whom the terms refers) seems to be important for many of the terms, since some of them refer only to males and others only to females. In several cases the sex of ego also seems to play an important part. For a few terms, it is also apparent that the relative age of the referent when compared to that ego is important. *Maraga* for instance can mean 'younger brother' or 'sister,' (as well as certain younger cousins) but quite different terms must be used for 'elder brother' and for 'elder sister.'

These rather simple criteria allow us to start to differentiate among the terms, but it is also apparent that the Njamal must use some other and less transparent criteria as well. The complexity of the array of kin-types shown with each term, might even make it appear that the Njamal have remarkable memories—for by usual English standards each term contains a strange mixture of kin-types. Furthermore the innocent looking "etc.'s" that appear after each list of kin-types imply additional kin-types for each term. The reader can only infer the use of the terms for more distant kinsmen if he understands the principles by which the kin-types are apportioned, and this itself suggests that it is the principles that are important rather than the simple list of kin-types. In fact, a Njamal can apply one of these kinship terms to any other Njamal however distantly he may be related. They recognize no boundary beyond which people are no longer counted as kinsmen. This makes it quite impossible to list *all* of the kin-types to which a term can refer, but even if kinship terms were not so widely applicable, anyone wishing to provide full and formal description of the system should find presence of the "etc." disturbing.

To understand how the terms are used, something must be known of Njamal kinship organization, other than their terminology. One point in particular is essential: every Njamal belongs to one or the other of two "moieties" and his membership is determined strictly by the membership of his father. That is, if we designate the two moieties as *A* and *B* a man will belong to the *A* moiety if and only if his father was also an *A*. The Njamal also insist that a man of the *A* moiety marry a woman who belongs to the *B* moiety, and vice versa. It follows from these two rules that everyone should belong to the moiety *opposite* to that of his mother, but a man's wife and his mother must be in the same moiety as each other. By using these rules, it is easy to count out in any direction and calculate whether a kinsman of any particular kin-type belongs to the same or the opposite moiety as oneself. FaFa must be in one's own moiety, for instance, but MoFa must be in the opposite one. WiBr must be in the opposite moiety to one's self, but WiBrWi is again in one's own. FaBr's children and MoSi's children (the parallel cousins) must be in one's own moiety, but FaSi's children and MoBr's children (the cross-cousins) must be in the opposite. It follows that cross-cousins are appropriate spouses, but parallel cousins are rather like siblings and they cannot marry. If the nature of Njamal moieties is kept in mind, it is possible to see more clearly how the kinship terms can be distinguished from one another.

It is easiest to begin with the generation of one's parents, where there are four terms, *Mama, Karna, Midari,* and *Ngardi*. It is at once apparent that *Mama* and *Karna* refer exclusively to males, while *Midari* and *Ngardi* refer only to females. To a westerner who is unaccustomed to reckoning kinsmen by moiety membership it takes a little longer to realize that *Mama* and

Midari refer only to members of one's own moiety, while *Karna* and *Ngardi* refer only to members of the opposite moiety, but to a Njamal, a man's moiety membership is probably almost as obvious as his sex. These four terms can therefore be precisely and briefly characterized by the generation, sex, and moiety membership of the kin-types to which they refer. A few rather obvious symbols allow the meaning of each term to be shown very simply. We can let capital letters stand for the various dimensions of semantic contrast and let superscript numbers or lower case letters indicate the component of meaning along this dimension. G^{+1} can then stand for the first ascending generation (to which all four of these terms apply); S^m and S^f can indicate male and female sex of the referent, and M^e and M^o can indicate membership in ego's moiety and in the opposite moiety. Thus:

$$
\begin{array}{ll}
\text{Mama} & G^{+1}\ M^e S^m \\
\text{Karna} & G^{+1}\ M^o S^m \\
\text{Midari} & G^{+1}\ M^e S^f \\
\text{Ngardi} & G^{+1}\ M^o S^f
\end{array}
$$

Since members of the second ascending and second descending generations are called by the same terms, it is most natural to consider them together. (These generations can be characterized as G^2 in which the absence of a plus or minus sign indicates that both of the "grand" generations are equally included.) The four terms for these second or outer generations are *Maili, Mabidi, Kandari, and Kabali*, and like those for the first ascending generation each can refer only to members of a single moiety: *Maili* and *Kandari* refer to members of one's own moiety; *Mabidi* and *Kabali* only to members of the opposite moiety. The assignment of kin-types by sex is somewhat more complicated than for the parental generation since every term can refer both to some males and to some females. The trick is to recognize that it is not always the sex of the person referred to nor the sex of ego that is significant, but rather it is the sex of the *senior* member of the pair, no matter whether he is the referent or ego. Thus *Maili*, for instance, is always used reciprocally between two members of the same moiety who are two generations apart, so long as the senior member of the pair is a man. The sex of the younger member is quite irrelevant, for a man uses the term for both his son's son, and his son's daughter (as well as a number of other more distant relatives), while both boys and girls use the same term for their father's father. The only reasonable thing to do, therefore, is to ignore the sex of the younger member of the pair and to recognize instead a new dimension of semantic contrast, that of the sex of the older member of the pair. This distinction can by symbolized as O^m, oldest member of the pair male and O^f, oldest member female. The other three terms for the outer generations are used in analogous ways. *Mabidi* like *Maili* is used when the oldest member of the pair is male, but for members of the opposite moiety, while *Kabali* and *Kandari* are used when the older member is female. Symbolically these can be shown as:

Maili	$G^2M^eO^m$
Mabidi	$G^2M^oO^m$
Kandari	$G^2M^eO^f$
Kabali	$G^2M^oO^f$

Six terms are used for members of ego's own generation—three for those in one's own moiety, and three for those in the opposite one. The three in one's own moiety require only that an additional distinction be made between elder and younger kinsmen, and the sex distinction is maintained only for those who are older. Thus *Maraga* is used both for younger brother and for younger sister as well as for many other more distant but younger kinsmen regardless of sex. Sex need not therefore be noted in the definition of *Maraga*. If the contrasting components of the semantic dimension of relative age are shown as A^e and A^y for elder and younger respectively, the terms for moiety mates of one's own generation (G^0) can be shown as:

Kurda	$G^0M^eA^eS^m$
Turdu	$G^0M^eA^eS^f$
Maraga	$G^0M^eA^y$

The three terms for those who belong to ego's own generation but to the opposite moiety have to be assigned by somewhat different principles. The most natural way to describe the situation is to note that one of the three terms is used reciprocally between pairs who are *not* of the same sex, (between cross-cousins of the opposite sex, spouses, and so on), while the second is used between men, and the third, between women. If we recognize a distinction of same or opposite sex of ego and referent (Z^s same sex, Z^o opposite sex) then this new distinction can be combined with that of the sex of the referent, which has already been used, and unambiguous definitions can be given:

Njuba	$G^0M^oZ^o$
Ngarbari	$G^0M^oS^mZ^s$
Julburu	$G^0M^oS^fZ^s$

Only two terms remain. These are *Ngaraija* and *Tjilja*, which are used only for members of first descending generation. *Ngaraija* is used by men for their sister's daughters and by women for their brother's daughters. This term raises a new problem, since these cross-nieces belong to the woman's own moiety but to the moiety opposite that of a male speaker. The other terms can all be characterized as referring either exclusively to moiety mates, or exclusively to nonmoiety mates, but this is impossible for *Ngaraija*. It would be possible to define *Ngaraija* as having one meaning for men (women of the *opposite* moiety, one generation down) and a different meaning for women (women of the *same* moiety, one generation down), though this seems rather cumbersome. It would force us to recognize dimension of semantic contrast (speaker's sex) that has not been needed before.

The situation can be clarified by recognizing that for kinsman of this first descending generation a man and his wife use the same term. For the other generations, a man always uses the same terms as his sister. A man and his wife must belong to different moieties, and only the man can belong to the moiety of their children, but both he and his wife use the same term when referring to their sons and daughters. One way to deal with this problem is to recognize a new dimension of contrast that takes as its point of reference not the moiety membership of the speaker himself but that of his or her children. Thus, if we let C^s mean that the kinsman referred to belongs to the same moiety as that of ego's child and C^d mean that the referent's moiety is *different* from that of his child, the term *Ngaraija* can be simply defined as "women of the first descending generation of the moiety opposite that of the one's children." The sex of ego is then irrelevant:

$$\text{Ngaraija} \quad G^{-1}C^dS^f$$

All other kinsmen of the first descending generation are called *Tjilja*. The range of this term is peculiar since it covers all one's own children of *either* sex and also cross-nephews (that is, sons of one's opposite sexed siblings). It does not seem possible to give a unitary definition for this term and indeed it turns out that it can be defined in two different though equivalent, ways: either as "children and cross-nephews," or "men of the first descending generation and daughters":

$$\text{Tjilja:} \quad G^{-1}C^s \quad \text{and} \quad G^{-1}C^dS^m \quad \text{(children and cross-nephews)}$$
$$\text{or:} \quad G^{-1}S^m \quad \text{and} \quad G^{-1}C^sS^f \quad \text{(men of the first descending generation and daughters)}$$

The formulas that I have given for the Njamal kinship terms, when used with the definitions of the various semantic dimensions, can define the terms far more succinctly than the list of kin-types originally given, but the formulas do more than just simplify and clarify the list. Assumptions about application of the terms are no longer hidden behind "etc.'s" as they were in the kin-type list. The formulas can be used to predict what term would apply to any kin-type, however remote, and not merely to those shown on the original list. Of course the only way to be completely certain that the term really does apply to these additional kin-types would be to find a Njamal and ask him, but the formulas do provide a way to make predictions back to the original data and to predict further testable data that was not given originally. Just as the analysis of Palaung pronouns by means of a number of intersecting components of meaning brought them into a reasonable and understandable arrangement, so the apportioning of Njamal kinship terms by similar techniques brings order into what may seem at first to be an unduly complicated system.

English

A sound technique for analyzing kinship terminology should be as valid for our own terms as for those of a distant tribe, but perhaps because we are so much more deeply aware of their subtilties and complexities, it is often surprisingly difficult to give satisfying analyses to aspects of our own culture. A consideration of modern American kinship terminology should test the method and bring the techniques of formal semantic analysis a little closer to our own experience. Of course not all Americans use kinship terms in exactly the same way. There may be a few ethnic and regional differences, and there is certainly variation among families. Many Americans for instance never use expressions like *once removed* or *twice removed* to distinguish the various distant cousins from one another, and even though they have heard such expressions, they may not know how others apply them. For an objective observer, no particular variety can be called more correct than another, and all we can do is to investigate actual usage. If people use such expressions as "once" or "twice removed", they must be included in the analysis, but they would have to be omitted from a description of a dialect that lacks them. In the description given here I will follow Ward Goodenough's account of his own terminology. Many Americans use slightly different patterns.

A useful way to sort English kinship terms into major categories is to note how they can be variously combined with different modifiers. One group of terms, that consisting of *mother, father, brother, sister, son* and *daughter* can be used with the modifiers *-in-law* and *step-*.[2] These six terms seem clearly to refer to those whom we consider to be our closest "blood relatives," the people with whom we expect to be joined in a family during part of our lives.

---

[2]In order to simplify my presentation somewhat I will omit the expression *foster*, which, as Goodenough points out, can be used with this same group of terms.

A second group of terms includes *grandmother, grandfather, grandson, granddaughter, uncle, aunt, niece,* and *nephew.* These can be used with modifiers *grand* or *great.* Notice that *grandfather, grandmother, grandson,* and *granddaughter* are regarded as basic unanalysable terms rather than as formed from a separate *grand* that is joined to a more basic underlying term. If this seems slightly artificial, it can be justified by observing that not all the terms of the first group (*father, brother,* etc.) can be used with *grand* for we have no such term as **grandbrother* or **grandsister.* Even more convincing perhaps, is the fact that *grandfather, grandson,* etc., are pronounced with the intonation appropriate to a single word, while expressions such as *great-grandfather, great-uncle,* or *grand-nephew,* are pronounced as two words. The initial *great* or *grand* is set off from *uncle* or *nephew* by the intonation appropriate to an adjective, as it is not in *grandfather.*

When the terms of this second group are joined to one or more adjectival *greats,* they refer to slightly more remote kinsmen than when they are used alone. If the terms of the first group (*mother, father,* etc.) are said to have a genealogical distance of one and the simple terms of the second group (*grandfather, uncle,* etc.) are said to have a genealogical distance of two, then the complex terms constructed from an adjectival *great* or *grand,* can be said to belong to a subdivision of group two, that can be called the "great-2 group" or, for short, "2g."

English has a single basic term, *cousin,* for still more remote kinsmen. *Cousin* is unique in being able to enter constructions with a *first, second, third,* and so forth, and some speakers, though not all, can use it with the expressions *once removed, twice removed,* etc. The term cousin together with its various modified forms refers to the most distantly related people whom we still recognize to be kinsmen. If a man is not even a cousin he is not related at all. *Cousin* can be said to refer to the kinsmen of the "third degree of genealogical distance."

Strictly speaking a categorization of English terms that depends upon their possible modifiers is based upon grammatical rather than semantic principles, but if the terms are arranged on a diagram in which the generations are distributed along the vertical axis and collateral distance along the horizontal axis, the same categories can be seen to be semantically reasonable. The various categories of terms will be seen to form concentric sets around ego. Each succeeding category includes relatives at an increasing distance. The concept of genealogical distance thus combines those of both generational and collateral distance. We can consider ego himself to be at a zero degree of genealogical distance. The significant degrees of genealogical distance can then be symbolized following the labels already given, as D^0, D^1, D^2, D^{2g}, D^3. They include the following terms:

0:    (ego)
1:    father, mother, brother, sister, son, daughter

2: grandmother, grandfather, uncle, aunt, niece, nephew, grandson, granddaughter

great-2: great-grandfather, great-uncle, grandnephew, and so on

3: cousin

Table 2–1   Degrees of Genealogical Distance

Generation Removed from Ego	Collateral Distance					Degree of Genealogical Distance
	4	3	2	1	0	
+3	.	.	.		Great-grand-parents	2g
+2	.	.	1st cousin twice removed	Great-uncle, Great-aunt	Grand-parents	2
+1	.	2nd cousin once removed	1st cousin once removed	Uncle, Aunt	Parents	1
0	3d cousin	2d cousin	1st cousin	Brother, Sister	ego	0
−1	.	2d cousin once removed	1st cousin once removed	Nephew, Niece	Son, Daughter	1
−2	.	.	1st cousin twice removed	Grand-nephew, Grand-niece	Grand-children	2
−3	.	.	.	.	Great-grand-children	2g
		3				

A second important distinction made by English kinship terms is that between consanguineal and affinal kinsmen, or as Americans express it, between "blood relatives" and "in-laws." The terms for the closest affinal kinsmen are *husband* and *wife* and these are the only English kinship terms that are incapable of combining with any modifiers at all. It is convenient to regard *husband* and *wife* as being, like ego himself, at a zero degree of genealogical distance. To place both ego and his spouse at the zero degree suggests that the marriage bond (unlike the sibling bond or the jump across generations) does not add to genealogical distance, and we will see this confirmed in a number of other ways.

If we skip group 1 for the moment, we find that the terms of group 2 apply most characteristically to "blood" relatives, but *uncle, aunt, nephew* and *niece* can also apply to certain affinal kinsmen. *Uncle,* for instance, can mean not only the brother of one's parent, but also the husband of one's aunt. *Nephew* can sometimes be used not only for one's own brother's or sister's son, but also for the son of one's *spouse's* siblings. Perhaps, however, those people who are *uncles, aunts, nephews* and *nieces* by marriage are not quite so clearly kinsmen as the "blood" relatives. Perhaps they are just a bit beyond the bounds of kinship. We may say *my wife's nephew* more naturally than *my nephew* for such an affinal, and even though *uncle* is surely the appropriate label for one's mother's sister's husband (at least if we have known him since our own childhood), the fact that *uncle* may also be used for a friend of one's parent who is in no way related, shows that the use of a kinship term does not necessarily insure that the person referred to is a kinsman. Most kinsmen are permanent—once a brother, always a brother—and nothing can completely dissolve the bond, though in particular cases it may amount to little in the way of either emotional or economic dependency. Even a former spouse is still one's *ex-husband* or *ex-wife*, but the term *ex-uncle* for a man who was once married to one's aunt seems implausible, for an ex-uncle is simply not a kinsman at all. We might also have trouble applying the term *uncle* to a man who married our *aunt* late in her life after we had long known her, though we would never have difficulty about using the term *stepfather* however late in life our mother might remarry. Our *uncles, aunts, nephews* and *nieces* by marriage, have, therefore a somewhat ambiguous status, but I will nevertheless assume that such people are in fact kinsmen and include them here, in spite of the complexities they introduce to the analysis. All terms in group 2, then, can be used for blood relatives and some can also be used for certain affinal relatives.

The utility of regarding the marriage bond as having no effect upon genealogical distance is demonstrated by these affinals of group 2. Here the same term is applied to males of the first ascending generation, whether they are related through a marriage bond or not. It is reasonable to regard them all as having the same degree (two) of genealogical distance. Nevertheless, we must give each of the terms, *uncle, aunt, nephew,* and *niece,* two separate definitions. A consanguineal *uncle* would be first degree of genealogical distance, consanguineal, first ascending generation, male, while the *uncle* by marriage would be first degree of genealogical distance, affinal, first ascending generation, male.

To be completely explicit we must also note that the use of these terms is limited in one other way. The terms *uncle, aunt, nephew* and *niece* are used for affinals of second degree of genealogical distance, but they apply only when the marriage bond is in the senior generation of those who are related. For example, I call my mother's sister's husband *uncle,* but I would not use this term for my wife's mother's brother, (even though he is *also* an affinal, male, of the second degree of genealogical distance one generation up) because the marriage bond (my own) is in the lower (my) generation rather than in the upper (my wife's mother's) generation. In fact, we have no term that applies specifically to people like the wife's mother's brother and we can only refer to them by descriptive phrases such as those I have used. We must therefore distinguish between those who are related to one through a linkage in which the marriage bond is in the senior generation (M^s) and those in which it is not (M^j).

Cousin seems to be used only for blood kinsmen. If it were to be used for the spouse of one of these kinsmen that would be an extension of its use hardly more significant than the application of the term to an unrelated friend, and for the most part the spouses of one's cousins hardly seem to be counted as kinsmen at all.

When we finally return to group 1, the situation is a bit more complex. The simple terms of group 1 are, of course, used only for blood relatives, but the *step-* terms and the *-in-law* terms are used for kinsmen who are related to ego through an intervening marriage bond and they must therefore be counted as affinal. Here again the marriage bond does not serve to increase the degree of genealogical distance, since people who are related by marriage (that is, mother's husband or wife's mother) are treated terminologically as if they were in some way courtesy relatives of the first degree.

The *step-* and the *-in-law* relationships are all affinal and all at the first degree of genealogical distance, but clearly the two types differ from one another. One way to see the difference is to note the unique position of the *step-* kinsmen within the ideal American family. Clearly our normal expectation is that every family will consist of a single married couple together with children over whom the couple shares biological parenthood. If this were always the case then the mother's husband would always be one's father, and father's son would always be equivalent to mother's son. When secondary marriages occur these equivalences no longer hold, but we still tend to act (both in terminology and in our other behavior) as if they did. Thus father's wife can be said to fill a structurally equivalent position to that of the real mother, and husband's son can be said to be structurally equivalent to one's own son. It is for such people that we use the modifier *step-*. The group of *step-* relatives, unlike other groups of affinals, therefore, can be said to be structurally equivalent to corresponding consanguineal relatives.

The *in-laws*, like the step relatives, are affinals at the first degree of genealogical distance (since the marriage tie does not increase genealogical distance), but, unlike the *steps*, they are not structurally equivalent to primary relatives. Thus *mother-in-law* and *daughter-in-law* are at the first degree of genealogical distance, but unlike one's *stepmother* or *stepdaughter* they are not structurally equivalent to one's own mother or daughter. We can therefore distinguish kinsmen along a dimension of consangunity as either "blood" (consanguineal) relatives (C^b); structurally equivalent affinals (C^s); or nonstructurally equivalent affinals (C^m).

The distinctions made among kinsmen along the semantic dimensions of genealogical distance, consanguinity, and generational location of the marriage bond allow a fairly fine sorting of the English kinship terms.

Zero distance, consanguineal (D^oC^b): (ego)

Zero distance, affinal (D^oC^m): husband, wife

1st distance, consanguineal (D^1C^b): mother, father, brother, sister, son, daughter

1st distance, structurally equivalent (D^1C^s): step-kinsmen

1st distance, nonstructurally equivalent (D^1C^m); in-laws

2d distance, consanguineal (D^2C^b): grandfather, grandmother; grandson, granddaughter; "blood" uncle, aunt, nephew, niece

2d distance, affinal, marriage bond in senior generation ($D^2C^mM^s$): spouse of uncle, aunt; nephew and niece of spouse

"2g" distance, consanguineal ($D^{2g}C^b$); great-grandparents and children, great-uncle and great-aunt, grand-nephew and grand-niece

"2g" distance, affinal, marriage bond in senior generation ($D^{2g}C^mM^s$): spouse of great-uncle and great-aunt; grand-nephew and grandniece of spouse.

3d distance, consanguineal (D^3C^b): cousin.

Having categorized kinsmen up to this degree, only two other distinctions are necessary—the two simple contrasts of generation and sex. Most of our terms indicate both generation and sex unambiguously. The generation of the kinsman to which a term applies can be simply the number of generations above or below that of ego and can be represented as G^o (own generation), G^{+1} (parent's generation), and so on, while sex can be shown as S^m (male) and S^f (female). Our term *cousin* is unique in being ambiguous on these two dimensions. It is a simple matter to add designations for components along those two dimensions to the components of the three dimensions given earlier and thus produce unique definitions for each of our more basic kinship terms.

These five dimensions of semantic contrast adequately distinguish the majority of our kinship terms from one another, but some modifiers remain to be defined. As already pointed out, *great* (or in some dialects *grand*, especially when immediately preceding *niece* or *nephew*) can precede any of the kin-terms of group 2, and, moreover, *great* can be applied recursively. With each use it simply increases by one the value of the sign of generational distance. Other modifiers can be applied to the term *cousin*. When used alone, *cousin* does not specify the degree of collateral distance except to show that it is beyond the second degree. By prefixing *first, second, third,* etc., to *cousin*, the exact degree of collateral distance can be specified. By itself *cousin* also fails to make the kinsman's generation explicit. Those speakers of English who use the expressions *once removed, twice removed,* etc., can add these to *cousin* to show how many generations separate the speaker from the man to whom he refers.

If these various dimensions of contrast and the components of meaning along them are carefully specified, they also show the limits beyond which kin-terms cannot be used. Beyond these limits we can only describe kinsmen by some sort of descriptive label, a complex term made up from simpler terms. For instance, the spouses of our more distant kinsmen, the secondary kinsmen of our spouse, and almost anyone related through two or more marriage bonds are too distant to rate a simple kinship term. Nevertheless, those kinsmen lying beyond the range of our ordinary kin-terms can be defined and even classified by the same semantic contrasts needed for the named kinsmen. Spouses of nieces and nephews, for instance, would be second degree affinals in which the marriage bond is in the junior generation, or symbolically, $D^2C^mM^jG^{-1}$; spouses of great nephews and nieces would be $D^{2g}C^mM^jG^{-2}$; spouses of cousins would be D^3C^m.

Taken together these dimensions of semantic contrast, the definitions of their various components, and a description of the operators *great*, *grand*, and *first*, *second*, *once removed*, and *twice removed* serve to distinguish our various kinship terms from one another and assign kin-types to them. One should probably retain some skepticism about whether such a description corresponds at all closely to the process by which Americans really go about selecting their terms, but the description does at least end by assigning terms to the appropriate kinsmen.

The treatment of Njamal and English kinship terms given in this chapter illustrates the technique of componential analysis in the cultural domain where it has been most successful. Kinship terminology is also a strategic area for experimentation with semantic techniques other than just componential analysis, and I will return to these in later chapters. First, however, I will turn to a few attempts to apply componential analysis, and some closely allied methods, to semantic domains other than kinship.

3 *Componential Analysis*

Further Applications: Jamaican Meals

Kinship terminology has lent itself to more detailed and precise analysis than has the terminology of any other semantic domain. Those who have worked with kin-terms find a special satisfaction in organizing them into clear and explicit patterns. But it is obvious that kinship terms occupy a small part of our total vocabulary, and the only real justification for lavishing so much attention upon them is the hope that the techniques useful for kinship might later prove to be applicable to other semantic domains.

In principle, one would suppose that the techniques should be widely applicable. Kinship is certainly not the only domain in which terms are distinguished from one another by distinctive semantic features. The terms of almost any set also seem to discriminate the different aspects of some range of observable phenomena. To describe the aspects to which any particular term applies should, it would seem, require operations similar to those used for kinship. People do learn to use terms, and they can learn to decide which term is appropriate on a particular occasion or for describing a particular event. This manifest ability strongly suggests that the criteria by which a speaker chooses among terms in any domain should be amenable to formal description. A few attempts along these lines are worth considering.

The small segment of vocabulary used by Jamaicans to name the meals they eat in the course of a day has been given a succinct analysis by David DeCamp. The English spoken in Jamaica is so different from that of Britain or the United States that it has generally been considered a creole and although Jamaicans use the same words for their meals as do speakers of English elsewhere in the world, they use them in subtly different ways. Jamaican English is extremely variable within the island. Even neighboring villages may use rather different dialects. The upper class, the merchants, and the laborers each have their own special forms. To account for the internal differences among the various classes, four class levels must be recognized each with its own special usage: (1) the urban and suburban upper-middle class; (2) the self-employed lower-middle class including shopkeepers; (3) estate laborers and those small farmers who live far from their fields; (4) peasant farmers who live near the fields in which they work. The terms that members of each class use is shown in Table 3–1:

Table 3–1   Jamaican Meal Terms

Dialect	5:00–7:00 A.M.	11:00– Noon	4:00–6:00 P.M.	7:00–8:30 P.M.	10:30–Md- night
Upper middle class	*breakfast* medium	*lunch* medium	*tea* light	*dinner* heavy	*supper* light
Lower- middle class	*breakfast* medium	*dinner* heavy	*supper* medium	*supper* light	
Estate laborer	*tea* light	*breakfast* medium		*dinner* heavy	
Peasant farmer	*tea* light	*breakfast* heavy	*dinner* medium	*supper* light	

Only two dimensions of semantic contrast are needed to distinguish the meanings of these various terms: (1) the time at which the meals are eaten, and (2) the size or heaviness of the meal. T can stand for the dimension of time and the segments of the day which must be recognized as distinctive can be symbolized as follows:

T^m morning—5:00–7:00 A.M.
T^n noon—11:00–noon
T^a afternoon—4:00–6:00 P.M.
T^e evening—7:00–8:30 P.M.
T^1 late—10:30–midnight.

Similarly H can stand for the dimension of heaviness of the meal. The three degrees of heaviness recognized by the Jamaicans can be shown as follows:

H^1 a light meal, usually including a hot drink, but lacking hot food
H^m a medium meal
H^h the heaviest meal of the day.

Table 3–2   Jamaican Meal Terms (2)

	Breakfast	*Lunch*	*Tea*	*Dinner*	*Supper*
Upper-middle class	$H^m T^m$	$H^m T^n$	$H^l T^a$	$H^h T^e$	$H^l T^l$
Lower-middle class	$H^m T^m$			$H^h T^n$	$H^m T^a / H^l T^e$
Estate laborer	$H^m T^n$		$H^l T^m$	$H^h T^e$	
Peasant farmer	$H^h T^n$		$H^l T^m$	$H^m T^a$	$H^l T^e$

The abbreviations can then easily be combined (Table 3-2) to indicate the meaning of the five words as used by each of the four Jamaican classes.

Displayed in this way it is easy to see not only the differences between words, but also the differences among the classes. *Tea* for instance is always a light meal, but it comes in the afternoon for the upper-middle class and in the morning for estate laborers and peasant farmers. Breakfast is an earlier meal for the two upper classes than for the two lower classes.

It is not difficult to offer similar definitions to the terms that residents of the United States use for their meals, although the time distinctions would have to be slightly revised (perhaps to morning, noon, and evening— T^m, T^n, T^e,) since we apparently recognize different significant blocks of time than Jamaicans. The light-medium-heavy distinction seems still to be appropriate. *Breakfast* then would be a medium morning meal ($H^m T^m$), and the hurried commuter who merely grabs a cup of coffee before rushing to work hardly deserves to call what he has consumed *breakfast*. *Lunch* is a medium noon meal ($T^n H^m$) and supper a medium evening meal ($H^m T^e$). *Dinner* is certainly the heaviest meal of the day, but the term can be used for a meal at any time from the middle of the day on into the late evening ($T^{n-e} H^h$). Perhaps a *coffee break* is simply a light meal, unmarked for time (H^l).

English Verbs

Of course terms for meals hardly get at the heart of general vocabulary any more than do pronouns or kinship terms, but applications of componential analysis to less restricted domains of meaning have been rather few. One intriguing attempt, however, has been made by Edward H. Bendix, who has studied a number of very common verbs in English. Bendix deliberately chose words from the general vocabulary rather than from the more specialized domains that always seem more amenable to systematic description. He managed moreover, to get along without needing *all* the terms in a single well-defined and delimited domain, for it would be quite impossible to handle all the members of a large class such as the one within which he works.

Bendix begins with an elaborate analysis of the English verb *have*. I will not attempt to summarize this analysis, but the meaning of *have* must be assumed when proceeding to the definitions of the remaining verbs, since all include the meaning of *have* as one component of their own meaning. These are verbs indicating that, at some point, somebody *has* something. Since these verbs express relationships, Bendix feels it is better to consider them within sentences along with subjects, objects, and indirect objects rather than in isolation. Since, however, he wants to avoid analyzing the subjects and objects themselves, he simply labels them by arbitrary letters. The verbs (or more properly the schematic sentences), which he seeks to define, are the following:

> A gets B
> A finds B
> C gives B to A
> C gets B for A
> C lends B to A
> A borrows B from C
> A takes B from C
> A gets rid of B
> A loses B
> A keeps B

To one accustomed to kinship, a less auspicious set of terms than these verbs is hard to imagine, but it turns out that they can be differentiated by a number of fairly simple distinctions. As an essential defining feature, all these verbs include the idea that A "has" B at one time or another. Beyond this common feature, the terms are differentiated from one another in several ways:

1. In all the sentences except *A gets rid of B*, *A loses B*, and somewhat ambiguously *C gets B for A*, the meaning includes the idea that A will have B, after or as a result of the indicated action. This will be true whether *A gets B*; *A finds B*; *A is given* or *lent B by C*; or *A borrows*, *takes*, or *keeps B*. In all these cases the resulting condition is that A has B.

2. Only two of the sentences, *A gets rid of B* and *A loses B*, explicitly indicate that after the time to which the verb refers, A does *not* have B. *C gets B for A* is unique among these ten sentences in not

explicitly indicating whether A actually has B or not, so this sentence alone can be regarded as unmarked along both of these first two dimensions of contrast.

3. All the sentences except *A gets B* and *C gives B to A* imply that B must already have been in existence before the time indicated by the action of the verb. One cannot *find* something if it does not already exist before the finding, nor can one *lend, borrow, take, get rid of, lose,* or *keep* something that doesn't exist first. But one can *get* a job or a jail sentence that was not in existence before its acquisition, and one can *give* someone a scare or *give* someone a black eye, where no implication of prior existence is made. These two sentences alone, therefore, are unmarked for prior existence.

4. *C lends B to A* and *A borrows B from C* are unique in explicitly stating that B does not belong to A. A *has* B after he *borrows* it from C, or after C *lends* it to him; but that does not make it his. In all the other cases B *may* belong to A although in no case *must* this be true. The other sentences can therefore be regarded as unmarked with respect to the feature of "belongingness," while *C lends B to A* and *A borrows B from C* are marked unambiguously as indicating that B does not *belong* to A, even though A does indeed *have* B.

5. *C gives B to A, C gets B for A,* and *C lends B to A* all imply some causation on the part of C. In these three alone, it is definitely stated that someone *other* than the A who has the B takes some positive action.

6. *A borrows B from C, A takes B from C* and *A gets rid of B,* imply that the causation is due to A. Just as C takes some positive action in the three sentences indicated in 5, so A takes some positive action for these three. A can *get, find, lose,* or *keep* B by accident. *Borrowing, taking,* and *getting rid of* are not accidental.

7. Finally, two of the sentences, *A finds B* and *A loses B,* indicate that the action was in some way accidental. One cannot *find* or *lose* something on purpose.

The meanings of these various verbs can be summarized in a table that looks very much like a chart of kinship terms. Table 3-3, which is based upon Bendix's summary, indicates only those features that are positively marked for each sentence.

It is clear that many of the logically possible combinations of semantic features needed to define these verbs do not occur. The seven required semantic features would be capable of supporting a much larger number of sentences than just the ones formed. Perhaps English has a few additional simple verbs Bendix omits that combine the same features in other ways, but it must be true that in this part of the vocabulary we simply do not have individual terms for all possible combinations of semantic features. When we need to express other combinations of these features, we usually require

Table 3–3 Analysis of English Verbs

	1. A has B after the action	2. A does not have B after the action	3. B has prior existence	4. B does not belong to A	5. C causes the action	6. A causes the action	7. There is chance or accident in the action
A gets B	x						
A finds B	x		x				x
C gives B to A	x				x		
C gets B for A			x		x		
C lends B to A	x		x	x	x		
A borrows B from C	x		x	x		x	
A takes B from C	x		x			x	
A gets rid of B		x	x			x	
A loses B		x	x				x
A keeps B	x		x				

longer and more complex expressions. Thus we can say *A kept B accident-ally*, combining the usual features of *A keeps B* with the accidental feature of dimension 7, and we can say *C got B for A but forgot to give it to him*, thus making clear that A does not have B. The absence of specific terms for some logically plausible combinations of semantic components certainly does not keep us from expressing such combinations when we need to or want to do so.

It may be that one of the ways in which kinship terminology differs from the terminology of most other semantic domains is in its tendency to carry out the logical possibilities for combining the various semantic components more fully. In kinship we typically have terms that cover a high proportion of the logically possible combinations of components. This makes kinship systems appear rather clean and symmetrical. In other domains it may be that most logically possible combinations of components require complex constructions. Outside of kinship terminology, a relatively high number of components in proportion to the number of terms will be needed, and many conceivable combinations will simply not be expressible by a single term.

Taxonomies

Componential analysis of the type used for pronouns, kinship terms, and more experimentally for meals and verbs is most clearly applicable in domains where the terms fall into paradigms, that is where the various semantic dimensions crosscut one another in such a way that all, or at least a high proportion, of the possible combinations of components combine with one another to define a term. More typical of many semantic domains are "taxonomies" in which terms are hierarchically related so that the meaning of more specific terms is included within the meaning of higher-level and more general terms. Perhaps the best-known analysis of a set of terms into a taxonomy has been Charles Frake's treatment of the terminology for various skin diseases known to the Subanun, a tribe living in Mindanao in the southern Philippines.

The Subanun have more than their share of illness. They recognize many different diseases and often discuss them. Treatment depends upon diagnosis, and diagnosis is made on the basis of symptoms, but since symptoms may be less than perfectly clear, the Subanun spend much time debating whether or not a particular disease name should be applied to some collection of symptoms. Since symptoms may be ambiguous, there can be disagreements about which particular disease term should apply in a particular case, though the debaters may agree closely on the abstract principles by which they feel the diseases should be distinguished.

Beyond the ambiguity of symptoms, however, a particular illness can often quite legitimately be called by several alternative terms, some of which are much more specific than others. For instance, the Subanun term *nuka* is a general term covering a wide variety of skin diseases, including all those labeled slightly more specifically—*meŋabag*, 'inflamation'; *beldut*, 'sore'; and *buni*, 'ringworm.' *Beldut* is further subdivided into such subvarieties as *telemaw*, 'distal ulcer,' and *baga?*, 'proximal ulcer.' *Telemaw* in turn includes both *telemaw glai*, 'shallow distal ulcer,' and *telemaw bilgun*, 'deep distal ulcer.' Thus in a particular case it might be quite correct to answer the question what disease does he have? by any of several disease terms: *nuka*, *beldut*, *telemaw*, or *telemaw glai*. Each of these answers would be correct but each varies in the specificity of information it conveys. To answer *nuka* would be to give only a general broad category. To answer *beldut* is to say the person has a particular kind of *nuka* that is not *meŋabag* or *buni*. To answer *telemaw* or *telemaw glai* would be to give an even sharper diagnosis. Each term can be said to diagnose the disease at a different level of contrast.

It can happen that the same term can appear at different levels of contrast. *Nuka* for instance can be used not only in the broad sense of skin disease in general but also in a very specific sense, to refer to a particular skin disease, a sense for which Frake uses the translation 'eruption.' In this more specific sense *nuka* contrasts with *telemaw glai*, for both terms are at the most delicate level of diagnosis. To know which sense of *nuka* is being used, the hearer must rely upon the broad context in which he hears the term, or else the speaker must modify the term to make his meaning clear. If ambiguity is a danger, the Subanun speaker can say *tantu nuka*, 'real *nuka*' (that is, 'eruption'), and show that it is not just any skin disease that is intended.

It should not be surprising to find the same term appearing at different levels in such a hierarchy of terms. The English term *man* can contrast at a very general level with *animal*, embracing all people of any age or sex. At a more specific level *man* contrasts with *woman*, and at an even more specific level it contrasts with *boy*. Even our word *sick* can be used both in a very general sense to describe someone with virtually any unpleasant symptoms and also in a much more specific sense for certain stomach ailments. Thus it could be perfectly proper to answer the question *has he been sick?* by saying *no, he hasn't been sick but he has had a high fever*, though in another sense of the word, anyone with a high fever certainly deserves to be called *sick*.

The Subanun disease terms can be said to fall into a taxonomy, and indeed they can be arranged very much like the terms of the biological taxonomies with which we are familiar, though of course with Subanun disease terms we are dealing with ordinary colloquial terms, not with an explicity organized and defined set. In a taxonomy we expect that some terms will be more general than others, and that there will be several levels of specificity. At the most general level a single term may cover an entire domain of meaning. (It has been suggested, if only half seriously, that the English word *thing* sits at the very top of an enormous taxonomy, which embraces all English concrete nouns.) Beneath the most general term, will be several more specific terms each labeling a subdivision of the total domain and contrasting with one another on that level. Then each of these terms may in turn be subdivided into smaller and smaller divisions, until the most specific lexical level is finally reached. It seems likely that the terms of many semantic domains can be usefully seen as falling into such taxonomies.

One likely possibility for a taxonomic study is the set of terms for plants and animals. The very fact that scientific taxonomies have been so readily devised for biological species suggests that the colloquial or folk terminology for the same phenomena might be arranged in a somewhat similar way. While a scientific taxonomy depends only upon the characteristics of the plants and animals, to work out a colloquial taxonomy, one must study how people use terms and not worry if their usage violates scientific principles. Nevertheless the colloquial use of terms does depend upon the characteristics of the species as observed by speakers of the language. It may reflect some of the same properties as a more formal scientific classification.

All languages include many names for varieties of plants, and perhaps they always have general terms that group similar plants under the same label. This should allow us to construct taxonomies of plant terms much like the one Frake offered for disease terms. It is easily suggested that in colloquial English (disregarding, of course, the nomenclature of taxonomic botany) our word *tree* subsumes several categories such as *palm*, *evergreen*, and so on. These in turn are divided into smaller groups such as *pine*, *maple*, and *birch*, until one finally reaches such minimally distinctive labels as *red pine*, *norway pine*, *white pine*, and *jack pine*. At each level of this hierarchy, we use different criteria to distinguish among the various members. Such a taxonomy differs from a paradigm, applicable to kinship, in that the semantic distinctions needed for one segment of a taxonomy typically do not apply in other segments. Thus the difference between a *jack pine* and a *white pine* has no applicability to oaks or maples, while the difference between *brother* and *sister* (that is, sex) crops up repeatedly in kinship, distinguishing *uncle* from *aunt*, *son* from *daughter*, and so on.

Still, the differences between a taxonomy and a paradigm are not profound. To sort terms in either way requires us to search for distinctive features of the observable world and to note how a terminology discriminates among these features and how various combinations of features are assigned to particular terms. It is easy to suppose that a similar analysis should be applicable to virtually any set of terms.

Cognition, Indeterminacy, and Methodology

In spite of many interesting experiments, the ability to provide convincing formal semantic analyses for more than a tiny proportion of the vocabulary of a natural language still eludes us. It has proved to be a good deal easier to make programmatic statements about the reasonableness of attempting semantic analyses than actually to provide them. A few of the problems that seem to have made formal semantic studies difficult need to be mentioned.

One problem hindering progress has been a lack of clarity about the goals of semantic analysis. The more modest goal, and the one I have been stressing in these chapters, is simply to produce a formal statement that will account for or *predict* the terms that can be appropriately used in various nonlinguistically-defined circumstances. This has been the minimum goal of most of those interested in formal analysis, and it is comparable in the semantic field to the linguist's grammatical goal of writing rules that will generate grammatically acceptable sentences. Since speakers can learn to use words appropriately, it hardly seems unreasonable to attempt to construct a formal statement that will duplicate a speaker's ability.

Some semantic analysts, however, have also had the further goal of discovering and then describing how the people *themselves* use their terms to classify the phenomena of their world. Since the use of terms implies a classification, and since classification can be regarded as an important aspect of the speaker's cognitive skills, the study of the use of terms has often been looked upon as a way of investigating cognition in the diverse cultures of the world. To investigate cognition is a far more ambitious goal than simply to provide a device that chooses the same terms a native would choose without pretending to duplicate his inner mental processes of classification and decision. To claim that one's analysis is the same as that used by the native speaker does not necessarily add to its powers of explanation. If the only clue to cognitive processes comes from knowledge of the use of terms, then little would seem to be gained by invoking cognition. Only if some independent test of cognition is available, a test so independent that it does not rely wholly upon the use of terms, does it seem likely to prove fruitful to add cognition to our conceptual baggage. Such independent tests have been exceedingly hard to construct.

There is a related problem: sometimes several different but equally workable ways of treating a set of terms can be devised. Any speaker of English should be able to formulate an analysis of English kinship terms, which differs in some respects from that given in the last chapter. So long as each analysis is equally able to account for the application of the terms, it is difficult, perhaps impossible, to demonstrate that any particular one is better or more correct than another. If one analysis is a great deal more complex, requiring complex definitions and many semantic features, that might provide adequate formal grounds for dismissing it in favor of a simpler solution, but the criteria for measuring complexity are not always clear. When two analyses predict the same set of data and have roughly the same complexity, it may be impossible to choose between them. If two solutions are so nearly equivalent as to be isomorphic (in the sense that one could derive one solution directly from the other without either adding or losing information), then one might argue that the two are entirely equivalent and that the differences between them are quite trivial. Either solution would be equally adequate to the task of predicting the use of terms. But if the goal is to specify how the speakers of the language use the terms themselves then the problem is not so easily dismissed. In practice it has been unclear just how we are to choose among various plausible solutions or how we can know whether people really choose their terms in a way that is at all similar to that given by a formal analysis.

One failing sometimes charged to the formal analysts has been an undue addiction to methodological nit-picking. The literature has been rather heavy with statements about how one ought to go about producing a semantic analysis and a bit thin on completed statements. Yet the arguments given by Chomsky and his disciples about the fundamental unimportance of discovery procedures with respect to grammatical theory are equally applicable in semantic theory. One's analysis may be the result of long and painful struggle, or it may be the result of a single flash of insight. What really matters is whether or not the analysis allows us to predict back to the data and to predict additional grammatical or semantic uses of the language. If a theory that describes how terms are employed makes use of extralinguistic criteria, it passes beyond grammar and into semantics, but no more than in grammar does it matter how the theory is reached.

The concern with methodology and the worry about the cognitive status of semantic analyses are, in my opinion, peripheral issues. At worst they have done no more than divert some attention from more productive tasks, and they do not, I think, raise serious questions about the reasonableness of formal semantics. One must grant that our natural use of language includes choices we make with reference to things and events outside language and that speakers are as capable of learning to make these choices as they are of learning grammar. It follows that it is just as reasonable to try to formalize a semantic description, incorporating extralinguistic variables, as it is to formalize a statement of grammar, depending only upon linguistic variables. In the face of widespread reluctance on the part of linguists to become embroiled with extralinguistic variables, the anthropologists have been left to struggle with the problem almost alone. If they have had less than total success, that simply indicates the difficulty of the problem. It does not mean that the objective is unreasonable.

4 *Literal and Extended Meanings*

Three Remaining Problems

Those who have undertaken componential analysis have made a number of assumptions that deserve to be made more explicit and, in a few cases, I believe they ought to be questioned. In particular, I see three assumptions that have led to difficulties. First is the assumption that the field to which a set of terms refers is a perceptual continuum, and that only by the use of our terminology do we introduce divisions within this continuum. This assumption misses the possibility that common human perceptual abilities might introduce similar distinctions in all languages. The second assumption is that the semantically meaningful linguistic choices to be investigated are confined to those that distinguish lexical items. This ignores the possibility that semantically meaningful choices might also be made at the syntactic or other levels of language. Third, componential analysts have tended to assume that lexical items must always be defined by more or less direct reference to extralinguistic phenomena, thus ignoring the obvious human ability to use previously defined words in building up the definitions of new words.

This and the following two chapters will each be devoted to one of these assumptions I will suggest some evidence that calls the assumptions into question and consider a few of the difficulties and opportunities that arise as a result. I turn first to the question of perceptual continua.

Color

The semantic studies so far considered have rested upon a more or less explicit assumption that events in the world present an essentially undifferentiated continuum to our most naïve perceptions. Only our language, we have presumed, forces us to divide up this continuum into lexically labeled classes that are mutually contrasting. It has been thought that each language makes its own distinctions, which need have little to do with the distinctions made by other languages. Our perceptual abilities are supposed to be too flexible and too complex to impose any particular categorization upon the world's events.

The classic domain used to persuade skeptics of this doctrine has been that of color. The color spectrum is surely a physical continuum, for the possible wave lengths of visible light show no sharp breaks from the red end to the blue end of the spectrum, only a continuous intergradation of ever changing hues. From this physical fact, it has seemed to follow that only the arbitrary characteristics of a particular language could impose divisions upon the continuum, and only the lexical labels for various segments would separate one region from its neighbors. Investigations by Brent Berlin and Paul Kay now suggest, however, that all languages share certain common features in color assignment, and even differences that do exist are by no means random.

If you offer a man a chart of colors, ranging across the spectrum from red on the left to blue on the right and varying on the vertical scale from the lightest to darkest shades so that they reach a maximum of white at the very top and black at the bottom, you can ask him to do two related but by no means identical tasks. Either task might be expected to indicate the meaning of his color terms. You can ask him to indicate the range of each of his terms by drawing boundaries on the chart that separate the areas referred to by each. To make this request is to assume that all of the thousands of discriminable colors can be assigned to one of the basic color terms of the language, though some colors will be much closer than others to a border. The request to draw borders seems a reasonable one, but people often have considerable difficulty with it. They debate about marginal colors and struggle over the exact range of some terms. If asked on a later occasion to repeat the task they may give quite different results from their first attempt. Their difficulties suggest that the bordering regions between the terms are not very well-defined.

If, instead, a man is asked to indicate the particular points on the chart that represent the truest *red*, the truest *green*, and so forth, he will generally have a much easier time. He can quickly indicate the spot that is a *real red*, (if he is a speaker of English) another that is a *real yellow* and still another that is a *real orange*. If asked later to repeat his performance he is likely to duplicate his own work quite closely, and different speakers of a language agree better with one another upon the designation of these focal points than they do on the location of the borders between the terms.

This much is consistent with the idea that our language imposes its own classification upon a continuous range of hues. Some colors (those near the center of a term's range) might be relatively easy to code, while those along the borders would pose more difficulties. The startling result of Berlin and Kay's study is that speakers of all languages seem to place the foci of their color labels at very nearly the same spots on the color chart. Borders are more variable from one language to another, though perhaps not a great deal more variable than from one speaker of the same language to another or even between repeated trials by the same person, but the foci remain in one place. Color terminology seems not to be assigned so arbitrarily as we have always imagined.

This identity of color foci does not mean that all color terminologies are identical. Some languages have more basic terms than others and thereby code more foci, but those terms that a language does have will have their foci at the same locations as other languages. Furthermore, if a language has, for instance, five basic color terms, these five will always have their foci at the same places (white, black, red, green, yellow), and if a sixth term is added it will always be added at the focus of blue.

We can hardly doubt that all people with normal vision are physiologically capable of discriminating the same colors. An impoverished color vocabulary does not mean impoverished vision, and whatever a man's language may be, he can refine his reference to color by forming complex phrases or by citing particular colored objects. But, to be counted as a basic color term, a word must be a single lexical item (not a construction such as *light blue*, *lemon-colored*, or *the color of the rust on my aunt's old Chevrolet*). It must not be merely a subdivision of a higher-order term (such as *scarlet* or *crimson*, which are unquestionably varieties of *red*); it must be applicable to more than a restricted range of objects (unlike *blond*, which is rarely used for anything except hair or wood); and it must be used and accepted readily by all speakers of the language or dialect (unlike *beige* or *chartreuse*). It is in their number of basic terms that languages differ, not in the foci of those they have or in the ability to give more precise descriptions of colors when this must be done.

Languages have been reported with no more than two basic color terms, and these always have their foci at black and white. It may help an English speaker to think of these terms as if they translate our own *dark* and *light*, but when a Jalé of the New Guinea highlands is asked for the truest *siŋ* he will indicate the color we refer to as *black*, and when asked for the truest *hóló* he will point to white. (An English speaker would presumably indicate black and white as the foci of his own *dark* and *light*.) The Jalé have more specialized terms that are used in restricted contexts. *Mut* means 'red soil.' *Pianó* is the name of a plant that can produce a green dye. But these are not basic color terms since they are not broadly applicable to all objects.

Languages with three basic color terms always add the third one at the focus that we call *red*. Most of the warm colors—yellows, oranges, and browns—may be included under red at this stage, but its focus is still a proper red. When a language has four basic color terms, three still have their foci at black, white, and red, but the fourth may be either at yellow or at green. The fifth term adds the one missed at the previous stage, so that all languages with exactly five terms have 'black,' 'white,' 'red,' 'yellow,' and 'green.' The focus of the sixth term is always at blue, which becomes differentiated from green and black, and the focus of the seventh term is brown, which refines the terminology for the warm colors. Up to this point, with the exception of variability in adding 'yellow' and 'green,' it appears that people do not have a term late in the list unless they have all the earlier terms. They do not have a term for brown unless they also have one for blue, and they do not have one for blue unless yellow and green are also labeled.

To these seven terms, English adds four others, which can be considered basic: *grey*, *pink*, *orange*, and *purple*. Terms with the same foci as these are also found in other languages, but it does not seem to be possible to arrange these final four foci in any fixed order of acquisition. None of these final four appear unless all of the earlier seven are also present, but they are not mutually ordered among themselves.

Perhaps the most astonishing and controversial claim about this sequence is that it correlates rather closely with the level of cultural and technological complexity. Languages with two terms are confined to people with the simplest level of technology, such as the New Guinea Jalé. At the other extreme, the only languages known to have terms for all eleven foci are from Europe and east Asia where the people have long histories, and great complexity in their culture and technology. Between these extremes are people like the Tiv, a rather simple African tribe of Nigeria with three terms, the Hanunóo tribe of the Philippines with four, the Eskimo with five, some rather complex African tribes with six, and the Malayalam of southern India and the Burmese with seven.

For present purposes, however, it is not so much the differences between the systems that are important, as their underlying similarity, for the common features of all color terminologies insistently suggest that the spectrum does not form a perceptual continuum after all. The physical determinants of color—wave length and degree of purity or mixture of different wave lengths—certainly vary continuously, but it is difficult to imagine how the world's languages could be so consistent in the colors they code by basic terms if our underlying perceptual skills did not impose a discontinuity upon the spectrum and break it up into perceptually distinct chunks. In a sense these chunks are sitting there, waiting for a label.

Crow and Omaha Kinship Terminology

The conclusion that our common human perceptions impose discriminations reflected in our color terminology and that we have a strong reason to suppose one red is indeed a truer red than another seems to be in conflict with the assumptions made in dealing with Njamal and English kinship terminology. In describing these systems I made an implicit assumption that all the kinsmen who are called by any particular term have an equal claim to that term. As terms were apportioned into smaller and smaller sets until every term was finally distinguished from every other along at least one dimension of semantic contrast, it was taken for granted that the important distinctions were those that separated sets called by *different* terms, while distinctions among various kinsmen called by the same term were ignored. But this assumption should not pass without question in kinship any more than in color. We ought to ask whether a term might not better be seen as applying most specifically to a particularly close relative, while its use for more distant kinsmen could be seen as an extension of this primary meaning. It might be possible, then, to shift attention from the differences *between* terms to the relationship that the various meanings of a single term have with one another.

The most substantial work along such lines is that of Floyd Lounsbury, who has worked with terminological systems, long of interest to anthropologists, that have come to be known as "Crow" and "Omaha" in honor of two tribes of Indians that have such systems. Crow and Omaha terminology is characterized most strikingly by grouping kinsmen of different generations under the same term, and Lounsbury has worked out precise rules to show how this grouping occurs. Instead of seeking criteria that divide one named group of kinsmen from a differently named group, as I did for Njamal and English terminology, Lounsbury constructs rules that join some kin-types to other equivalent kin-types by "reducing" the more distant kin-types to closer ones. The more distant kin-type is shown by these reduction rules to fall into the same set as a closer one.

The simplest of the rules is perhaps the half-sibling rule, which states that half siblings can be grouped with full siblings, as in English, where *brother* and *sister*, for instance, can be applied to half brothers and half sisters as well as to full siblings. It appears that this half-sibling rule is needed for the kinship terminology of almost all people, not merely for Crow and Omaha systems. The rule does not mean that people *cannot* make a terminological distinction between full brother and half brother but only that such a distinction can be ignored so as to allow half brother and full brother to fall together into a larger set.

The half-sibling rule can be given a precise formulation by stating that father's son and mother's son (the more distant kin-types) fall into the same terminological set as brother, while father's daughter and mother's daughter are classed with sister. The four parts of this rule can be conveniently symbolized as follows:

$$FaSo \rightarrow Br$$
$$MoSo \rightarrow Br$$
$$FaDa \rightarrow Si$$
$$MoDa \rightarrow Si$$

The second rule, the so-called merging rule, also has a wider occurrence than just Crow and Omaha systems, though it is not as widespread as the half-sibling rule, not being, for instance, a feature of English terminology. The merging rule expresses the terminological equivalence of siblings of the same sex. It says for instance, that for certain purposes, father's brother falls into the same class as father, while mother's sister falls into the same class as mother. The merging rule would be required for Njamal terminology since (except where age distinctions are made in one's own generation and moiety) siblings of the same sex are always given the same term.

Part of the merging rule can be stated succinctly by the following formulas:

$$\male \; Br... \rightarrow \male...$$
$$\female \; Si... \rightarrow \female...$$

The first of these two expressions is to be understood to mean that a man's (shown by the Mars symbol: $\male$) brother (Br) who is a linking relative (...) to a more distantly related kinsmen, is equivalent to ($\rightarrow$) the man himself ($\male$) as a linking relative (...). The linking requirement simply means that the man's brother *himself* need not be regarded as equivalent to the man, but rather that it is the more distant relatives of the brother who will always be regarded as equivalent to similar relatives of the man. Thus FaBrDa would be equivalent to (reduces to) FaDa, since the Br in the first term is a linking relative and is himself the brother of a man (that is, the man indicated by Fa). The second expression parallels the first except for the change in sex, and it states that a woman's sister as linking relative is equivalent to the woman herself.

The reciprocals of these merging rules are also true: just as a man's brother (as linking relative) is equivalent to the man, so also a linking relative's sibling of the same sex is equivalent to the linking relative. These reciprocals can be written as:

$$\ldots \male \ Br \rightarrow \ldots \male$$
$$\ldots \female \ Si \ \rightarrow \ldots \female$$

Taken together, the four parts of the merging rule state that siblings of the same sex are equivalent so long as *one* of them is a linking relative. If neither of the siblings was a linking relative, then the merging rule would have the effect of saying that a speaker's own brother is equivalent to himself, and it is to avoid such an unlikely result that the limitation to linking relatives must be introduced.

The third and final reduction rule needed for Crow and Omaha systems is known as the skewing rule. It is this rule that brings people of different generations together, and it is thus the distinctive characteristic of Crow and Omaha systems. Several slightly varying forms of the skewing rule are needed for different terminological systems. The varieties distinguish Crow from Omaha as well as subvarieties of each of these. I will outline just one of these varieties, that known as the type II Omaha skewing rule, a rule needed, for instance, for the terminology of several Tzeltal Indian communities of Chiapas Mexico. The Omaha II rule states quite simply that one's father's sister is terminologically equivalent to (reduces to) sister, and reciprocally that a woman's brother's child is equivalent to her own sibling of the same sex. The Omaha II reduction rule can be given formal expression in three parts as follows:

$$FaSi \rightarrow Si$$
$$\female \ BrSo \rightarrow \female \ Br$$
$$\female \ BrDa \rightarrow \female \ Si$$

The power of these three reduction rules can only be realized when it is seen how they can work together to reduce a great (even infinite) array of distant kin-types to the terminological position of a few close kinsmen. Such reductions can proceed in several stages. FaFaSi, for instance, can be seen to be equivalent to FaSi by one operation of the skewing rule, and the resulting FaSi is then reducible to a simple Si by a second application. Similarly FaBrDa reduces to FaDa by the merging rule (since father's brother as a linking relative is equivalent to father), and then FaDa reduces to Si by the operation of the half-sibling rule. The result of these reduction rules is to put FaBrDa, FaDa, FaFaSi and FaSi into the sister category. These three rules can state precisely how a very large number of kin-types can be organized into a much smaller number of terminological categories.

Strictly speaking, however, these rules do not join together only those kin-types that rate the same term, but, instead, they produce what we can regard as superclasses of kin-types that may then be further subdivided by some other dimensions of semantic contrast into two or more subclasses. It is these smaller subclasses whose members are actually designated by a single term. For instance, the rules I have given will reduce MoSi, MoBrDa, MoBrSiDa, and many other kinsmen to the mother category, but it might still be the case that one's own mother is terminologically distinguished from everyone else in this class. This fact could be easily expressed by a rule stating that the lineal member of the mother superclass is given one term while all other members of the superclass are called by a different term. The logic of such a division is exactly the same as that already used in describing Njamal and English, but the need to subdivide the broad class defined by the reduction rules need not cause us to reject the reduction rules as inaccurate. Rather, they lay out precisely those classes that are capable of subdivision, and their reasonableness is often confirmed by other aspects of the system. For instance, even if the real mother receives a term distinct from all of the other kinsmen of the mother class, the real mother and the other mothers may all use the same term for the reciprocal kinsmen. That is, both a woman and her sister (as well as all other kinsmen of their class) may reciprocate to the varied terms by which they are called, by using the same term for their daughter and sister's daughter.

Lounsbury's reduction rules raise a number of possibilities that seem to go beyond those of the simpler componential analyses such as were used for Njamal and English. First and most obviously, the reduction rules give a firm basis by which we can say that a word (a kinship term in this case) has one meaning that is more central or basic than its other more extended meanings. A term that can be applied to one's mother, to one's mother's sister, and even to one's mother's brother's daughter can now be reasonably said to have the central meaning of *mother*, and its other uses constitute extensions of this central meaning to kin-types related in specific ways to mother. Suddenly it can be respectable once more to say that tribesmen in some part of the world call their mother's sister, mother, for at last we can give a reasoned explanation for the centrality of its use for one's real mother. No longer do we need to look upon such a statement with contempt as so many anthropologists have tended to do, for it need not simply be an imposition of our ethnocentric ideas of kinship upon an alien culture.

It is not difficult to foresee that by recognizing even greater extensions we might finally be able to give a formal account of the extension of kinship terms to nonkinsmen, as when we speak for instance of a "mother-superior" or of a "fraternity brother." So long as we confine our attention to kinsmen we leave such people out of consideration, but surely these more extended meanings must ultimately be treated in some way, and it seems likely that they should be seen as extensions of their more literal use for kinsmen. Only by some such device can we distinguish metaphoric extensions of meanings from narrower literal meanings.

From the more limited viewpoint of kinship systems these reduction rules have other implications. Recent work on kinship terminology is often thought to have demonstrated the need to take sociological phenomena into account when describing kin-terms. In defining the Njamal terms, for instance, I pointed out that the terms could be partially differentiated by the moiety relationships of the kin-types involved. Moiety membership is a sociological phenomenon, something that a society may or may not recognize. Lounsbury's reduction rules, on the other hand, are strictly genealogical, for in no place do they rest upon the recognition of any sociological grouping. The wide applicability of these rules suggests that all men share a common genealogical core in their techniques of reckoning kinsmen.

The rules also permit subtle manipulation so as to take account of varied systems. By varying the details of the skewing rule, a remarkable array of kinship systems can be accounted for, and by dropping the skewing rule or by adding other rules, similar treatments can be given of terminological types other than just Crow and Omaha. This makes it possible to compare a wide variety of terminological systems with great precision. By comparing the rules necessary for different systems one can reach a minimal but adequate statement of exactly how one system differs from another. By contrast, the implication of a componential analysis such as I used for Njamal and English is that each system must be examined in its own right, and the prospects for precise comparison seem a bit more remote. Of course, the reduction rules too must first be applied to individual systems and adjusted so that they account accurately for all of the data of each. But it has turned out that such similar rules are needed for so many systems that we have a real prospect for conducting a genuinely comparative study in at least one domain of human lexicon.

Lounsbury's study of Crow and Omaha kinship terminology and Berlin and Kay's study of color terms allow parallel conclusions. In the study of both color and of kinship, we seem to be moving past an insistence upon extreme relativism, in which we felt that each system had to be seen only in its own terms and with rather little reference to the kinship terms or color vocabulary of other people. For both color and kinship terms we can now begin to see ways of comparing one system with another and of relating all systems by means of underlying universals, universals that depend, presumably, upon our common humanity.

The parallel with linguistics and the linguists' recently renewed interest in other kinds of linguistic universals is obvious. In linguistics too, this interest in universals has followed a period of descriptive particularism and has led to a new interest in the contribution of our inherited human potential to the production of language. Just as it is now believed that the grammars of all languages share a great deal, so perhaps do the kinship terminologies and color vocabularies of all people. The details of each system can be expected to vary, but just as we can find certain grammatical rules that are needed for all languages, the half-sibling rule seems to be needed for all kinship terminologies. The variability introduced by each language's particular rules or by nonuniversal semantic rules like the merging and skewing rules operate within strict limits, imposed presumably, by the nature of the human animal.

In Lounsbury's analysis of kinship and in Berlin and Kay's treatment of color, moreover, we are led away from what we formerly imagined to be a homogeneous field and toward a view that insists some locations in this field must be selected as more basic than others and more specifically coded into our vocabulary. Thus in kinship, certain positions (mother, father, and so on) can be seen to be more basic than others and these rate the unambiguous use of a term. Similarly, certain locations on the color chart appear to be more focal than others and more ready to be named. Other locations either on a kinship chart or on a color chart are further from a focus, and although they can be named, this naming is not quite so literal. Their names can be regarded as almost analogical, or at least given by extension from the most explicit reference of the term. For areas far from the focus of our interest—for distant kinsmen or for colors along the borders—we have difficulty assigning terms accurately and consistently. Some reds turn out to be *redder* than others, and some aunts more certainly to be *aunts*. It is difficult to know exactly how these findings should apply to other semantic domains than kinship and color, but the implications for semantic study are surely far-reaching. After studiously trying to define terms by drawing boundaries between one term and the next, it now seems that a more satisfactory way may be to define a term first in its most literal sense and only then to describe how that term is extended to increasingly metaphorical usage. The range of applicability of a single term can no longer be looked upon as an internally homogeneous field.

5 *Semantics and Syntax*

Grammar and Meaning

The examples given in earlier chapters have dealt primarily with lexical choices. It is natural to consider these first, since it is in the choice among lexical items that meaning seems most characteristically to enter language, and lexical choices have received far more careful investigation than other types of semantic choices. As was suggested at the beginning of the last chapter, however, too exclusive attention to lexical choices can lead one to ignore the possibility that meaningful choices might be made at the syntactic or other levels of language. Semantic choices—whether lexical or other-wise—are unquestionably intimately intertwined with grammatical choices, and sooner or later linguists will have to consider how the two varieties of choices can be related to each other. How, in other words, can semantic rules (defined as those that relate language to things outside of language) be shown to relate to syntactic rules (which relate linguistic items only to one another)? The question is fraught with enough difficulties to make any answer extremely tentative, and, before going too far, it will be well to consider in somewhat more detail the way in which the two kinds of rules can be kept conceptually distinct. There is no point in relating things unless the difference between them is first understood.

I have written of semantics and grammar as if the difference between them were simply a matter of definition. But if "grammar" could simply be defined so as to include only those aspects of language that can be described independently of extralinguistic events, then any protracted argument against admitting meaning into the study of grammar would seem to be quite pointless. Meaning would simply be excluded by definition from all considerations of grammar. Yet linguists have often felt obliged to argue at length for the independence of grammar, and it may be useful to clarify my own viewpoint by considering a few examples in which the two phenomena, the internal or grammatical constraints upon language and the external or semantic constraints, seem to be intertwined. One way to proceed is to consider sentences that somehow deviate from normal usage. We can ask how the anomaly of such sentences is best described. In particular we can ask: when do we want to describe something as semantically deviant and when would we rather call it grammatically deviant?

In some cases the decision is easy. Consider for example the sequence /kætz/ in which the English word *cat* is followed by the voiced form of the plural. Such a sequence does not, of course, occur in normal English, and to exclude it we can easily construct a rule that says the plural is formed by a voiceless sibilant /s/ when it follows voiceless stops (including /t/). The voiced form of the plural is used only when it follows vowels and certain voiced consonants. A rule of this sort includes no reference to the world outside of language, and, indeed, in this case it is difficult to imagine that knowledge of the extralinguistic world could be of any help. Here is a decisively grammatical rule. Or, consider the sentence *John found sad*. Here we have a transitive verb (*found*), which ought to be followed by a noun object, but instead it is followed by an adjective. Once again we can explain a deviation from normal usage entirely by means of items within the sentence itself. Knowledge of the world outside of language would appear to be of no help whatsoever.

On the other hand, we also have sentences like *men have three eyes* and phrases like *purple cow*. The peculiarity of these examples can hardly be explained by reference to the nature of the language. If we feel they are peculiar, it is only because our empirical experience of the world has taught us that the things we call *men* do not really have three of the things we call *eyes* and cows do not come in the color purple. There would seem to be no conceivable way to describe the anomalies of these examples if we had to limit ourselves to the linguistic forms from which they were constructed. Both examples are surely grammatical in any reasonable sense of the term. Their deviance is certainly semantic, and only semantic, for they can be shown to be deviant only by an appeal to our knowledge of the events outside of language.

We have no problem in discarding /kætz/ on grammatical grounds and *men have three eyes* on semantic grounds, but it is easy to think up examples that are not so clear. Consider for instance the sentence *he went tomorrow*. Surely there is something wrong with this sentence, but does it violate a grammatical rule or a semantic rule? Or does it even make sense to ask which rule is violated? Perhaps we could say that it violates *both* kinds of rules. More precisely, perhaps we could construct both a grammatical rule and a semantic rule, either of which would explain its anomaly. We could say, for instance, that *tomorrow* refers to events in future time, while the past forms of the verb (such as *went*) refer to past time, and in our empirical experience the past and the future do not coincide. This would amount to the same sort of statement as the claim that cows and purple do not coincide in our experience, and to characterize the anomaly in this way would be to formulate a semantic rule that calls upon our empirical experience outside of language. But we might also say something like the following: English has a class of adverbs (of which *tomorrow* is one), and this class does not occur with verbs of certain types (such as *went*). This would be a statement much like the ones formulated earlier, which forbade nouns ending in some kinds of consonants from occuring with the voiced form of the plural or which forbade a verb like *found* from occurring with an adjective like *sad* instead of with a noun object. It turns out that a sentence like *he went tomorrow* can have its peculiarity described either by the disharmony of the events to which it refers or by the disharmony among its linguistic constituents.

Many expressions are like *he went tomorrow*. Their error can be explained either by drawing upon extralinguistic variables or by excluding them. With a sentence like *the man are here* most linguists would certainly find it more natural to describe its peculiarity as being grammatical. They might say that some forms of a noun subject can occur only with certain forms of the verb, and in particular the form represented by *man* cannot occur with the verb form *are*. It is also possible, however, to point out that as part of its meaning *man* refers to a single object, while as part of its meaning *are* refers to more than one object. Since these are incompatible in the world outside of language, there is something semantically peculiar about a sentence in which the two are juxtaposed. On the other hand, a phrase such as *male daughter* seems to be described most easily in semantic terms. *Male* refers to one kind of object in the world, and *daughter* refers to another kind. Empirical techniques can tell us that these two kinds of objects are mutually exclusive. To reject *male daughter* on such grounds is reminiscent of our rejection of *men have three eyes*. But one might also characterize the anomaly of *male daughter* in grammatical terms. One would have to set up grammatical classes for adjective like *male* and for nouns like *daughter* and then specify that this class of adjective could not occur with this class of noun. Such a grammatical rule would require no reference to extralinguistic phenomena.

The point of this discussion is that it is a false question to ask whether any particular anomalous or deviant example is grammatical or semantic in its deviance. In some cases (such as /kætz/ or *men have three eyes*), it may be impossible to explain the anomaly except in one way. In other cases (*male daughter, the man are here*), it may be a good deal easier to do it in one way even though the other is not impossible. In still other cases (consider *the boy hit herself* or *John persuaded the table to move*), it may be difficult to decide which mode of explanation is easier and utterly impossible to claim that either mode is wrong.

Nothing inherent in these sentences dictates the choice between semantic description and grammatical description, but the type of anomaly lies entirely in the kind of description we choose to give. If for some sentences it is difficult to see any way by which two different explanations could be given, there is still a large area where both formulations are possible. For many sentences, therefore, it is simply a silly question to ask whether the anomaly is grammatical or semantic. Rather, the proper question would be "is the rule that I formulate grammatical or semantic?" The distinction lies in the eye of the linguist, not in the sentence that he observes. The distinction is in the type of rule and specifically in the kind of variables upon which the rule depends. When extralinguistic variables are not included, our rules can be regarded as grammatical. When they are included, the rules will be semantic. Trying to distinguish the grammaticality of a sentence from its semanticity, apart from the rules that we devise to describe it, is futile.

Burmese Numeral Classifiers

I will try to clarify the distinction between semantic and grammatical rules by means of a somewhat elaborate example from Burmese. It will prove possible to provide a semantic analysis to account for a set of linguistic data that might first be imagined to require grammatical treatment.

In Burmese, as in most of the languages of southeast Asia, a number is rarely used without being accompanied by one of the special class of morphemes generally known as numeral classifiers. The choice of classifier depends in a rough way upon what is being counted, but it is difficult to know whether to phrase the rules for choosing a classifier by reference to the noun with which it occurs (a grammatical rule) or by reference to the object to which both noun and classifier refer (a semantic rule). For instance, in Burmese, a special classifier is used for counting people, and it is never enough simply to say the equivalent of 'one woman,' but one must also include the classifier for people. The resulting phrase has three parts: noun to be counted, number, and classifier. Burmese has about 200 classifiers, and somehow the speaker must choose just one of these each time he uses a number. The question we must ask is: what kind of rules can we formulate that will duplicate the speaker's behavior? What sort of rules will account for the speaker's ability to decide what classifier should be used on any particular occasion? In some respects the choice seems similar to the choice among nouns: one picks the term that corresponds to the extralinguistic situation, the situation to which one wishes to refer (a semantic choice). In other respects, the choice of numeral classifier seems to resemble more closely such choices as that among the various plural forms in English (a grammatical choice).

First, we can consider the extent to which the choice among classifiers can be dealt with grammatically. Classifiers might be thought to indicate something rather like the noun classes of Bantu, or even the gender classes of Indo-European. One could say, for instance, that the Burmese nouns *khwêi*, 'dog'; *shín*, 'elephant'; *myîn*, 'horse'; *nwâ*, 'cow', and many others, all belong to the same noun class, because in counting they are all commonly accompanied by the same classifier, -*káun*:

kwêi hnakáun	'two dogs'	(dog, two animals)
nwâ leikáun	'four cows'	(cow, four animals)

Such a view has been implied in occasional suggestions that each noun entry in a dictionary of a language like Burmese should include a notation of the classifier that accompanies it. If this were done in a Burmese dictionary, then the word *khwêi*, 'dog,' for instance, would be accompanied by a note showing that it belongs to the class of nouns that take the classifier -*káun*. If one objects that this information is a trifle superfluous, since -*káun* is used for all animals, and only for animals, from mosquitoes to elephants, he simply demonstrates his misunderstanding of what a grammatical rule amounts to. From a strictly grammatical viewpoint, we have no way of knowing whether or not a noun refers to an animal. Since we can set up grammatical classes only by grammatical criteria, it is only a stroke of luck when the classes have semantic correlates, and even a very close semantic correlation does not allow us to define the class by semantic criteria. It would make better grammatical sense to say that we know *khwêi* is an animal because it is used with -*káun* than to say we use it with -*káun* because it is an animal. For every Burmese noun, one might attempt to indicate the appropriate classifier, all without reference to the meaning of either noun or classifier.

Nevertheless, a number of problems would arise if one seriously attempted this. Perhaps the most obvious problem is that a single noun can, on different occasions, be accompanied by different classifiers usually with more or less varied meaning. Thus, to give an extreme example: *ŋapyóθî*, 'banana,' can be accompanied by a large number of classifiers: *ŋapyóθî talóun*, 'one banana'; *ŋapyóθî tamyóu*, 'one kind of banana'; *ŋapyóθî tashé* 'ten bananas'; *ŋapyóθî tawe⁊*, 'one half of a banana'; *ŋapyóθî tatwê*, 'a bunch of bananas'; *ŋapyóθî takháin*, 'one big bunch (arm) of bananas'; *ŋapyóθî taphî*, 'a small bunch (15–20) of bananas'; *ŋapyóθî tathân*, 'one shoulder-pole load of bananas'; *ŋapyóθî tapèiθâ*, 'a viss (about 3½ pounds) of bananas.' Similarly, *lóunjí*, 'Burmese sarong-like skirt,' can be variously classified with -*thé*, which is used for any article of clothing, or with -*kwîn*, which is used for things that can encircle something else. Pairs of these skirts are classified with -*ou⁊*, a common usage since they are frequently sold in pairs. Probably no other word in Burmese regularly occurs with this unique trio of classifiers. *Êinjí*, 'shirt,' for instance, can be classified with -*thé* (clothing), but *êinjí takwín* is forbidden. "Shirts," it seems, do not encircle the body unambiguously enough to take *-kwîn*.

Even animals occur with other classifiers than just *-káun*. *Šîn* is used for pairs of animals but only with certain species. *Nwâ tašîn*, 'a pair of oxen,' and *cwê tašîn*, 'a pair of buffaloes,' are entirely proper phrases, but *-šîn* is not used with the word for 'horse' let alone with that for 'mosquito.' It is impossible to make any simple generalization, allowing *-šîn* to be used with all nouns that can take *-káun*; *-šîn* simply defines a separate (although overlapping) class of nouns. The point is, of course, that *-šîn* is used only with animals used in teams, and Burmese do not happen to use teams of horses. Since knowledge of the extralinguistic context such as the nonoccurrence of teams of horses in Burma is irrelevant to a strictly grammatical description, the only structurally sound procedure would be to note in the lexicon under *nwâ*, 'cow,' that it can be classified not only with *-káun* but also with *-šîn*. The implication of these examples is that each noun listed in the lexicon would have to be followed by not just a single notation of the class to which the noun belongs, but by a list of several classifiers, any one of which might be used with that noun. To do this is to open up a truly formidable prospect. Native speakers say with utter conviction that *ceʔ tataun*, 'a basket of chickens,' is acceptable but *nwâ tatâun*, 'a basket of cows,' is forbidden. This difference between 'cows' and 'chickens' is semantically transparent, but it is awkward to work it into a grammatical rule. Must we coldly indicate that *-tâun*, 'basket,' can be used with *ceʔ*, 'chicken,' but not with *nwâ*, 'cow'? Such a procedure is surely far-fetched but it is not quite impossible. One could treat even these relationships grammatically, but it seems more reasonable to treat them semantically and forbid 'a basket of cows' only by reference to the ethnographic fact that Burmese do not carry cows in baskets. If we decide to treat *nwâ tatâun*, 'a basket of cows,' as a semantic anomaly, then why not treat *einjí takwîn*, 'a circle of a shirt,' and *lú takáun*, in which *lú*, 'person,' is erroneously used with the classifier for animals, in the same way? Why indeed should we exclude any combination of noun and classifier as ungrammatical? Why not consider the entire problem as semantic?

The possibility of using several different classifiers with a single noun is not, however, the only problem when we attempt to specify the choice of classifiers on syntactic grounds. Classifiers are also regularly used with no antecedent noun whatever. *Lêiyauʔ sâjínté*, 'four people wish to eat,' is impeccable Burmese, but the fact that it is people, rather than animals, who wish to eat, is indicated only by the choice of *-yauʔ* as the classifier. If one desired to be more specific and say, for instance, 'four women wish to eat,' a noun would have to precede the numeral: *mêinmà lêiyauʔ sâjínté*. But if such precision is not required, then it is unnecessary and a bit redundant, though not forbidden, to introduce the sentence with a noun such as *lú*, 'person.'

After realizing that no antecedent noun need be present, the only possible way to salvage the view that the choice of classifier is grammatically governed by a noun is to suggest that the noun can be deleted after its required classifier is introduced. Such a view is awkward, for upon hearing the sentence *lêiyauʔ sâjínté*, it is quite impossible to judge what particular noun has been removed. It could have been *lú*, 'person,' *mêinmà*, 'woman,' *yauʔcâ*, 'man,' *khalê*, 'child,' or any one of many other nouns. Even if one surmounts that difficulty, what is to be done about the few classifiers that never take any antecedent noun at all: *-yeʔ*, 'day'; *-paʔ*, 'week'; and so on. With no antecedent noun to govern the choice of some classifiers, it becomes increasingly difficult to regard them as grammatical markers whose use depends upon the grammatical features of the noun.

It is obvious that the choice among Burmese numeral classifiers carries a far greater semantic load than the purely grammatical choice among plural forms in English. The phrases given earlier with ŋapyóθî, 'banana,' do not *mean* the same thing, and the wide variety of meanings is imparted only by the choice of classifiers. If classifiers do carry this much meaning, an analysis reflecting that fact and explicitly incorporating factors of the world outside of language may be more satisfying than an analysis that attempts to be purely grammatical.

Nevertheless, the relationship between nouns and their classifiers does again raise the question: is the relationship most conveniently described grammatically (without reference to the world outside of language) or semantically? In principle both types of analysis might be possible. An anomalous classifier phrase is not merely grammatically or merely semantically peculiar. It is both. But to work out fully the limitations on cooccurrence of nouns and classifiers as a syntactic phenomenon would be enormously complex and, in the end, not particularly interesting. One could prove conclusively that 'mosquitoes,' 'dogs,' 'cats,' 'elephants,' and 'snakes' belong to one syntactic class, but that 'women,' 'children,' 'shopkeepers,' 'carpenters,' and 'beggars' belong to another. Certainly, as a practical matter, such information is quite useless. One who is learning the language finds it relatively easy to learn the appropriate classifier for any situation, precisely because the classifiers make such good semantic sense. No Burmese would ever hesitate about which classifier to use for a new animal upon hearing its name for the first time.

In the end, the problem resolves itself into whether it is simpler to specify the criteria of choice by the linguistic or by the nonlinguistic environment. The latter is surely more promising, but that does not make the former incorrect.

It seems reasonable to conclude that the difference between grammar and meaning lies in the kind of rule we construct, and we can use the term "semantic" to describe those rules that depend upon extralinguistic variables. It is also reasonable to ask whether such variables bear only upon lexicon, as the examples used up to now would suggest, or whether they also bear upon the syntactical and phonological levels of language.

I will begin to approach this question with another look at a system of kinship terminology. In the kinship systems considered earlier the implications of the rules did not extend beyond the choice of lexical items. The extralinguistic criteria defined by various semantic dimensions served to distinguish terms from one another, but these semantic choices seemed to be without influence on other features of the language. It turns out, however, that semantic criteria can have implications that go beyond the simple choice of a term. Once again, Burmese can provide an example.

Burmese Kinship Terminology

In many respects, Burmese kinship terms are rather like those of English, but I am concerned here primarily with a small set of suffixes that are added to the base terms in order to modify or limit their range of application. No topic is ordinarily felt to be more grammatical (as opposed to semantic) than the rules that state how suffixes can be combined with their preceding bases, but for Burmese kinship terms it proves easier to state some affixation rules semantically.

It is first necessary to specify certain semantic criteria by which the base terms are distinguished from one another. Four dimensions of semantic contrast must be recognized in order to understand the meaning of the consanguineal terms. (These are the terms for blood relatives. For present purposes, we can ignore terms for kinsmen related by marriage.) The four dimensions and their components needed to define the terms are:

1. Generation. Every Burmese term expresses unambiguously the generation of the kinsman relative to that of the speaker.
2. Lineal *versus* collateral. A few terms are applied to both lineals (direct ancestors and direct descendants) and to collaterals (kinsmen descended from one's own ancestors, but who are not lineals: uncles, brothers, nephews, and so on). Some terms, however, can refer only to lineal kinsmen, while others can refer only to collaterals.
3. Elder *versus* younger. Certain kinsmen, particularly siblings, uncles, and aunts, are distinguished by their age relative to the speaker or to the age of the connecting lineal relative.
4. Sex of kinsman.

Using these four dimensions, a small selection from a much larger number of kin-terms can be defined:

1. pí	Third ascending generation. Collaterality, relative age, and sex are irrelevant (great-grandparent or other kinsman of that generation.)
2. dólêi	First ascending generation, collateral, younger, female (younger "aunt," that is younger sister or younger female cousin of one's parent).
3. akóu	Own generation, collateral, elder, male (elder brother or elder male cousin).
4. θâ	First descending generation, lineal, male. Relative age is inapplicable (son).
5. myî	Second descending generation. Collaterality, relative age, and sex are irrelevant (grandchild, or other kinsman of that generation).

The meanings of these terms can be readily displayed as in Table 5-1:

Table 5–1   Burmese Kinship Terms

	Generation	*Lineal versus Collateral*	Relative Age	Sex
pí	+3	(either)	(either)	(either)
dólêi	+1	collateral	younger	female
akóu	0	collateral	elder	male
θâ	−1	lineal	(inapplicable)	male
myí	−2	(either)	(either)	(either)

In a number of respects these terms are ambiguous, but the Burmese have suffixes that they can attach to their base terms to clear up some ambiguity. The meaning of the suffixes can be specified with the same four semantic dimensions that were used for the base terms together with one additional dimension:

5. Degree of collateral removal. For certain collateral kinsmen the distance of their collaterality can be made unambiguous. For instance, siblings can be distinguished from first cousins, first cousins from second cousins, and so forth, but these distinctions are shown only by a suffix.

Other suffixes can be used to specify the sex of a kinsman in those cases where the base term leaves that ambiguous. The suffixes are:

-aphôu	Male, used only for elder kinsmen.
-aphwâ	Female, used only for elder kinsmen.
-yauⁿcâlêi	Male, used only for younger kinsmen.

-mêinkhalêi	Female, used only for younger kinsmen.
-tawûnkwê	When suffixed to terms for collateral kinsmen, this designates those who are first cousins, first cousins of parents, or first cousins' children, that is, in the first collateral line. Literally, "one womb removed" (*cf. ta*, "one").
-hnawûnkwê	Designates parent's second cousins, ego's second cousins and their children. "Two wombs removed" (*cf. hna*, "two").
-θôunwûnkwê	Designates third cousins of parents, ego's third cousins and third cousins' children, "Three wombs removed" (*cf. θoun*, "three").

These suffixes are shown in Table 5-2.

Table 5–2   Burmese Suffixes of Kinship

	Generation	*Collaterality*	*Sex*	*Degree of Collateral Removal*
-aphôu	+3, +4		male	
-aphwâ	+3, +4		female	
-yau?câlêi	−2, −3, −4, −5		male	
-mêinkhalêi	−2, −3, −4, −5		female	
-tawûnkwê	+1, 0, −1	collateral		one
-hnawûnkwê	+1, 0, −1	collateral		two
-θôunwûnkwê	+1, 0, −1	collateral		three

The bases and suffixes cannot be joined together with complete freedom, but the definitions already given, allow the restrictions on their co-occurrence to be stated with ease: *No term can be used with a modifier if a component of the definition of one is contradictory with a component of the definition of the other*. The compound that results from joining a base and a suffix can be simply defined by the sum of the components of the base, together with those of the suffix. For example:

píaphôu	Third ascending generation male; that is, great-grandfather, or his brother, or classificatory brother.
dólêihnawûnkwê	First ascending generation, female, younger than connecting parent, second collateral line; that is, younger female second cousin of one's parent.
akóutawûnkwê	Own generation, collateral, elder, male of first collateral line; that is, elder, male, first cousin.
myîmêinkhalêi	Second descending generation, female; that is, granddaughter, or other girl of the second descending generation.

Many combinations of base and suffix are impossible because of the incompatibility of their definitions. For instance, **θâmêinkhalêi* is impossible because *θâ* refers only to males, while *-mêinkhalêi* refers only to females. **θâtawûnkwê* is similarly impossible because *θâ* can refer only to a lineal kinsman, while *-tawûnkwê* is restricted to collateral kinsmen. **píyauʔcâlêi* is impossible because *pí* refers to elder kinsmen, while *-yauʔ-câlêi* refers only to younger generations. Other examples could easily be multiplied.

If the complete list of Burmese kin-terms were defined by means of these dimensions and their semantic components, it would be easy to tell which suffixes could be used with which term. But the rule by which the bases and suffixes are allowed to combine is, by usual linguistic standards, a peculiar one, for it depends upon the meaning of the items, that is upon the way in which the language refers to phenomena in the extralinguistic world. Linguists ordinarily taboo such rules completely.

It would be possible to avoid such rules and to phrase the restrictions in grammatical terms, for here, as in the examples given earlier, either grammatical or semantic rules can be constructed to account for the data. To do this grammatically, one would have to set up grammatical classes of kin-terms and of the modifying suffixes and then specify which classes of each could be combined. These grammatical classes would turn out to have very obvious semantic correlates, however, and anyone who is not in the grip of linguistic dogma is likely to feel that it is far more straightforward to admit that avoidance of semantic nonsense, rather than adherence to complex grammatical rules, prevents Burmese (and English) speakers from talking about a 'female son.'

I have given this example from Burmese in an attempt to demonstrate how knowledge of the extralinguistic world can help us to understand even the relationships among linguistic items such as bases and suffixes. Burmese speakers do not use kinship terms without knowing what they mean, and it seems arbitrary for a linguist to exclude this knowledge in his examination of the language.

Semantic and Syntactic Choices in the Deep Structure

Examples from kinship terminology may be suggestive, but they derive from an exceedingly limited segment of a language. If we are to gain any real understanding of the interrelation between the grammatical and semantic aspects of language, we will have to examine more basic linguistic phenomena. As linguists have extended their investigations further in the direction of what they have been calling the deep structure of sentences, they have approached areas in which it has seemed more and more difficult to disentangle the two. Charles Fillmore, for instance, has considered the relationship among such sentences as these:

The door opened.
John opened the door.
The key opened the door.
John opened the door with a key.
The door was opened with a key by John.

In all of these sentences, *door*, *John*, and *key* seem to have some sort of constant relation to the verb *open*, though this is not a relationship that has been made clear by conventional grammar. The three nouns alternate quite freely, for instance, in such conventional grammatical roles as subject and object. But in whatever part of the sentence they appear, it is always John who is the agent and who sets the action into motion, always the key that is the instrument by which the action is accomplished, and always the door that moves as a result of the action. To some degree these constant relationships seem to be semantic in the sense that I have used that term, for they describe constant relations that hold in the world of real doors and real keys. On the other hand, the words that stand for these objects also have interrelationships, and these can be described without resorting to the extralinguistic environment of doors and keys at all. One can, for instance, point out that one, but never more than one, of the nouns always occurs in the subject position before the verb. It is also true that the noun that stands before the verb never occurs with a preposition, but some do have prepositions when following the verb. Such generalizations seem to have little relationship to the extralinguistic environment. In the relationship between noun phrases and their verbs, therefore, we have an area of language where grammar (the relationship among linguistic items) and semantics (the relationship between linguistic and nonlinguistic entities) seem to be thoroughly intertwined. Is there any point in even trying to disentangle them?

The answer, I believe, is to return to the idea that in the description of a language certain rules can be regarded as grammatically obligatory while others are always left as grammatically optional. We must also recall that the semantically relevant choices can come only at those points in the generation of a sentence where the grammar allows freedom. To sort out the grammatical and semantic aspects of the sentences with *John*, *door*, and *key*, we would have to list a sequence of rules by which they can be generated. We would also have to note carefully which choices are the result of obligations imposed by grammar and which are optional, selected because of subject matter.

In Fillmore's formulation, for instance, one of the most basic rules expands the major part of the sentence into a verb, on the one hand, and into what Fillmore calls its cases, on the other. These cases represent the constant aspect of the relationship between the noun phrases and the verb. Thus Fillmore speaks of the three nouns in the examples as representing the objective case (*door*), the instrumental case (*key*), and the agentive case (*John*), respectively, and even though these nouns can get shuffled about in position, their case remains constant. Any of the three cases can occur as the subject of the sentence. No particular case is obligatory in English, but some sentences may have a half dozen or more cases. A sentence such as *it's raining* can be regarded as having no cases at all, if we interpret the *it* to be a dummy filler for the subject position. *John gave the book to me for Mary with the tongs in the park* can be regarded as having six cases: agentive (*John*), objective (*book*), dative (*me*), benefactive (*Mary*), instrumental (*tongs*), and locative (*park*).

One way of formulating rules that will account for these matters is to say that one of the very first options when generating a sentence is the choice of what cases to include. All are optional, but several may be used together, and they may be used in virtually any combination. If this is an open choice, then we would expect it to have the potential for carrying meaning, and, in fact, it is this choice that is reflected in the differences among the first four sentences with *key, door,* and *John.* If these four sentences differ in meaning, the difference lies in their changing combinations of cases. Since the fourth and fifth sentences have the same cases, however, any differences in meaning between these two must lie elsewhere.

If we suppose that the choice of cases is made before the choice of a particular verb, then to some extent the first choice limits the second. For example, if the agentive and objective cases have been selected (as in *John opened the door*) then such verbs as *open, close, hit, break,* and many others are available, but *come* and *sleep* are not, since **John came the door* and **John slept the door* are deviant. In other words, each English verb can occur only with certain limited combinations of cases. We can say that the choice of a particular verb is partially limited by the previous choice of cases, and this would be a grammatical characterization, since it is phrased as a limitation imposed by one aspect of a sentence upon another. However, since any constellation of cases can occur with a considerable array of verbs, some choice among verbs remains optional at this point (such as the choice between *open* and *close*), and choices of this sort are therefore capable of carrying meaning.

Such dual constraint is characteristic of any set of generative rules. At every point choices made earlier impose some restraint on later rules, but other options remain open. Another example, occurring somewhat later in the sequence of rules, is the choice of prepositions to accompany some of the nouns. Here again syntax and semantics seem to be deeply intertwined, for prepositions are used in part to demonstrate the relationship between their nouns and the verb. This is a syntactical function, but prepositions sometimes carry meaning as well.

The syntactical constraints, limiting the choice among prepositions, include at least the following: (1) Some cases have their own characteristic preposition. The dative is ordinarily indicated by *to*, as in *I gave the book to John*. The agentive, under certain conditions, is marked with *by*, as in *The door was opened by John*. The objective usually has no preposition at all. (2) Prepositions must sometimes be deleted. Whichever case is placed in the subject position before the verb always looses its preposition. Since a likely candidate for the subject position is the agentive case, its characteristic *by* is usually deleted and appears only when the agentive is placed after the verb in a passive sentence. The case immediately following the verb also usually has its preposition deleted. This accounts for the difference between *I gave John the book* and *I gave the book to John*, since the dative (*to John*) loses its preposition when it occurs immediately after the verb, while the objective (*book*) never has any preposition at all. (3) Some verbs and some nouns force the choice of particular prepositions. The verb *blame* is associated with both *for* and *on*. We can say *I blame John for the accident* or *I blame the accident on John*. The noun phrase represented by *John* requires the preposition *on*, and that represented by *accident* requires *for*, except that in accordance with the deletion rule the preposition is dropped from whichever noun phrase immediately follows the verb. Also, we ordinarily say *on Monday*, *at noon*, and *in the afternoon*, in which the particular nouns tend to govern the choice of the preposition.

I have phrased these limitations on the choice of prepositions in grammatical form, for they have been seen as limitations imposed by one feature of the sentence upon another feature. But, after all these constraints are taken into account some degree of freedom still remains, particularly in what Fillmore calls the locative case. Nothing in the sentence *I looked for the cake_____the table* limits our choice among such prepositions as *on, in, inside, next to, beside, underneath, behind*. This choice can only be made in accordance with what one wishes to say. It is limited not by other features of the sentence, but only by features of the world being described. Semantic description, perhaps by some such device as a componential analysis, would be a more suitable way of dealing with such choices than the construction of grammatical rules. In the choice of prepositions then, as in the choice of a particular verb for our sentence, both grammatical and semantic criteria converge, and the choice of preposition cannot be fully described without considering both internal and external variables.

It is easy to write a sequence of grammatical rules and imagine it to be the one actually followed by real speakers as they construct real sentences. Of course, we have little idea what the processes of natural sentence production are, and it is safer to take the rules as simply a convenient and plausible mechanism in describing sentences. Nevertheless, once we have a sequence of rules and once we sort out their obligatory and optional aspects, we can see in a striking manner just how deeply grammatical and semantic constraints interpenetrate one another. In particular it is worth emphasizing that in the sequence of rules, decisions that are optional at one level and that can therefore only be made on semantic grounds, regularly impose restrictions on later levels, and these then have to be considered as grammatically binding.

Careful scrutiny of a sequence of rules should also demonstrate that lexical choices have no unique role in semantics. Not all lexical choices carry meaning, and, reciprocally, not all meaningful choices are made at the lexical level. But to argue that semantically relevant choices are scattered over all the steps in the generation of a sentence, from the deepest syntactic rules to the selection of lexical items and even on into the phonological component, in no way implies that the analytical distinction between grammar and semantics has become muddled.

So long as we take seriously the idea that it is the extralinguistic variables that lie within the domain of semantics, and that these variables can affect language only at those points at which the grammar allows options, we have a reasonable way of distinguishing semantics from grammar. This view suggests that it is less useful to view grammar as somehow lying between semantics at one end and phonetics at the other than to regard semantics as paralleling grammar at all levels. One can then look for points at which meaning penetrates the sentence at any time in its generation all the way from its deepest level of syntax to the last stages of its surface phonology.

6 *Verbal Definitions*

Kinship Once More

At the beginning of Chapter 4 I pointed out that componential analysts tend to assume that lexical items must always be defined by direct reference to extralinguistic phenomena and that this seems to miss the obvious human ability to define some terms by means of other, previously defined terms. In daily life we often define terms verbally, but neither componential analysis nor the reduction rules of Lounsbury make use of verbal definitions. Both seek in somewhat different ways to relate terms rather directly to their referents, but, in avoiding verbal definitions, it may be that something important about our linguistic abilities is missed.

In describing English kinship terms in Chapter 3, I defined *uncle* by much the same type of operation as *father* or *mother*. The meaning of *uncle* was expressed by the intersections of several semantic components or features. In the case of *uncle*, this definition amounted to assigning the following semantic components: second degree of geneological distance, consanguineal, first ascending generation, male; *or* second degree of geneological distance, affinal, marriage bond in senior generation, first ascending generation, male. So long as we know what is meant by first ascending generation, second degree of geneological distance, and so on, this is an adequate definition. It serves to distinguish in a precise and explicit way those men known as *uncle* from all other kinsmen. But the definition is surely a complex one, and millions of English speaking people are able to talk about their *uncles* without difficulty even though they can hardly subject the term to such an analysis. One suspects that most speakers simply asked what *uncle* meant would say something like "the brother of your mother or father," and perhaps most of us first learned the term by having it explained to us in this way. This should make us ask whether we

70

might not incorporate such definitions into a semantic theory. We might first define a limited set of terms by assigning them semantic components, but then use these terms to define additional terms and in this way build up an ever more elaborate vocabulary. Surely children learn many of their words by having them explained, or at least by hearing them used in a way that allows meaning to be inferred from verbal context alone. As adults, most of the words we add to our vocabulary come in a verbal context rather than directly in association with nonverbal phenomena. Perhaps it has been the recognition of our ready ability to give verbal definitions that has led many linguists to suppose they could ignore the nonverbal context entirely.

A slightly more complex example, demonstrating the utility of verbal definitions, can be taken from Garo kinship terminology. Most Garo kinship terms can be defined by a limited number of crosscutting semantic dimensions. The most important are the following: (1) sex, (2) generation, and (3) moiety membership. Garo moieties are similar to those of the Njamal described in Chapter 2, except that Garos belong to the moiety of their mother rather than to that of their father. Thus one's mother, mother's mother, mother's brothers and sisters, and mother's sister's children all belong to one's own moiety. As among the Njamal, everyone must marry into the moiety opposite to his own, and so spouse, father, father's brothers and sisters, and many others always belong to the opposite moiety. Garos use the term *mama* for all men who are one generation older than themselves but in the same moiety. *Mama* applies most directly and specifically to one's own mother's brother, but it is readily used for all other men of the same moiety and generation—mother's mother's sister's son, father's sister's husband, and so forth. *Mama* can also be applied to wife's father, since father-in-law and son-in-law will always be in the same moiety as one another, so long as both men abide by custom and marry a woman from the other moiety. However, besides *mama*, the father-in-law can also be called by a much more specific term, *obide*. This term can be used for a number of other kinsmen besides father-in-law (all of whom can also be called *mama*) but it is not extended to all men of that generation and moiety as is *mama*. The *obides* are a subclass of the *mamas*, and *obide* means most explicitly the 'father of one's husband or wife.' In order to explain the use of *obide* for more distant relatives, further description of Garo kinship practices is needed.

It is the Garo custom for each married couple to choose just one of their daughters for a special role, distinct from the role of her sisters. This chosen daughter and her husband are expected to care for her parents in their old age, and in return they will inherit all the property of the older couple. The Garos have special terms for this chosen daughter (*nokna*) and her husband (*nokrom*). These terms differ from those used for other daughters and other sons-in-law. For the sake of simplicity, I will translate these special terms as 'heir' and 'heiress.' The chosen daughter and her husband must always belong to the same kinship groups as her mother and father respectively, and in a sense they step into the sociological role of the older couple. This is expressed terminologically by allowing some kinship terms to be inherited from the older couple along with their property.

For instance, if a man has two daughters and two sons-in-law, only one of the latter will become his 'heir.' While the older man lives, both sons-in-law will refer to him as their *obide*. Once the older man dies, however, the son-in-law who is *not* the 'heir' will refer to the other son-in-law (the 'heir') as *obide*. In effect, the 'heir' will have inherited the term and the status of *obide* from his father-in-law. The term can be inherited a second time or even more often so that if the nonheir son-in-law should survive the 'heir', the survivor will still be able to use the term *obide* for the 'heir' of his own father-in-law's 'heir.' It would seem difficult to set off the men to whom the term *obide* can refer by simple semantic dimensions analogous to 'generation' or 'sex,' but there is no problem in defining the extended use of the term by means of previously defined words: *The 'heir' (nokrom) of a deceased obide is called obide.*

There is an additional complication. Not only is one's own father-in-law called *obide*, but *his* father-in-law is also *obide*. In other words one's wife's father, one's wife's mother's father, and for that matter one's wife's mother's mother's father (and so forth) are equally entitled to the term. Of course most of these gentlemen can be expected to have died, but since the term is inheritable each of them may have a living 'heir' (or 'heir's heir') and so it is entirely possible for a man to use the term *obide* correctly for several different living men, the various 'heirs' of the men who, like himself, have married into the line of women extending backwards from his wife. It would seem hopelessly complex to try to define this set of *obides* by relating them to directly observable nonlinguistic criteria. But once certain basic terms are understood, such as the Garo terms for 'wife,' 'father,' 'heir,' and the relationship of possession (which in English we symbolize as " 's"), it is not difficult to define *obide* as meaning first of all one's wife's father, second the *obide* of any *obide* (which extends the term backward through the generations), and third, the 'heir' of any deceased *obide* (which brings the term back down again to living men).

The logic by which a term used for a close kin-type is extended to cover more distant kin-types is clearly very much like the logic of Lounsbury's rules for Crow and Omaha terminology in which distant kin-types were reduced to closer ones. Both rules relate varied kin-types to each other, though they do so from opposite directions. Here I mean, however, to suggest a more purely verbal formulation in which terms themselves are used in definitions. Lounsbury's rules operate entirely on kin-types and make no use of the words of a language. By starting with close kin-types, those at the focus of a term's meaning, we can exploit the definitions given first by using them at later stages of our analysis.

These examples suggest that definitions by direct reference can be supplemented by verbal definitions, either in defining entirely new words or in extending the meaning of old words. This possibility has barely been raised by anthropologists who have worked with componential and formal semantic analysis, but a few linguists (who are usually more interested in the relationship among words than in their reference) have struggled with the problem of verbal definitions. These studies have grown out of more general grammatical and semantic considerations, in particular out of an interest in the way lexical meanings are combined to form the meaning of phrases or of entire sentences. I will consider some of the problems of such combinatorial semantics and will then return to the question of verbal definitions.

Combinatorial Semantics

The discussion of case grammar in Chapter 5 was an attempt to show how the semantic (optional) and grammatical (obligatory) choices can be seen as interwoven in the generation of a sentence. This viewpoint takes what can in a loose sense be seen as a speaker-oriented position, for it asks how semantic choices affect the formation of a sentence. A listener has a somewhat different task. He must take the sentence as he hears it, all constructed and already formed, and he must then disentangle both its meaning and grammar. Not only must he understand the meanings of the individual words, but he must interpret the way in which the grammatical constructions permit these individual meanings to converge to form the meaning of the whole sentence. Typically, of course, words are not used in isolation, but are combined into sentences. It is sentences that we hear and that we must interpret, not simply individual lexical items. Any reasonably complete semantic theory ought to show how the meanings of these lexical items can be productively built up into longer expressions.

The simplest way for meanings to be joined is by a simple sort of addition. If we have somehow defined the meanings of *blue* and of *house* then the meaning of *blue house* can be reasonably looked upon as simply the sum of the meanings of its parts—the phrase refers to whatever is both blue and a house. Similarly, *the man walks* seems to refer to whatever is both *the man* and *walks*. If individual terms having mutually incompatible meanings are joined together we find these resulting phrases to be anomalous. *Male daughter* is anomalous because part of the meaning of *daughter* is that it does not refer to males, so an anomaly results when *male* is used with it. Similarly the phrase *pretty boy* is at least a mild anomaly because *pretty* ordinarily implies femaleness (or at least nonmaleness), while *boy* certainly has *male* as one of its semantic components.

We use the incompatibility between the meanings of individual parts of constructions as a means for choosing an interpretation of what might otherwise be an ambiguous phrase or sentence. For instance, when used alone *story* and *dull* are both ambiguous. *Story* can mean either a narrative of some sort, usually fictional, or one level of a building. *Dull* can mean either 'blunt' or 'tedious.' *Dull story* would ordinarily be interpreted only as 'tedious narrative,' because the other possible meanings of the individual parts are mutually incompatible.

Not all constructions allow such an easy derivation of meaning from their parts. Clearly sentences such as *cats chase mice* and *mice chase cats* do not mean the same thing, nor does *three cats chased a mouse* mean the same thing as *a cat chased three mice*. Since the parts of these sentences are identical, the meaning of a sentence is certainly more than a simple summation of the meanings of its parts. More precisely, the manner in which meanings are combined is dependent upon the grammatical nature of the construction, and it may be that several different ways of combining meanings will have to be recognized.

Uriel Weinreich has recognized several kinds of constructions with different semantic implications. He uses the term "linking" for the simple additive constructions, which result in the meanings of phrases such as *blue house*. He uses the term "nesting" for a more complex type of construction in which the meanings of the individual parts retain an ordered relationship instead of being merged into an unordered heap. The meaning of *fix teeth*, for instance, is hardly reducible to a simple addition of the meanings of *fix* and *teeth*, in the way that the meaning of *white teeth* or even *fixed teeth* (in the sense of 'teeth which have been fixed') might be reducible.

Distinct from such nesting constructions are those that somehow limit the class of referents of a sign. In these constructions the general meaning of a word such as *sheep* is reduced to a restricted sense—*these sheep, some sheep, five sheep, one sheep*, or even *all sheep*. Some of these "delimiters" quantify the general notion of *sheep*, either numerically (*five*) or non-numerically (*some*); others delimit the range of application with reference to the discourse in which they are mentioned or the range of focus of attention at the time of the utterance (*the, these*). These delimiting constructions seem to differ from the linking constructions of adjectives (as in *white house*), since no meaning can be attached to **the house is five*, or *house is the, while we can easily say *the house is white*. In a great many languages the devices for delimitation (quantifiers, determiners) have unique syntactic roles. Reference to time by such means as tenses and adverbs and indication of quantity by adverbs (*a lot, very, completely*, and so on) seem more closely related to delimitation than to the simpler kinds of linking or nesting constructions.

Still another type of construction is recognized by Weinreich, one used to indicate that some statement should not be taken literally, or to disclaim certainty, or to show that the contrary of a statement is true. Words like *perhaps, certainly, so-called, like*, and *resemble*, belong to a variety of syntactic classes but are all somehow involved in the assessment of the truth, falsity, or likelihood of some statement. To this extent they fill a different role from the simpler linking constructions of many adjectives with their modified nouns.

Weinreich also suggests that any full account of the way in which meanings of individual items are joined together in larger constructions must allow for the possibility that semantic features from one constituent of the construction are transferred to another constituent. If one of the semantic features of the verb *sail* is that it is used only for water vehicles, and if *craft* is ambiguous as to whether it is a water vehicle or not, then the feature of "water vehicle" can be said to be transferred to *craft* in the expression *sail a craft*.

The various kinds of constructions proposed by Weinreich and mentioned here, would need a far lengthier discussion to justify them fully. But perhaps the main point will be granted—a great deal of complex structure must be admitted into any description of how meanings of individual terms are combined into the meanings of entire constructions. It is far too simple to imagine that meanings are simply merged as an unordered heap of semantic features or components. Once this is recognized, it must also be conceded that to give an accurate verbal definition even of a single term, we must allow for every type of semantic construction available to an entire sentence. The word *dentist* means roughly 'one who fixes teeth,' and if to define 'fix teeth' requires us to recognize a nesting construction, then so does the word *dentist*. The term *chair* cannot be taken simply as the unordered sum of features such as "sit" and "furniture," but must be recognized to express a particular relation between the action of sitting and the piece of furniture. This can be clearly seen if we compare the word *chair* to a word such as *parent*. The meaning of *parent* can be regarded as consisting of a simple and unordered linking of the semantic features, first ascending generation and lineal. This allows us, when modifying the term *parent* with the adjective *male*, to understand the semantic feature of male linked as easily to lineal as to first ascending generation. A "male, lineal" or a "male of the first ascending generation" are both reasonable, and all three components can be linked together, without ordering, to produce the meaning of *father*. On the other hand, if the semantic features of *chair* are something like "sit" and "furniture," and we wish to add the meaning of "black" to these, we cannot freely choose either individual feature of *chair* to add it to. "Black furniture" makes sense, but there is no plausible way in which "black" can be combined directly to the feature "sit." The conclusion must be that the features of *chair* are not joined in the same simple unordered manner as the features of *parent*.

As a matter of fact the syntactic form that we give to verbal definitions differs in no way from the syntactic form of other sentences. This can be seen in the following pairs of examples all of which were given by Weinreich.

> A chair is a piece of furniture for one person to sit on.
> A concert is an event for music lovers to enjoy.
>
> To munch is to chew with a crunching sound.
> To vote is to perform a civic duty.
>
> A plumber installs and repairs pipes.
> A prophet exhorts and castigates his people.

There seems no way in which definitions like the first of each of these pairs can be distinguished syntactically from statements of fact like the second members of the pairs. If the first sentence is a definition of the word *chair* and if its meaning is a complex construction formed from the meanings of all the individual constituents of that sentence, then *chair* alone would seem to require the same complexity for its definitions. Verbal definitions must be allowed an essentially sentential form, and it is this fact that allows us to add new words to our language with such ease. We can easily define a new word by means of a sentence and then carry on with the new word in lieu of the entire sentence. Sentences, of course, can be generated productively and it seems that whenever we begin to use one phrase or sentence repeatedly we can, in a sense, generate the meaning of that sentence into a word, carrying within itself the entire meaning of a syntactically far more complex expression.

The syntactic identity of definitions and nondefinitional sentences allows us to talk about a language in the same language, or, as it is sometimes phrased, to use a language as its own "metalanguage." We easily slip back and forth between using a language to describe itself and using it to describe other things, and the confusion that this occasionally entails is one of the things that makes the study of language and of its referents so difficult.

Componential and formal analysis of meaning has been most successful in lexical domains in which the items can be largely defined by simple linking constructions. Kinship terms can generally be defined by means of an unordered set of semantic features or components. Occasionally a description may be simplified by allowing some terms to be defined by means of other previously defined terms, but for many kinship systems it seems possible to avoid these complex definitions. The same may be true of most pronoun systems, of color terminology, and possibly of a few other semantic domains, but the majority of our vocabulary would seem to require some provisions for a far more complex type of definition than the simple unordered linking of features, which is the only mechanism really allowed by simple componential analysis. Weinreich's demonstration of the great syntactic complexity that may be required to define a single term is an essential corrective to the simplistic and unordered heaping up of features to which componential analysis has usually been limited.

Weinreich takes an extreme position in one respect, however, and it may be that in the interest of demonstrating the complex interrelationships between semantics and syntax, he has gone even further than necessary in his insistence upon the need to give a sentential form to all definitions. Like many other linguists, Weinreich is determined to keep reference and denotation out of his theory, and he says nothing about how terms or constructions might be shown to reflect phenomena in the world. He goes so far as to claim that, in the independence of semantics from reference, natural languages differ from the artificial language of logic. Logicians distinguish between syntax, which covers the relations among the symbols of their logistic language, and semantics which refers to the relation between the symbols and certain entities outside the symbolic system. Weinreich grants that this distinction is workable within a logical language, but he says ". . . in natural language, semantic relations, too, are relations between symbols." He argues that all of the terms of definitions must be elements of the language itself and not of some metalanguage that is outside the system. He says that "the logistic dichotomy is inapplicable to natural languages."[1]

At the same time, Weinreich is forced to admit some irreducible circularities into his definitions. If all words are to be defined by constructions made from other words, then sooner or later one will reach a point where two or more words can only be defined by means of each other. If one is willing to regard semantics as involving only the relationship among symbols, there is no way to escape this circularity. Furthermore, the difference between semantics and syntax continues to be an elusive one, for semantics like syntax involves only the relationship among symbols, and in Weinreich's system they interpenetrate so extensively that it is quite impossible to imagine any sense in which semantics can be said to begin

---

[1]Uriel Weinreich, "Explorations in Semantic Theory," in Thomas Sebeok, ed., *Current Trends in Linguistics*, Vol. III, *Theoretical Approaches* (The Hague: Mouton, 1966), pp. 468–469.

"where syntax leaves off." The question still remains open: exactly which relationships among symbols are to be handled as part of semantics and which as part of syntax?

Referential and Verbal Definitions

I have argued that we can describe many linguistic phenomena in two ways. We can either include the relationship of symbols to phenomena outside of language, or we can limit ourselves to the relationship among the linguistic units. But while entirely willing to grant the interest and importance of many analyses that exclude the nonlinguistic setting of language, we should, I believe, remain uneasy about the desire, which linguists like Weinreich seem to have shown, to exclude the setting *in principle* from all linguistic considerations. Surely language is used to refer to things, and surely we must sooner or later come to the point of investigating the relationship of language to these things. If this is an interesting or worthwhile subject, it seems unnecessary to go to such lengths to stay within the confines of language. Weinreich's work brilliantly demonstrates how large a part verbal definitions do play in our ordinary language and how large a part they might play in more formal linguistic analysis. Many words, perhaps most, can most easily or only be defined by means of other words. But this need not imply that every single word in a language has to be or even can be defined by other words. In fact, if one will admit that *left* and *right* are different in meaning and if one will grant that part of the task of a semantic analysis is to investigate and describe this difference, it can be demonstrated that at least some portion of our vocabulary can *only* be defined by an appeal to nonlinguistic evidence.

Imagine that we have established radio communication with a distant planet so enshrouded in clouds that we can see nothing in common with its inhabitants. Somehow we have learned most of their language, but a few crucial terms elude us, among them their words for *left* and *right*. We know that they have words for both *left* and *right*, but we do not know which is which. It does us no good to have *right* described as the hand with which the majority of them write, because, even if we knew their bodies were constructed like ours, we could not know without looking at them whether the majority were right-handed or left-handed. They cannot describe astronomical phenomena since we can see nothing in common, but even if they were on the earth, to understand *left* as being the direction of the sunrise when one faces the sun at midday would make the unwarranted assumption that the people were living in the northern hemisphere. They cannot describe some spacially asymmetrical rule of physics, such as the left-hand rule for magnetism and current flow, because unless we already have a definition of *left* and *right*, we cannot know whether they have defined *north* and *south* magnetism as we have or the other way round. They cannot transmit television pictures to demonstrate which is *right* or *left*, because we cannot know whether our receiving sets are constructed like theirs or in mirror image. Only by referring to the atomic asymmetrics revealed by the absence of physical parity could one successfully define *left* and *right*, and even this would not work unless we could be certain that their world was not constructed of antimatter. One is forced to conclude that *left* and *right* cannot possibly be defined except by appealing to a context outside of language. Surely that is the way children learn these terms. We point to their left eye or their right hand and we tell them in which direction they are turning.

If *left* and *right* must be learned within a nonlinguistic context, one loses nothing by admitting that the same is probably true of many other terms. Even the meanings of the logical operators of a natural language are probably first learned through their total context and not just within their linguistic context. A child hears *no* repeated many times until the difference between the use of *no* and its absence can finally be abstracted from the settings in which it has occurred. The difference between *eat your meat and your potatoes* and *eat your meat or your potatoes* is correlated closely with the behavior of a child's parents, but it is hardly predictable from the surrounding linguistic context. Anyone who has struggled to make a child understand the elusive meaning of *tomorrow* or to disentangle the shifting meaning of pronouns when used by various speakers, can hardly doubt that all these meanings are more or less laboriously abstracted from the contrasting aspects of the nonlinguistic environments in which they are used.

To insist that the meaning of some terms must necessarily be learned in the context of the extralinguistic environment does not mean that *all* terms are learned this way. We all know that children go through a stage when they constantly ask the meaning of words, and verbal definitions are probably essential for certain aspects of language learning. Most children probably have little direct experience with God, but they learn what *God* means and they can learn the meaning of *London* and *Paris* without ever visiting those cities. The more abstract nouns and many verbs and adjectives are surely learned by verbal explanation. Eventually children even learn to use dictionaries, and, as we grow older, an increasing proportion of our new words are probably learned in a linguistic context, but we have to begin with the extralinguistic setting.

The work of anthropologists and linguists, then, should be complementary. Linguists have usually been reluctant to incorporate nonlinguistic criteria into their rules. Instead they have busied themselves almost exclusively with rules whose only variables were linguistic ones. However justified on practical grounds this limitation may have been, it has meant that serious attention to reference has been left to others, and linguists have failed to grapple with one important aspect of language. Anthropologists who have worked in formal semantics have shown little of the linguist's fear of reference but, I believe, they have also missed something important about meaning by going too far to the opposite extreme and insisting upon too direct a relationship between the terms they investigate and their referents. I suggested at the beginning of Chapter 4 that this too exclusive anthropolgical concern with reference risks overlooking our ready ability to define some words by means of other words. If most linguists have ignored nonlinguistic factors in their investigation of language, most anthropologists have ignored the possibility of defining some words by other words rather than by relating them directly to the world of sensory experience.

The conclusion seems clear: any theory of meaning must provide for two essentially different ways by which we can learn and define the meaning of words. *Mother* must almost always be learned in context, while *second cousin once removed* could probably never be learned without some degree of verbal explanation. *Water* is learned in context, *hydrogen dioxide*, with an explanation, and so on. Does the fact that we learn terms like *second cousin once removed* or *hydrogen dioxide* with the help of other words mean that they lack relationship to the extralinguistic environment that is characteristic of those terms that we first learn by contact with the world? I think not. Having learned the extralinguistic contexts of *mother*, another set of extralinguistic contexts for *brother*, and still a third set for possession as shown by *'s*, one may then learn part of the meaning of *uncle* by being told that it includes the *mother's brother*. But if the meanings of *mother, brother*, and *'s* lie in their relationship with the nonlinguistic environment, then these meanings hardly lose their extralinguistic relationship when combined as the meaning of *uncle*. *Uncle* can be defined as *mother's brother* but these words still give *uncle* an extralinguistic referent. Both logically and ontogenetically, associations between terms and observable phenomena must come first. Once some minimum set of terms and operations have been learned, however, we are able to use these terms to define a vocabulary of larger and larger proportions, and, to construct such definitions, we have at our disposal the entire grammatical resources of our language. Indeed to generate new sentences requires much the same sort of process as to generate new meanings of terms. The one proceeds with hardly more difficulty than the other. Whether or not it would be possible in principle to define all terms by their relationship to nonlinguistic phenomena (the example of *left* and *right* shows that the exclusive use of verbal definitions is not possible), the task would be hopelessly complex in practice. What proportion of words in our language could best be given referential definitions and what proportion best be defined by means of other terms is a question that is open to empirical investigation. But, however indirectly, even words that are defined at several stages removed from any direct relation to the nonlinguistic environment can be said to rest ultimately upon reference. This dependence upon reference gives a reasonable and secure basis for drawing a distinction between syntax and semantics. All of semantics can be seen as ultimately based upon relations between language and other things. Syntax deals only with those relations between linguistic signs that do not involve reference outside of language. This is the same distinction that logicians make between syntax and semantics, and it is the distinction with which I began this discussion of meaning in Chapter 1.

7 *The Social Situation*

Lexical Choices

In the earlier chapters, I asked how we choose words and constructions so as to convey information about subject matter. It is now time to turn to other factors that influence our choices, for reference is by no means the only influence upon language. Beyond reference, we also choose our words so as to express something about the situation of the conversation itself: the mood of the speaker, the relative social positions of the speaker and the man to whom he speaks, the formality of the occasion. We have many words that are referential synonyms, words that refer to much the same phenomena, and the choice among such synonyms cannot depend upon their reference but must depend, instead, upon such factors as their social connotations. From the viewpoint of reference, *pop*, *dad*, and *father* can all be regarded as synonyms, but they express quite different attitudes on the part of the speaker or perhaps differences in the formality of the conversation. From this point of view, they can hardly be regarded as synonyms.

A striking example in which speakers have a wide choice among alternatively elegant or plain styles is found in Javanese and has been well described by Clifford Geertz. It should first be said that Javanese society has rather sharp social divisions, and, at least in the region from which Geertz drew his example, three distinct social groups can be distinguished. At the bottom are the farmers, who form the majority of the population, live in the villages, do most of the hard manual work of the society, and grow the food that all three groups eat. At the top are the aristocrats, heirs and descendants of the ancient Javanese nobility. Before the Dutch conquered Java, the ancestors of these aristocrats had formed the social and political elite, and, even under the Dutch, some continued to hold responsible positions as civil servants. Today the aristocrats still try to maintain a gracious and cultured way of life, but it is a style, however admired, that is quite beyond the reach of most ordinary villagers.

Between the peasant and aristocratic extremes are townsmen—men and their families who engage in business or in petty manufacturing. The townsmen occupy an intermediate economic and social nitch, clearly higher than villagers but lower than the aristocracy. They also differ from both in their more vigorous devotion to Islamic practices. Peasants, townsmen, and the aristocrats each have their own work and their own main interests, but they must all deal with one another too. All three groups speak Javanese, and all can easily understand each other, but they also regularly indicate their own social affiliation by the particular details of their language.

Any one who speaks Javanese must first choose among three levels. These levels are called stylemes by Geertz. Stylemes are distinguished by a large number of contrasting items of vocabulary. For instance, the word 'now' can be translated by *saiki*, the lowest and roughest of the three alternatives—by *saniki*, a little fancier—or by *samenika*, the most elegant choice. Javanese has many such triads, so many that one cannot speak for long without having a choice forced upon him, and he must then decide how plain or how elegant he wishes to be. Once having made a choice among these three levels, a speaker, for a while at least, is fairly consistent. If he chooses to be elegant and use *samenika*, he will make the same elegant choice when he comes to other triads. It is quite impossible for a Javanese to speak without choosing one of these three basic levels.

There is a complication. Javanese has a number of special terms, chosen in partial independence from the more basic choice among the triads. Most of these refer to people, to body parts, to possessions, or to human actions. Geetz calls this group of terms honorifics, and by using them a speaker can raise his speech to some extent, without boosting it a whole level. The honorifics, however, are generally added only to the lowest and highest of the three basic stylemes and not to the intermediate one. To complicate matters even more, not even the top and bottom levels are treated identically. One group of words (we can call them low honorifics) can be added only to the bottom level. Another group (high honorifics) are most characteristically added to the top level but can occasionally be added to the bottom level, instead. All together, then, Javanese must choose among at least six styles: the unadorned lowest level (1); the lowest level with low honorifics (1*a*); the lowest level with high honorifics (1*b*); the middle level (2); the top level (3); and most elegantly of all, the top level with high honorifics (3*a*). An example, taken from Geertz, is displayed in Table 7-1, and it shows how a single sentence can vary from level to level. The words that translate 'are,' 'going,' and 'now', in this example, are triads, and the choice among these indicates the basic level on which one wishes to speak. To translate 'rice,' one has only two alternatives, but this can be looked upon as an incomplete triad, in which the same form happens to be used on both the second and third levels. 'And,' on the other hand, is translated by the same form on the first and second levels, but has a special elegant form on the highest level. Honorifics can be used to translate the words for 'you' and for 'eat.' The level 1 word for 'you' is *kowé*, but, by using the low honorific *sampéjan*, one can boost a basically level 1 discourse to a slightly more elevated style. It happens that '*sampéjan*, is also the basic form for levels 2 and 3, but when used without other level 2 or 3 words as in level 1*a*, it functions as an honorific. There is also a high honorific form for you—*pandjenengan*—and this can be used either on level 1 or 3. The alternatives for 'eat' are the same as those for 'you.' Only one word in this sentence—*kaspé*, 'casava'—is unchanged throughout.

Not all Javanese sentences are quite so unstable, but this one dramatically illustrates the possibilities with which a speaker must cope. On any particular occasion, he must decide which forms to use and his choice inevitably conveys information about his attitudes. The lowest level (called *ngoko*, the levels being distinct enough to have explicit names) is the ordinary rudimentary form of speech. It is the language that children learn first, whatever the social class of their family, no doubt because that is the form adults generally use in addressing them. *Ngoko* is considered rough and down to earth, and although it may be most appropriate for the peasants, everybody uses it on some occasions. It is really the basic language upon which the fancier forms of the higher levels can be added as flourishes. People use *ngoko* when they are not worrying about courtesy. Two close friends (who always belong to the same social class) may use it with each other, but a man of high rank also uses this basic speech when addressing someone who is clearly his social inferior. A high government official, for instance, might use this level when speaking to most townsmen, and he would certainly use it when addressing peasants. In fact, anyone of a higher rank customarily uses this plain speech when talking to a peasant.

Low honorifics are added to this basic language by villagers or sometimes by lower ranking townsmen, when they speak to others of their own rank with whom they are not particularly intimate. The use of these honorifics is a courtesy, which indicates some degree of social distance, though not much status inequality. High honorifics, when added to the basic *ngoko* level, tend to be a specialty of the aristocrats. This form is also used between people of equal status, most often between aristocrats who are fairly well acquainted, but who feel themselves to be too elevated to use either plain *ngoko* or *ngoko* with merely low honorifics. High honorifics, when added to the lowest of the three main levels, achieve something of a compromise between the need to show both respect and familiarity at the same time.

The second main level is used symmetrically between ordinary townsmen who are not close friends, and occasionally by similarly nonintimate

Table 7–1 Level Differences in a Javanese Sentence

	Are	*you*	*going*	*to eat*	*rice*	*and*	*casava*	*now?*
3a	menapa	spandjenengan	baḍe	ḍahar	sekul	kalijan	kaspé	samenika
3	menapa	sampéjan	baḍe	neḍa	sekul	kalijan	kaspé	samenika
2	napa	sampéjan	adjeng	neḍa	sekul	lan	kaspé	saniki
1b	apa	pandjenengan	arep	ḍahar	sega	lan	kaspé	saiki
1a	apa	sampéjan	arep	neḍa	sega	lan	kaspé	saiki
1	apa	kowé	arep	mangan	sega	lan	kaspé	saiki

peasants. It is also used by peasants when addressing their social superiors, for this is usually the most elevated form of speech the peasants master. Villagers have little opportunity to hear or to learn the more elegant forms of the third level, and so when speaking to people in higher classes or when showing great courtesy to other villagers, they cannot expect to pass level 2.

Level 3 is used primarily between aristocrats who are not well acquainted, but any time that either an aristocrat or an educated townsman wishes to be really elegant, he will add high honorifics to level 3. Townsmen may speak in this way to a high government official, and particularly elevated aristocrats may use these forms when speaking to each other. These higher levels generally have longer words and sound more elaborate than the lower levels, and they should be spoken with a formality that demonstrates the grace and breeding of the speaker. When speaking at a high level one should speak more slowly, more softly, and with even rhythm and pitch. Taken together, these traits serve to give the language "a kind of stately pomp which can make the simplest conversation seem like a great ceremony."[1]

When set out in such a fashion, rules like these sound wooden and mechanical, as though one merely needed to know certain simple facts about the status of the speaker and hearer in order to predict confidently what forms would be used. The situation is really more complex and fluid. For one thing, the setting of the particular conversation may influence a speaker's choice. The same two men speaking about the same topic would be likely to use more elevated forms when attending a wedding, for instance, than if they had met casually on the street. People are also more likely to use more elevated forms when speaking of an elevated subject like religion than, for instance, when speaking of ordinary commercial affairs. Finally, many individual traits may be reflected in a person's use of language. His sex, age, education, occupation, wealth, family background, and his own idiosyncratic attitudes all make a difference. Some people are formal and rather ceremonial in their personal behavior, and they are likely to use relatively elevated forms. Others tend to look at more elaborate forms as just a bit silly, and they are likely to prefer somewhat lower and simpler forms.

Even within the family, one is expected to use different levels of respect with different kinsmen. Children learn the lowest level first, and it always seems the easiest and most relaxed form. The more elevated levels always involve a bit of a strain. When children first begin to speak, they are allowed to use the familiar style with their parents and even their grandparents, but before long they are expected to assume a more respectful style, even when addressing their own parents. This inevitably introduces a strain into the relationship between parent and child, or perhaps it is fairer to say

[1]Clifford Geertz, *The Religion of Java*, (New York: The Free Press 1960) p. 254.

that this becomes one aspect of a relationship that can be strained. Children are sometimes permitted to delay using respectful forms with their grandparents until somewhat later, an example of the uniquely intimate relationship that grandparents in many parts of the world so often have with their grandchildren. But an adult whose grandparents still live is likely to shift to more respectful forms when speaking with them. With more distant relatives, respectful forms are certain to be used, and the rules are, in some ways, quite rigid. No two kinsmen in Java ever have exactly equal status so it is never easy for two kinsmen to address each other symmetrically with the lowest and most basic form of speech in the way that two close friends can do. Aristocrats, for instance, are expected to address members of their parents' generation by forms of level 3, though not generally with honorifics. These are reserved for those in one's grandparent's generation. Most of those in one's parent's generation are comfortably older than one's self, but even if an uncle or a parent's cousin should be younger than his nephew or cousin's child, this is not felt to be sufficient reason to deny him the respectful forms of speech.

The strain of speaking the more elevated levels is particularly acute in certain modern situations for which cultural traditions provide no clear patterns. Students, when living away from home, sometimes find it almost impossible to write letters to their parents for fear of making glaring errors in the elaborate linguistic forms that they must use. Spoken language is ephemeral and even if a mistake is momentarily embarrassing it may soon be forgotten, but when a boy commits himself to paper, he may feel that his mistakes become a permanent record. The only solution may be not to write home at all unless he can write in the familiar style to a younger brother or sister, who will then be able to relay the message orally to their parents.

Similarly, modern politics brings events in which it seems impossible to make a happy choice among the styles. When a political party holds a meeting, a speaker faces a difficult decision. He is surely at a formal gathering, and this seems to call for elevated terms. Moreover, he may be soliciting support from those he is addressing, and he may wish to honor them with respect. On the other hand, he is likely to be a high official and his constituents are obviously lower than he on the social scale. This would seem to call for a less elegant form of speech. The traditional rules simply have no provision for such a situation, and the only solution has sometimes been to use the national language—Indonesian—which lacks the complex choice among styles that characterizes Javanese. Indonesian, however, is a foreign language to most Javanese, so it is hardly an ideal medium. Moreover, the introduction of Indonesian does not really liberate the people from their dilemma. Instead of allowing them to use a language with no situational connotations, Indonesian comes simply to offer an additional choice, a new style, which becomes appropriate for certain new occasions. In some respects this new style is perhaps even more difficult to learn than the most elevated form previously available, but any Javanese who wishes to participate in politics may have to add Indonesian to his arsenal of linguistic skills.

Address Forms

An American, on first hearing of the Javanese alternatives, is likely to conclude that the language is not only absurdly complicated but tragically undemocratic. Even the relatively simple choice among the familiar *tu* and more formal *vous* of French or the similar pronoun choices in German or Spanish often make an English speaker acutely uncomfortable. He wonders how he should decide whether he knows a person well enough to use *tu* or whether only *vous* will do. Yet in their choice among first names, last names, various titles, Americans make distinctions that are similar to those shown by second person pronouns in the European languages, and, to some extent, they express sociological relationships rather like those expressed by the Javanese speech levels.

As Roger Brown and Marguerite Ford have shown, Americans have two main patterns with which they address one another, title together with the last name (*Mr. Brown, Miss Smith, Dr. Green, Professor White*, and so on) or the first name alone. A nickname, even when based upon a man's last name, unquestionably acts as the equivalent of a first name, certainly not as a substitute for the title plus last name. Whenever we wish to address somebody by name we must make a choice between using his first name or some title together with his last name. The criteria by which we make this choice are in some ways rather like those the Javanese use in deciding among the levels of their language. The choice depends upon the kind of relationship that the speaker and hearer have with one another and how long and in what connection they have known each other. The two modes of address allow three possible patterns: both speakers may use the other's first name; both may use title plus last name; or, finally, one can use the other's first name, but be addressed in turn by his title and last name. All three patterns are widely used, and, of course, the principles by which we choose among them are well known to all fluent speakers of American English, though we may have difficulty describing them explicitly.

The most common pattern, of course, is for two people mutually to use first names. Americans are even a bit proud of the speed with which they get on "a first name basis," though this does not really mean that Americans are friendlier than people of other nations but only that they use first names in situations where many Europeans would continue to use a more formal address. Where a first name seems called for but where it is not known,

Americans may even substitute a sort of generic first name: *Mack, Jack, Buddy*.

Title and the last name are generally used symmetrically between newly introduced adults, but only a small increment of intimacy need develop before first names are substituted. One could well argue that the very ease with which first names are substituted makes it difficult for Americans to demonstrate real warmth and growing friendship, since they have so often vulgarized the use of first names by using them with casual acquaintances. Younger people probably move to first names more rapidly than older people, and those of the same sex more rapidly than those of the opposite. A common occupation or nationality, or any common experience at all, encourages the rapid use of first names.

The nonreciprocal pattern is used only when people differ rather markedly in either age or occupational status. Children are often expected to address adults as *Mr.* or *Mrs. so and so*, though they themselves are always addressed by first names. As adults, we may continue to use the title and last name for people who are fifteen years or so older than ourselves, even if they call us by our first name. Asymmetrical address may also occur between master and servant, employer and employee, officer and enlisted man, or professor and student. Even after the two people come to know each other well enough to allow the person of superior rank to use the other's first name, the difference in status can still make it difficult or impossible for the junior-ranking person to reciprocate.

Age alone or occupation alone can be enough to force an asymmetrical address pattern, but when the two criteria are in conflict, the occupational criteria seem to predominate. In the rare home that still has a servant, an adolescent girl might call the family's middle-aged cook by her first name but be addressed in turn by a title. The young navy ensign may address the middle-aged enlisted man by his first name, but he can expect a title in return and so can the young executive, who speaks to an elderly janitor. But the nonreciprocal pattern is most common when age and occupational status both point the same way.

Although first name and title plus last name are by far our most common address patterns, a few others are also occasionally used. Sometimes, for instance, we use a title without any name at all: *Sir, madam, ma'am, Miss, Dr., Captain*, and so on. The title alone probably shows even more deference and less intimacy than the title joined with the last name. A near superior might be called *Lieutenant Smith*, but a more remote superior could rate the title *Colonel* by itself. Occasionally, we also use the last name without any title at all, though today this often has a rather old-fashioned connotation. To use the last name alone seems a bit more intimate than title plus last name but not quite so intimate as the first name. Army officers may address the enlisted men by last name alone but receive in turn their title plus last name. Enlisted men often seem to use last names alone for one another, and this usage is not uncommon among high school boys, but to continue using last names for a long period seems to imply some degree of mutual antagonism, a holding off of intimacy. The closest friends among enlisted men or high school boys are likely to use first names.

For our very closest friends, we have still another possibility, that of switching among several alternative names and nicknames for the same person. For very good friends, we may alternate between a nickname, a full first name, and other playful designations. For some kinsmen we have the possibility of using kinship terms, and even the choice among a considerable array of alternate terms, (*mother, mom, mama,* and so on). At the most intimate extreme for our husbands and wives, we have a truly formidable array of alternatives, not only among those forms based upon their name but among what have been aptly labeled the saccharine terms (*honey, sugar, sweety*) and the animal terms (*kitten, lamb*).

At the formal extreme, then, we may call a person by a generalized title such as *Miss* or *Sir* or *Dr.* and so identify him only by a very broad category, one which does not even distinguish him clearly from the many other people who rate the same title. At the opposite extreme, for those with whom we are most intimate, we can use several alternatives names, and in a sense we are not only able to set them off from all other people but give names to their various facets. The alternative names would seem to indicate the variety and complexity of our relationship with these people. If Arabs need many words for camels, because camels are important to them, and if Eskimos need many words for different types of snow, so we too need many alternative words for our closest personal relationships.

The distinctions we make, by using these various forms of address and in particular our most pervasive distinction between first name and title with last name, express two quite different features of our social relationship. On the one hand, we choose a form to express something about the degree of personal intimacy we feel with the other person; on the other hand, we use terms to show something about our relative status. We are so firmly habituated to using the same form (title with last name) both to grant higher status and to express social distance that we find it hard to imagine the opposite situation might in principle be possible. Yet with some effort, we *can* imagine a culture in which addressing a superior demanded intimate forms and addressing an inferior required a formal term. Empirically, however, English forms are simply not used that way, and it turns out that speakers of other languages also associate formality with the recognition of superiority. Like Americans, the Javanese use their more intimate speech levels when addressing people of lower status, while their more elevated forms are used not only for those of high status but also for equals with whom one is not intimate. The same is true in French for the choice between *vous* and *tu* and in German for the choice between *sie* and *du*. Even in English we make other linguistic distinctions that express the same association between formality and social distance. In the choice between *hi* and *good morning*, for instance, *hi* is the more intimate form, and *good morning* can be used either to show social distance or to show respect. Thus the boss may say *hi* in the morning, but his employees may return his greeting with a respectful *good morning*.

As friendships develop, people can express their changing relationship by using new forms of address. Most often the change is in the direction of increasing intimacy. Since the superior or older person in a relationship can sometimes use a more intimate term than he gets in return, the superior person always seems to be expected to make the first move in the direction of increasing intimacy. If two people have been addressing each other symmetrically by their titles and last names, it is practically obligatory for the superior to be the first to shift to the first name. It may require some time before the inferior or younger person can readjust and re-establish a symmetrical pattern with first names. Germans, who express much the same distinction by the contrast in their pronouns *sie* and *du*, may even go through a little ceremony in which the superior person must formally initiate the symmetrical use of *du*. Even the change from one reciprocal pattern to another may well have an asymmetrical aspect.

Not infrequently we find ourselves in a situation where there seems to be a conflict in criteria. The younger member of a university department may face an impossible choice with respect to the senior professor. As a colleague, he cannot possibly use the other man's title and last name, but the age difference may make the first name seem embarrassingly chummy. In the same way, a good many Americans never arrive at any satisfactory way to address their parents-in-law. As kinsmen they cannot possibly be addressed by title, but simply to call them by their first name implies an intimacy that many sons- and daughters-in-law never quite manage. The only solution may be to use no name at all when addressing one's parent-in-law or one's senior colleague. Here an English speaker has an option, though an awkward one, that is not available to a Javanese. In an impossible situation, we can avoid using any form. In speaking Javanese, the points where choices must be made among speech levels are so frequent that it is quite impossible to say anything at all without indicating unambiguously the level one has chosen.

Phonological Choices

The choices among English forms of address, like the choices among Javanese speech levels, involve lexical items, but similar distinctions are often made in phonology as well. American English can once again provide an example, and while the particular example I give is limited to a minority of American dialects, comparable choices are probably found everywhere.

As is well known, one of the many ways in which English dielects differ from one another is in the degree of constriction with which final and pre-consonantal *r* is pronounced. In popular terms, some speakers seem to "leave out the *r*" in words like *card*, *sort*, or *burn* and also in words like *ear*, *air*, *are*, or *poor*, unless these are followed immediately by a word with an initial vowel. A superficial generalization is sometimes made to the effect that British English lacks this *r*, while American has it. This is roughly true of standard British as represented by B.B.C. announcers when compared to the English used by their American counterparts. But many British dialects have vigorous constriction of the *r* in this position (that is, an *r* is present), while many American speakers lack it as completely as any Englishman. Except for Philadelphia, most of the major cities, of the eastern seaboard, for instance, have traditionally lacked *r* in final or preconsonantal position, or more precisely they have not had the articulatory constriction that char-acterizes the same words in other dialects. In these *r*-less dialects, there may be no distinction between such pairs of words as aunt/aren't, paw/pour, god/guard, sauce/source, or bad/bared, though in some cases the vowel preceding the absent *r* is pronounced so differently from any other vowel that the words remain in contrast.

To a considerable extent the presence or absence of final and pre-consonantal *r* is simply a matter of the geographical provenance of the speaker. In some parts of the English-speaking world people use the con-stricted *r*, while in other areas they do not. In a few places, however, gen-erally where different geographical dialects have come into contact, the presence or absence of an *r* has taken on connotations other than simple geography. Sometimes a single speaker shifts between using and omitting his *r*, almost in the way a Javanese shifts between speech levels.

In earlier styles of New York English, including the older upper-class dialect, final and preconsonantal *r* was missing, just as it has been absent in the speech of eastern New England. In recent decades, however, another form of English has gained prestige in New York, a form patterned on the more general American speech such as that used rather uniformly on radio and television and most often in our movies. Among other things, this type of English differs from older New York forms in having a vigorous *r* construction in all the positions where it is found orthographically. As a re-sult, many New Yorkers today look upon dialects which have *r* as in some way "better" or "nicer-sounding" than the older *r*-less dialects. They sometimes try to imitate what they regard as a more elegant form of speech, but they may not completely succeed. As a result, the *r* comes and goes from present day New York speech with remarkable ease. In a painstaking study of speakers from the Lower East Side of Manhattan, William Labov found that the higher a man's socio-economic class and the more careful his speech at a particular moment, the more likely he was to produce constricted *r*s. Labov divided his population (all of whom were native speakers of English and not immigrants) into six socio-economic levels and tested them under five conditions: in casual speech, in careful speech, when reading connected prose, when reading word lists, and when reading possible minimal pairs such as *god* and *guard*. The results can be displayed in graphic form if the percentage of words with historical and orthographic *r*, which were actually constructed, is plotted for various conditions of speech, as in Fig. 7–1.[2]

It is obvious that everyone, from the top to the bottom of the socio-economic ladder, uses more constriction (that is, he pronounces more of his *r*'s) as he is pushed toward increasingly careful styles of speech. It is equally

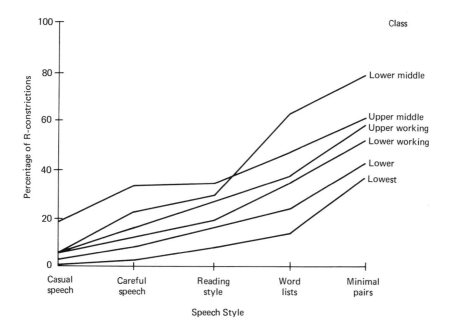

Figure 7–1.

[2]From William Labov, "Phonological Correlates of Social Stratification" in John J. Gumperz and Dell Hymes, eds., *The Ethnography of Communication*, Special Publication of *American Anthropologist*. Reproduced by permission of the American Anthropological Association from the *American Anthropologist*: Vol. 66, No. 6, 1964, p. 171.

clear that people who are relatively high in the social scale use *r* a good deal more readily than do those lower down. To the extent that the higher classes set the standard, it is obviously prestigious to use the *r*. There is, however, one curious exception to the regularity shown on this graph: in the two most careful conditions of articulation, the line for the group that Labov calls lower-middle class crosses the line for the upper-middle class showing that in these conditions alone members of one class use more *r*'s than their superiors. It looks as though the upper-middle-class speakers are more confident of their own speech and are willing to leave out a good many *r*'s even in their most careful reading of potentially minimal pairs. It is speakers of the second-highest group (no speakers in Labov's sample could really be assigned to an "upper class") who made the widest swings, between few *r*'s in their most casual speech to the highest proportion of *r*'s used by anyone when comparing minimal pairs. Sociologically, members of the second highest group are the ones who are classically supposed to be uncertain of their own position. In their uncertainty they may overcompensate in some respects and go even further than the highest class in trying to demonstrate prestigious forms.

The variables that bear upon a speaker's use of the *r* are not unlike those determining the speech level of Javanese. Of course, Javanese choices are made more self-consciously than those of New Yorkers, who may be barely aware of their vacillation in pronunciation. At most, New Yorkers are likely to feel that some pronunciations sound better than others, but not many can say precisely what characteristics make one pronunciation seem superior. Nevertheless, class level and the degree of care with which a person speaks converge to affect the New Yorker's linguistic choices just as they do those of the Javanese.

Of course, nothing inherent in the nature of *r* is either good or bad. People do not communicate more effectively with it. It has simply happened that social connotations have become attached to varying forms, and this has made one form seem better than another. Indeed, in some other parts of the country, the connotations of the constructed *r* seem almost reversed from those in New York.

In South Carolina, Raven McDavid has shown that among white speakers, those with more education tend to have less *r* constriction than others. Moreover, urban informants generally have less constriction than rural, and younger speakers less than older. By and large, white speakers from the parts of the state with a relatively low Negro population have relatively strong constriction. This means, in a general way, that the white communities from the areas of the state with poorer soil and with no history of plantation agriculture generally have more of an *r*, while those old plantation areas, populated by a combination of slaves and aristocracy, generally used less constriction.

This pattern seems to have come about in the following way. Originally most people in the state used the constricted *r*, but in the cities of the tidewater areas, particularly Charleston, the elite groups were strongly influenced by the *r*-less speech of southern Britain, and they developed a dialect without the final or preconsonantal *r*. The urban upper classes were closely tied to the plantation owners, and all maintained close ties with England. Whenever possible, they sent their sons to England for their education, and, though they formed only a small numerical minority, they occupied powerful economic and political positions in the state. The speech of these aristocrats lacked the preconsonantal and final *r*, and this speech became the prestige dialect.

The dialect gradually spread inland as plantation agriculture and the social system that went with it spread to displace the small farmers. Those upcountry farmers who became plantation owners would imitate the language of the older families just as they emulated all of their behavior. When inland towns arose, they tended to become cultural outposts of the cities, particularly of Charleston, and their business and social leaders looked to Charleston for guidance, in speech as in other ways. To a considerable extent these *r*-less dialects must have spread as unconsciously as have the dialects with *r* in New York, nevertheless this form of speech became a matter of great social pride for some speakers. In South Carolina, the social connotations of the constricted *r* seem nearly reversed to their role in New York, but perhaps a good many upper-class South Carolinians would share the observation of one southern youth, presumably of upper-class background, who said, "The reason we southerners resent the way the Yankees roll their *r* is that it reminds us of the way the crackers talk."[3]

—ing and —in

The phonological choices of the various forms of *r* allow speakers of some American English dialects to express their claims to social position or their judgement of the situation in which they speak. Indeed, it seems that virtually any feature of a language is potentially available for this use. One final English example, this one from an area closer to grammar, may round out the range of possibilities.

The English verbal suffix that we spell "ing" has two alternative pronunciations, *-ing* and *-in*, and most speakers, though hardly aware of what they are doing, can shift back and forth between them with considerable ease. From a strictly grammatical point of view, *-ing* and *-in* can only be called free variants, for nothing in the linguistic environment has

[3]Raven I. McDavid Jr., "Postvocalic -r in South Carolina: A Social Analysis," *American Speech*, 23 (1948), 194–203.

any bearing upon which is chosen. Wherever one can be used, so can the other. However, John L. Fischer has demonstrated that even before they are ten years old, some American children have become so sensitive to the social situation that they can switch between *-ing* and *-in* in close conformity with a number of rather subtle social variables.

While studying child-rearing in a New England community, Fischer came to know a number of children rather well and he interviewed several of them under a variety of conditions. The most formal condition was the administration of a Thematic Aperception Test (T.A.T.), but the children also answered a less formal questionnaire, and they participated in even more informal interviews in which they were asked to tell about their recent activities. The children were equally divided among boys and girls and among the age groups 3–6 and 7–10. Almost all made use at different times of both *-ing* and *-in*.

It turned out among other things, that girls had considerably more tendency to use *-ing* than boys. While taking the T.A.T., ten of the twelve girls but only five of the twelve boys used *-ing* more often than *-in* (see Table 7-2). It seems that to some degree *-in* is associated with masculinity.

Table 7–2   Numbers of Children Favoring *-in* and *-ing* in T.A.T. Protocols.

	-ing > *-in*	*-ing* < *-in*
Boys	5	7
Girls	10	2

Sex was only one variable, however, and idiosyncratic personality traits could also make a great difference. Fischer compared one child who was described as a "model" boy by his teachers with another whom they described as "typical." The "model" boy "did his school work well, was popular among his peers, reputed to be thoughtful and considerate." The "typical" boy was "physically strong, dominating, full of mischief, but disarmingly frank about his transgressions." It may come as little surprise to most Americans that the "model" boy used far more *-ing*'s than the typical boy, under the same conditions of the T.A.T. responses (Table 7-3).

Table 7–3   Numbers of *-ing* and *-in* Used in T.A.T. Protocols of Two Boys.

	-ing	*-in*
"Model" boy	38	1
"Typical" boy	10	12

Fischer found only a very slight tendency for children of different family backgrounds to use different proportions of the suffixes, but the community in which he worked was rather homogeneous, and lacked clear class lines. Quite possibly class differences would appear in a more heterogeneous community. He did find that children used markedly different proportions of -*in* and -*ing* in different situations. Here it is again instructive to consider the speech of the "model" boy. As can be seen in Table 7-4, he used -*in* far more often in the informal interview than in the T.A.T. protocol, while the formal interview produced an intermediate ratio.

Table 7–4   Frequency of -*ing* and -*in* in the Speech of a Ten-Year-Old Boy in Situations of Varying Formality.

	T.A.T.	*Formal Interview*	*Informal Interview*
-*ing*	38	33	24
-*in*	1	35	41

As Fischer points out, these three situations by no means exhaust the range of circumstances in which boys speak. In all likelihood, when this boy speaks casually with his friends, the ratio of -*in* to -*ing* would go even higher, particularly since Fischer himself conscientiously stayed with -*ing* throughout the interviews. In their T.A.T. protocols, Fischer also noticed that most of the children seemed gradually to increase the proportion of -*in* in their speech, probably a sign of their increasing relaxation, and they also had a tendency to use -*ing* with markedly formal verbs but to use -*in* with less formal verbs. They would say *criticizing, correcting, reading, visiting,* and *interesting,* but *punchin, flubbin, swimmin, chewin,* and *hittin.* Common words like *play* or *go,* might be used equally easily with either. Fischer concludes:

> In brief, then, the choice between the -*ing* and the -*in* variants appear to be related to sex, class, personality (aggressive/cooperative), and mood (tense/relaxed) of the speaker, to the formality of the conversation and to the specific verb spoken.[4]

No doubt the choice would also depend upon the person spoken to, though Fischer did not test that variable. Once again, the variables of situation, personality, and of the speaker's sociological nitch (sex, very likely class) come to bear upon specific linguistic alternatives, just as they often do on the lexical and phonological levels of language.

Diglossia

The lexical, phonological, and grammatical choices so far considered in this chapter, operate more or less independently of one another and each constitutes but a rather small segment of the language. It can happen that a

[4]John L. Fischer "Social Influence in the Choice of a Linguistic Variant." *Word,* 14 (1958), 51.

large number of variables act together so that speakers are able to shift rather drastically between two quite different forms of their language. This seems to happen most dramatically when the speakers of one dialect recognize a very divergent form of their language as appropriate for most written literature and on certain occasions for formal oral use. When a written language has a highly codified grammar and has served as the vehicle for a respected body of written literature, it can survive for a very long time, even in the face of a markedly divergent colloquial language. The superimposed written standard can either be a classical form of the language, no longer spoken anywhere in casual daily conversation, or the written form of a language whose colloquial form is found elsewhere. Classical Arabic was rendered immortal by the Koran, and, however divergent the modern spoken forms of colloquial Arabic have become, the classical language retains its prestige. Classical Arabic or a fair approximation to it continues to be used on most formal occasions. Latin had much the same position in the Romance language areas of medieval Europe. Latin was spoken natively by no one, but it was widely used and admired. Classical or written Chinese has had the same relation to the colloquial Chinese dialects, as has French in relation to the Creole of Haiti, or written German in relation to the colloquial German of Switzerland.

The similarity of these linguistic situations was recognized by Charles Ferguson who has aptly called them by the term "diglossia." In all these cases there is a clear and sharp functional division between the formal and the colloquial varieties of the language. Typically, the formal variety is used in religious ceremonies, in political speeches, in university lectures, and in most writing. The colloquial form is used for ordinary conversations within the family and with friends, in giving instructions to workmen or to servants, and often for certain special and restricted types of folk literature. To use the formal variety in casual conversation would be considered absurdly pretentious, but the colloquial form would be just as misplaced on a formal occasion. As long as the functions of both varieties are kept clearly distinct, a speech community can retain its diglossia for many generations.

Where diglossia occurs, speakers usually regard the formal variety as in some way superior to the colloquial, and they may even deny that the colloquial variety constitutes a real language. To them, the formal language may seem more logical, or more beautiful, or more capable of expressing important thoughts, and they are likely to prefer to listen to a speech in the formal language, even if they cannot fully understand it. On the other hand, children are always addressed with the colloquial variety, so it is that form which they learn first. As a result, it always remains the most natural language, the one that is easiest to use when at ease with one's intimate friends. The formal variety must come through formal education, and few speakers ever achieve the easy mastery over it that they have over the colloquial. The formal variety must always be approached to some extent as a system of learned rules, a norm to be striven for. As one would expect, the formal language can remain more stable and can even be perpetuated with little change from generation to generation. It can also be taught and learned in much the same form throughout a wide area, however diverse the colloquial speech may be. Grammars, dictionaries, and instructions for normative pronunciation and style can be produced, and all of them encourage the stability of the formal variety. The colloquial language is generally ignored by such descriptive or normative studies, and so it is left free to vary and to change.

The linguistic details that can distinguish the formal and colloquial varieties in diglossia are without limit. The more formal variety often seems to have a rather more complex grammar or at least to have more obligatory grammatical concord. There seem always to be synonymous lexical pairs, one formal, one colloquial, chosen like the forms of the Javanese lexical sets, and the phonology of the two styles may be quite divergent.

Ferguson gives some examples of how speakers can switch between the members of these pairs:

> In Arabic, the [formal] word for 'see' is *ra'ā*, the [colloquial] word is *šaf*. The word *ra'ā* never occurs in ordinary conversation and *šaf* is not used in normal written Arabic. If for some reason a remark in which *šaf* was used is quoted in the press, it is replaced by *ra'ā* in the written quotation. In Greek the [formal] word for 'wine' is *ínos*, the [colloquial] word is *krasi*. The menu will have *ínos* written on it, but the diner will ask the waiter for *krasi*.[5]

The phonology of the two varieties is sometimes quite divergent as in the case of colloquial Swiss German and the formal standard German dialects used in Switzerland, but in other cases there is little phonological difference. Where diglossia is well established, it can happen that speakers use what amounts to a single phonology for the two varieties. If the acknowledged "pure" form of the formal variety has articulations or phonological contrasts not found in the informal style, then colloquial habits are likely to be carried over when attempting the less familiar forms. Articulations familiar in colloquial speech may be substituted for the strange ones in the formal variety. This transfer of habits can help to ease the hurdle for speakers as they move between the colloquial and formal varieties of the language, but, in other respects, the two forms can still be remarkably diverse.

Bilingualism

In a community where two entirely different languages are spoken, a speaker frequently faces a choice between two languages, and the same variables that bear upon choices of lexical or phonological details can also

[5]Charles A. Ferguson, "Diglossia," *Word*, 15 (1959), 325–340.

influence the choice of language. A striking case is provided by Joan Rubin's study of the choice between Spanish and Guarani in Paraguay.

Paraguay is unique among Latin American nations in the vigor with which a native American Indian language—Guarani—has survived, and indeed, Guarani is a serious competitor with Spanish for the loyalty of the population. This is the result of Paraguay's unique history. Before the Spaniards arrived, its territory had been occupied by a relatively homogeneous population with a single dominant language. This placed Guarani in a much stronger position than any of the indigenous tongues in areas like Mexico, where languages were so numerous and diverse that no single one of them could seriously compete with Spanish. Unlike Argentina, on the other hand, enough Indians survived in Paraguay to keep the language very much alive. At the same time, the country lacked exploitable natural resources, and its geography limited the extent of international trade. The result was that Paraguay long remained relatively isolated from Spain and even from the neighboring Spanish colonies, where the Spanish language and Spanish culture were gradually becoming established. The few Spaniards who came into the country were for many years not even sufficient in number to establish a viable and self-perpetuating Spanish-speaking elite such as developed in other parts of the continent. The Guarani Indians also cooperated more effectively with the Spaniards than did Indians in most parts of the continent. The few Spanish-speaking men who did come to Paraguay generally married Indian women and raised children who were at least as fluent in Guarani as in Spanish. Indians and Spaniards had a relatively peaceful period of mutual adjustment, and throughout the colonial period Guarani remained the language of the great majority of the population.

Independence came to Paraguay in 1811, but contacts with the rest of the world remained limited. When, finally, after the middle of the 19th century, Paraguay began to come into more intense contact with its neighbors, Guarani had survived so vigorously as the language of the majority that it could serve as a symbol around which to rally nationalist loyalty. In the century since that time, Spanish has made considerable inroads in Paraguay. It has been encouraged by the schools, fostered as a necessary medium of international communication, and frequently valued as a symbol of sophistication. At the same time, however, a Guarani literature has been able to develop, and in recent years there has even been some official governmental encouragement for the indigenous language.

Today Spanish is the official language of the government, and it is the medium of most education, but the people of the country usually continue to speak Guarani. The 1951 census listed fifty-two percent of the nation's population as bilingual, and the great majority of monolinguals lacked Spanish rather than Guarani. In the capital city of Asunción, bilingualism reached ninety percent, but the proportion dropped to sixty percent in the suburbs and to only forty-eight percent in the interior. In the countryside many people speak nothing but Guarani, and, in fact, only a few sophisticates speak anything like pure Spanish. As would be expected, Spanish is the more formal language. It is used in schools, in businesses, in government offices, and it tends to be used with strangers, and, of course, with foreigners. Guarani, on the other hand, is used when speaking to friends, with servants, in making love, when offering confession to a priest, and as the Paraguayans say "between ourselves."

One who knows how will use Spanish with a high government official, and even social equals who do not know each other well may use Spanish. It is said that men first address their sweethearts in Spanish so as not to appear presumptuous, but when they later switch to Guarani, they are demonstrating the increasing intimacy of their relationship. Men speak to their wives, to their brothers, and to their close friends in Guarani. With servants or other social inferiors, even when not on intimate terms, one usually uses Guarani, and since the poorly educated members of the lower class are generally monolingual, nothing else may be possible. Social superiors with whom one is expected to be on close or intimate terms may pose a problem. Even a father or a grandfather is superior enough that the use of such an intimate language as Guarani may seem slightly presumptuous, but, for most Paraguayans Guarani is the language for family use.

The social ranks of the participants in a conversation are important in the choice of language but not the only factor. Under similar social circumstances, Spanish is more likely to be used in the cities than in the country, where Spanish may even appear to be a little presumptuous. The language of the schools, however, is Spanish, and parents are urged to speak in Spanish with their school-aged children, so as to help them with their school work. Despite the homely connotations of Guarani, a few parents manage to use Spanish with their children, though they may switch back to Guarani once the children have finished their education. Jokes, politics, sports, and women are said to be most easily discussed in Guarani, while school subjects and legal and business affairs go more easily in Spanish. Among upper-class bilinguals, men are more apt to use Guarani with each other, while women are more likely to use Spanish. Upper-class speakers use Spanish among themselves more freely than do lower-class speakers, to whom Guarani almost always comes easier. It is said that some countrymen switch to Spanish when they are drunk since Spanish is the language of power, and alcohol confers a sense of power. On the other hand, even upper-class Paraguayans generally like to speak Guarani if they go abroad, for then Guarani becomes a sign of distinction, a point of national pride. Spanish is used by a score of nations and is nothing unique to the Paraguayans, but they alone in Latin America have their own national language.

Perhaps language is always a crucial symbol of ethnic or national affiliation. The difficulty of learning a new language gives continuity to linguistic traditions, and it becomes easy to identify a language with a people, a nation, or even a race. Certainly language is one of the most obvious ways by which we classify people. Yet people can learn new languages, and the fact that a group of people speak a common language can hardly be taken as proof that they share a common ancestry. Indeed, the very ease with which language serves as a convenient symbol of cultural identity may allow people to switch their ethnic identity simply by learning a new language. The children of immigrants to this country, if not the immigrants themselves, have been able to become Americans almost in direct proportion to their ability to assume the American language.

In the mountainous parts of upland Burma, the tribes appear to be divided into an utterly bewildering array of diverse linguistic and ethnic affiliations. Dozens of tribes, each with its own distinctive language, jostle for space and sometimes for power. At first it can be imagined that this distribution of tribes could be the result of extraordinarily complex migrations and the continuous interpenetrations of people whose origins were diverse. On closer examination, it turns out that the people in this part of Burma are often bilingual or multilingual, and they switch from one language to another with considerable ease. A man rarely has difficulty in citing one language as his first language, but he may be fluent in several others. The language he gives as his own is offered as much as an ethnic identification as a real statement of linguistic skills. In the flux of shifting political and social power, some people may find it advantageous to identify with a new ethnic group, and to do so they need only change their language. In some cases this may simply mean that a man begins to cite a different language as first among his already available linguistic repertory. Statistics of linguistic distribution, therefore, tell us little about the past history of migration, but they are still important clues to the present attitudes toward ethnic identification.

Variables like those discussed in this chapter are probably important to all people. People everywhere are sensitive to the type of social situation in which they find themselves, and some sort of status difference always seems to mark people off from one another. Everywhere, it would seem, these sociological variables find their way into language use. In one place they may be expressed by the minutiae of phonetic detail, in another by lexical alternatives, and in a third by the choice among entirely separate languages, but some choices of this sort must always be made.

8 *India*

Dialect Differentiation

In language, as in so many other ways, India provides an admirably complex situation upon which to test generalizations first formulated for other areas. As one might expect, its intricate social organization is reflected in its intricate use of language. Throughout north India and in both east and west Pakistan, as well, most people speak one of the many dialects or languages of the Indo-Aryan branch of Indo-European. All these languages are descended from the speech of the Aryan invaders, who first came out of the Middle East and into India more than a thousand years before the time of Christ. In the three or four millenia since their arrival, the language has spread, come under the influence of neighboring languages, and diversified. Its daughter languages in their turn have spread, diversified, and reacted upon one another, until today these Indo-Aryan languages are distributed from the Arabian Sea in the east all the way westward to the Bay of Bengal.

The passage of time, the great size of the area, and imperfect transportation made it inevitable that north India would come to be divided among innumerable dialects and languages. Indeed, it is hardly an exaggeration to say that every village has its own special dialect, distinct in at least a few details from that of its neighbors. In some cases, differences of dialect divide even fellow villagers from one another. Neighboring villagers rarely have trouble understanding each other, but the further a man goes from his home, the more difficulty he is likely to have with the local speech, until at last it becomes so different as to warrant being called a different language. The different languages, however, are linked by a chain of gradually changing village dialects where neighboring forms are always mutually intelligible. One can travel all the way from Bombay in the west to Assam in India's far northeast without once crossing a sharp linguistic boundary that prevents neighbors from freely conversing.

The confused history of India has not given any single dialect the chance

103

to win a dominant position throughout all of this region. No city, for instance, has had the importance of Paris in setting a linguistic standard the entire hinterland would be willing to emulate. Nevertheless, local centers have arisen from time to time and have sometimes provided standard dialects for their own region. Before the British conquest, a number of these regional dialects came to serve as the basis for local literary traditions. Some devotional literature and court poetry were written in these dialects, although a single regional standard might not serve as a basis for all linguistic purposes. Local administration, poetry, and religious movements might each adopt a distinctive style of its own. Spoken forms similar to these regional standards were often the native speech for the town dwellers and for some trading castes, but they also served as mutually understandable mediums for the villagers of a region, since they tended to avoid the most divergent localisms of the village dialects. A good many Indian villagers came to be bidialectical, using their own village dialect at home but switching more or less successfully to the regional standard when visiting town or when speaking to a man whose village dialect was significantly different from his own.

Though these regional dialects served an important role in local trade and communications, their influence rarely extended beyond their own locality, and no single standard was recognized over more than a limited fraction of north India. Each trading caste was likely to have its own linguistic specialties, and each religious cult to have its own literary tradition. These could be based upon one of the local or regional dialects, but none ever achieved universal recognition. For many sacred purposes, Sanskrit retained great prestige long after it had ceased to be used colloquially. Even when the Moguls finally brought unity to much of north India by their conquest in the latter half of the 16th century, they used Persian for their administrative language rather than any of the indigenous forms of speech.

Soon after the consolidation of Muslim rule, however, a trade language based upon the local speech of the area just north and northwest of Delhi grew to particular importance. This language was widely used as a practical lingua franca in the courts, the army camps, and the trading centers throughout north India. It even penetrated the south to some extent as a trade language, especially in the Muslim kingdoms. Literary styles based upon this medium began to develop, though at first they were of limited scope. Only in the second quarter of the 19th century, after the British had replaced the Moguls as the dominant power in India, did a written prose form based upon this trade language really come into its own. This form made use of Arabic script and was known as Urdu. For official purposes the British replaced Persian with Urdu, giving the language a new prestige and initiating its wide use in schools. The script, however, led many Hindus to resist it, since its Arabic letters inevitably carried connotations of Islam.

Hindus would accept Urdu as a practical written form in government administration and in business, just as they had already come to accept the spoken form of the language as a practical lingua franca, having found it more useful in business than any other language of northern India. However, for literary use many Hindus came to prefer a second written style based upon the same spoken form but using the Devanagari script already in use for Sanskrit. The same spoken language, then, came to be written with two utterly different alphabets. When written from left to right in Devanagari characters, the language was called Hindi, which came to be a symbol of reform Hinduism. Hindi vernacular schools were developed to parallel and rival the Urdu schools, where writing proceeded from right to left with Arabic letters.

These different scripts obscured the essential original identity of their spoken forms, and, from the first, one script was associated with Islam, the other, with Hinduism. Then as written literature became more developed, each language's written styles had some tendency to draw apart. Urdu writers felt relatively free to draw upon Persian or Arabic for loan words, while those writing in Hindi were more apt to look to Sanskrit for inspiration. Particularly in the less colloquial literary styles these alternative sets of borrowed words brought a considerable linguistic difference to the two styles, and the result was a situation just opposite to that of English where speakers of quite divergent spoken dialects recognize a single written tradition. In India speakers of a single language came to be divided by two different literatures.

Throughout the 19th century, the unified rule that the British had imposed, together with ever more efficient transportation, encouraged these two literary standards to spread. Gradually they supplemented and then began to replace the earlier regional written styles of most of northcentral India. In Gujerat and Maharastra on the west, and in Bengal and Assam in the east, the earlier literary styles managed to survive with considerable vigor, though even at these geographical extremes, Bazar Hindustani, essentially a practical spoken version of literary Hindi or Urdu, was sometimes accepted as a medium for mundane business purposes. In the villages, of course, the spread of a new literary standard at first made little difference. Only a small proportion of the village population had ever been literate in any language, and most villagers went right on speaking as they always had. Their own village dialect that had survived from the past would seem more useful than a more formal, stilted, and often quite foreign literary standard. Even regional standards could survive as spoken forms, while their literary versions would be more likely to be displaced by a more nearly national standard.

Today, village dialects remain so diverse and so different from the written standards that it is impossible to give realistic figures for the number of speakers of each language. Language has been a subject of lively political debate in India, and the decennial census has always collected information about each person's native and second languages, in the hope that the information would assist those who were planning India's linguistic future. However, when an illiterate villager lives near the boundary dividing the Hindi and Bengali languages and tells the census taker that his native language is Hindi, that information is essentially worthless as a linguistic datum. His dialect could be as close to the Bengali literary standard as to the Hindi, and in many respects it may well be different from either. Sociologically, however, the answer may not be meaningless, for in giving a name to his own speech he also identifies himself with one social group. For a man to call his native language Hindi, may really mean that if his children were to become literate, he would want them to learn the writing conventions of Hindi. In the meantime he identifies with others who also claim Hindi as their language, and he is likely to support men who are literate in that language as political leaders.

After Indian independence, Hindi replaced Urdu as the official local medium in northcentral India, and, although Urdu literature continues to flourish, Hindi is now universally taught in school. Some Hindi enthusiasts have argued that it should replace English throughout the nation. But in parts of south India, where non-Indo-Aryan languages are spoken, Hindi has been violently opposed, and even in the eastern and western extremes of the Indo-Aryan area resistance has been strong. In the states of Rajasthan, Delhi, Himachal Pradesh, Uttar Pradesh, Madhya Pradesh, Bihar, and Haryana, Hindi has come to be widely accepted as a legitimate linguistic standard, a reasonable medium for all educational and governmental purposes, and a linguistic ideal toward which speakers are willing to move as they acquire more education.

The Hindi area is larger than that of any other Indian language, and the spoken forms continue to be extremely diverse, for the rise of a national standard has by no means eclipsed the ancient regionalisms. In most Hindi speaking areas today one can distinguish at least three co-occurring spoken stylistic strata. First, villagers continue to speak to each other in their own way, so village dialects continue their usefulness for communicating within the village and among immediately neighboring villages. Second are the regional dialects, which avoid the most extreme localisms of the villages, but they are not so cosmopolitan as standard Hindi, the third and most widespread linguistic stratum. With increasing urbanization and ever better communication, standard forms seem destined to make growing inroads upon the local dialects. Native speakers of standard Hindi are still a minority, but the minority is growing. It includes many of the most westernized and urbanized people of the region, men and women who will surely have an influence in the coming decades quite out of proportion to their numbers. Speakers of standard Hindi tend to be more urbanized, more innovating, and to have contacts at a greater distance from their own home than those who speak only a village or regional dialect. A few particularly widespread caste and religious groups such as the Sikhs and the Marwaris often use the standard language to communicate with each other over wide distances. The active, innovating groups, spurred by ideals of national unity, economic development, or religious reform, have been most in favor of the standard. Hindi has become a symbol of these nationalistic movements so that anyone who strives for these goals is likely to learn Hindi as part of his political maturation. Such men, of course, form a relatively literate segment of society, but the radio and cinema now provide spoken examples of the same language, making it widely available even to illiterates. Members of the relatively urbanized elite, even when scattered in distant cities, are probably in closer and more constant communication with one another than are villagers who live much closer to each other. The urbanized elite can be said to form something of a speech community, however scattered it may be geographically. To supplement the older geographical distinctions, which might once have been drawn over the map of north India and which would have divided village and regional dialects from each other, one must now add sociological distinctions that have little relationship to geographical regions.

For most people, standard Hindi remains a second or third spoken style, a style to be used in school, in college, in the office, or on formal occasions or when speaking with people of a different regional background. Even those who speak or understand little of the standard can expect to hear it used at political rallies, at meetings concerned with economic development, and at some religious ceremonies and more and more in the cinema and on the radio. Even when the people attending these functions understand little of what is said, they still may acknowledge the prestige of the language. Since it has prestige, its forms seep slowly but progressively into regional and village dialects. Loan words and even phonological and morphological borrowings filter down from the Hindu or Urdu standard. In the long run, this may bring a degree of linguistic unity to northcentral India that it has never before had. But real unity still lies in the future, and, if people are to make themselves understood in varying contexts today, they must often switch from one dialect to another. Even the written forms are by no means entirely uniform. With varying success, people shift from their village dialect to the regional dialect and from the regional dialect to the standard, and both standard Hindi and standard Urdu might best be characterized not so much as real colloquial languages but as sets of ideals toward which people aim, but which they do not always hit.

Dialects and Social Stratification

This broad picture of linguistic variability can be made more concrete by considering a few situations in more complete detail. The dialects of a village known as Khalapur have received a meticulous study by John Gumperz, and these dialects can provide examples of linguistic variability at its most local level. Khalapur is about eighty miles north of Delhi. The village dialect can be distinguished from the regional dialect of the area, and both differ from standard Hindi. The village and regional dialects happen to be close enough to one another to allow ready mutual intelligibility, and while all villagers use their village dialect for local purposes, most of the men, particularly those who do any traveling, sometimes use the regional dialect as well. A few of the more educated villagers can also speak standard Hindi, but this never makes them reluctant to use their familiar village dialect at home. However, even villagers in this region who do not habitually use standard Hindi can understand it. The forms of Hindi are close enough to local habits, so that the opportunities that all villagers have to hear the standard from time to time allow them to become used to its peculiarities. The reverse is not true for speakers of the standard language. Those not native to this region are unlikely to have much experience with the local forms of speech, and without such experience they are unable to follow the village idiom. The most interesting aspect of Khalapur speech, however, is not its relation to regional and standard forms of Hindi, but rather its internal variation within the village. To understand this variation, it is first necessary to know something of the organization of the villagers into castes and of the village's territorial divisions.

About ninety percent of Khalapur villagers are Hindus, the rest, Muslims. The Hindu majority is divided among several distinct castes or, to use a local term, "jatis." Each jati has a traditional occupation that many or most of its members follow, and each has at least some of its own special customs and rituals. A man must always take his wife from his own jati, and the jatis are ranked on a clear social scale. The top five percent are the Brahmans, who traditionally serve as priests and who are granted an unambiguously superior ritual position by all Hindus. Just below the priests are the Rajputs, the largest single group in Khalapur with forty-two percent of the total population. The Rajputs consider themselves to be warriors and rulers. They own ninety percent of the village land, so that, both by weight of numbers and by economic strength, they wield the predominant power within the village. The Rajputs group themselves into seven lineages. These are kinship groups, each of which includes a number of related families. The seven lineages serve as the nuclei of seven territorial divisions—wards—into which the village is divided. Members of other jatis are often dispersed among the various wards, but it is Rajput kinship and Rajput ownership that defines the territorial divisions.

Below the Rajputs are a smaller group of merchants who claim membership in the third traditional caste level, the Vaishyas. The Brahmans, Rajputs, and Vaishyas together constitute the so-called twice born castes, and in a number of ways they are ritually distinguished from all the jatis below them. Perhaps the most obvious symbol of their special position is that their men alone may wear the "sacred thread," a loop of string worn suspended across the chest from one shoulder. Below these three highest jatis are several jatis of artisans and laborers. None of these is numerous, but together they form sort of a middle group, not exalted enough to be included among the twice born but still safely above the untouchables.

The bottom of the social scale is formed by three Hindu groups: a fairly large group of Chamars (twelve percent of the village), who are landless laborers; a smaller group known as Jatia Chamars, who are leather workers and shoemakers; and finally the Bhangis or sweepers. These three lowest groups are classed as untouchables, and they suffer a number of disabilities. More than any of the higher jatis, each of the three untouchable groups tends to live in a geographically discreet section of the village. These untouchable neighborhoods are even enclosed by walls, which add a physical isolation not imposed upon other jatis. Members of the higher, or touchable, jatis all move with some freedom throughout the village, and their children, for instance, can play in groups of mixed jati membership. The untouchables more often stay in their own neighborhoods, unless they have a specific errand that calls them away. Each untouchable group has its own well or water pump and its children usually play only with their own caste-mates.

In addition to these Hindu groups are the ten percent of the population who are Muslims. The Muslims themselves are divided among several groups, which are rather like jatis; Muslim Rajputs and oil pressers being the most important. The colloquial speech of the Muslims is not sharply distinguished from that of the Hindus, and the linguistic details to be described here refer primarily to the Hindus.

Strong social restrictions divide jati from jati. The prohibition against intermarriage means that all of a man's kinsmen belong to his own jati, so the jati is something of a kinship group. Each jati has its unique rituals, and severe sanctions restrict a man's associations across jati lines, though the restrictions are more stringent between certain pairs of jatis than others. All members of the village do have to communicate with one another, of course, and their language is homogeneous enough so that they have no difficulty in understanding. But, where social relations are so restricted, one might expect that slight differences, characterizing the dialects of the various groups, could arise, which would come to be somewhat symbolic of the social differences. This does turn out to be the case.

The linguistic distinctions among jatis are in part lexical. Each jati has some special terms for technical or ritual items of its own subculture not shared with other jatis. But the more striking dialect differences are in phonology, and these fall into three types: (1) differences in phonological contrast in certain positions; (2) differences in the pronunciation of particular words; (3) phonetic differences not affecting the phonemic distribution. I will give just one example of each.

(1) The majority of speakers in Khalapur contrast certain simple vowels on the one hand with a set of diphthongs on the other. Members of the sweeper jati, however, fail to make this contrast except in word final position. For example the words *bal,* 'ear of corn,' and *lal,* 'red,' rhyme for sweepers, while members of the other jatis say *baɪl* and *lal,* which do not rhyme.

(2) Most villages make a contrast between /ə/ and /u/, but shoemakers and many Chamars are content to use /ə/ everywhere. Those Chamars who use only /ə/ are regarded as old-fashioned and in an apparent attempt to imitate the speech of higher jatis, some Chamars introduce /u/ into their speech, where they hope it will be appropriate. The speech of the higher jatis has come to be regarded as more prestigious but with only a limited chance to associate with higher castes, accurate imitation is not easy for the Chamars and they sometimes go too far. Chamars sometimes substitute /u/ for the supposedly old-fashioned /ə/, even in words where the upper jatis all use /ə/. This continues to keep Chamar speech distinct from that of other jatis, even though all now make the same phonological contrast. The word meaning 'blanket' is pronounced by the higher jatis as /dutə́i/, while most Chamars say /dətə́i/, and this seems to represent the "old-fashioned" Chamar speech. However, the word for a particular type of village building, which most upper caste men pronounce as /dəlán/, is pronounced as /dulán/ by many Chamars. In this case there seems to have been an erroneous substitution of /u/ which, while possibly sounding quite elegant, happens, by upper jati standards, to be out of place in this particular word. The result of Chamar imitation then is more likely to be funny than impressively high class. It is risky to imitate one's superiors.

(3) All dialects have a final vowel which can be regarded phonemically as /æ/, and which contrasts with all other final vowels. In the speech of most villagers this is pronounced phonetically as a low front vowel [æ], but shoemakers pronounce it higher and not so far front [əᵛ]. In some neighboring villages, the latter pronunciation is used even by higher jatis, but in Khalapur it is characteristic only of the shoemakers.

These three examples are but a small selection of a large number of phonological differences that collectively serve to emphasize the social distinctions found in the village by symbolizing them linguistically.

The most important social distinctions in the village are those of caste, and most dialect distinctions follow caste lines. But in one respect the residents of two of the village wards, whatever their caste, are set off linguistically from people elsewhere in the village. In some cases too, people felt to be old-fashioned use slightly different forms than others. Collectively, these linguistic details serve to map out the sharp social divisions in the village with considerable accuracy. Members of the touchable jatis have rather uniform speech, except for the characteristic that sets off the two wards as unique and except for a few special forms that are widely regarded as old-fashioned. The sharpest linguistic distinctions divide the touchables from the untouchables, but each of the three untouchable groups has its own unique forms, so that it is quite impossible to speak of a single untouchable dialect. Unlike the speech of the untouchables, that of the Muslims is not clearly set off from that of upper-caste Hindus. This reflects the higher status of the Muslims and their relatively free association with Hindus.

It may seem surprising that in most respects the sweeper dialect is the closest of any village form to the regional dialect. The sweepers are thought to have first moved to this village about a hundred years ago, and possibly they brought speech patterns characteristic of nearby regions with them and have been successfully enough segregated to maintain them through several generations. If these happened to approximate the regional dialect, then the century of segregated residence in the village has not given them sufficient chance to adjust completely to the speech of other villagers, though in some respects they may have borrowed upper-caste forms and thus modified their speech *away* from the regional standard. It appears too simple to suppose that all dialect borrowing occurs from the standard to the non-standard dialects. Whatever the history of the sweeper dialect, however, it puts the upper castes in this particular village in a rather uncomfortable position with respect to the regional dialect. To use the regional dialect might seem in some respects to be a mark of sophistication, a sign of moving beyond the limited confines of village life, but if it makes one sound like a member of the lowest caste in the village, the regional dialect might be quite consistently avoided except for the most mundane purposes, like marketing or business, where it is essential for practical communication.

In a few respects both Chamars and shoemakers appear to be somewhat conservative or old-fashioned in their speech, as if their language had shown fewer innovations. It is not impossible that members of the higher jatis have innovated more or less on purpose, just to make their speech a bit distinctive and less like that of the lower castes. If the lower castes regularly imitate their superiors, one can imagine that upper castes would regularly have to modify their speech in order to keep it distinct. This need not be a self-conscious process of innovation, but however rapidly the lower castes pursue, the elite can always keep ahead of them so long as they are willing to introduce a new form from time to time.

The linguistic criteria dividing one caste from another are but a minute part of the whole language, but like other symbolic differences that distinguish castes, such as clothing and ritual, they surely help to support caste distinctions, and they will probably persist as long as caste affiliation remains important. Comparable differences (though certainly not the same ones) are no doubt found in most Hindi-speaking villages of north India, and collectively these details add enormously to the complexity of Hindi dialectology. To a Hindi speaker who comes from some distance away, the internal differences found in the village would probably seem trivial. He could imagine everyone in the village to have much the same village dialect. But for those who have grown up within a village, the internal differences serve to map out and help to perpetuate the social structure.

Formal Standards of Hindi-Urdu

On a much broader scale, other linguistic distinctions also characterize social groups that are scattered all across north India. One of the most pervasive social distinctions found here is that which divides Hindus from Muslims. The differing literary forms of Hindi and Urdu, associated with this division, are for the most part simply different written forms of the same spoken language, but among literate speakers, a few distinctions have also crept into the spoken language. As in writing, the most important differences are in borrowed words. Words of Persian and Arabic origin are plentiful in all spoken dialects, and no speaker of Hindi or Urdu could get along without them. But just as they are more frequent in Urdu literature than in Hindi, they are also more common in the speech of Muslims than of Hindus. Regardless of the religion of the speakers, words of Persian and Arabic origin are also more frequent in the western portion of the Hindi-Urdu speech areas than in the east, for the impact of the Middle Eastern conquerors was felt more strongly in the west. Not only do Muslims and westerners tend to use more Persian and Arabic terms than Hindus or easterners, but they are also more likely to maintain something of the original pronunciation of these borrowed words.

Hindi literature as contrasted with Urdu often uses words formed from Sanskrit originals, and literate Hindu speakers are more likely to use such terms orally and to adhere to presumed Sanskrit pronunciations. The Middle Eastern languages and Sanskrit are not the only sources of borrowed terms, for English words have also flooded all varieties of Hindi-Urdu. Here again some speakers, generally the more educated, are particularly likely to use many English terms and more likely to approximate English phonology than their more poorly educated compatriots. Various styles of spoken

Hindi-Urdu can therefore be recognized, styles which show varying influences from Persian-Arabic, from Sanskrit, or from English.

All styles share a common phonological core. One can look upon them as having a stock of common phonemes, those listed in Table 8-1. To this common core, each style adds a number of its own special phonological distinctions, which were first introduced through borrowed terms but by

Table 8–1   Common Hindi-Urdu Phonological Core

p	t	ṭ	c	k	i		u
ph	th	ṭh	ch	kh	ɪ		u
b	d	ḍ	j	g	e	ə	o
bh	dh	ḍh	jh	gh	æ		ɔ
	s				h		a
v			y				
m	n		∼ (nasalization)				
	1						
	r (thrill)						

now have become so well established that they occur naturally as part of the everday language. Styles influenced by Sanskrit have a retroflex nasal /ṇ/, distinct from the dental /n/, and both /š/ and a retroflex /ṣ/ distinct from the ordinary /s/ that is used by all speakers. Styles influenced by Persian and Arabic may have several gutterals lacking in the other styles /ḳ,x,g/, and several distinct fricatives /f,š,z/. Styles influenced by English may have distinct /z/ and /f/, as in borrowed words based upon "razor" and "farm," and two new vowels, a front mid-vowel /E/ as in "check" and a low back unrounded vowel /a/ as in the borrowing based upon English "ball." A speaker who uses English borrowings freely may also contrast a retroflex stop /ḍ/ with a flap /ṛ/, although in some other varieties of Hindi-Urdu the flap [ṛ] is simply the allophone of /ḍ/ that occurs medially. English borrowings such as "soda" introduce a medial [ḍ] which contrasts with the flap in that position.

A few speakers make *all* these contrasts, but most do not. In normative spoken Urdu /ṇ/ (from Sanskrit) is not distinct from /n/, and /ṣ/ is pronounced /š/. In normative Hindi /ḳ/ is merged with /k/, and the fricatives /x/ and /g/ are assimilated to /k/ and /g/. Some Hindi speakers keep /f/ and /z/ (both from Persian-Arabic and English) distinct, but others merge these with /ph/ and /j/ respectively. A normative westernized style of Hindi-Urdu has yet to emerge as clearly as normative Hindi or normative Urdu, but possibly one could recognize at least an incipient westernized style in which /E, a, z, f, s ṛ/ are distinct, but in which /ṇ, s, x, g, k/ may be merged with other sounds. The alternatives allowed by these variables mean that any northcentral Indian is likely to demonstrate his religious and educational background by the details of his phonology, just as on a much smaller scale the villager from Khalapur is likely to demonstrate his caste membership by other phonological details.

By still other variables, the speaker of Hindi-Urdu demonstrates his geographical origin. Like many other Indian languages, all varieties of Hindi-Urdu distinguish a series of dental stops from the retroflex or "cacuminal" stops. The former are made with the tip of the tongue placed on, or near the upper teeth; the latter (those written with a subscribed dot) have the tongue curled more or less up and backward toward the roof of the mouth. This distinction is phonetically most extreme in the west, and as one moves eastward across the Hindi-Urdu area the phonetic separation between the two series of stops becomes progressively less, although it is never quite lost. If one proceeds still further east out of the Hindi-Urdu area and into Bengal and then finally to Assam, the distinction disappears entirely, for Assamese, the eastern most Indo-Aryan language, has but one series of appical stops, the only Indo-Aryan language to lack the contrast. The religious or caste identification of the speaker is irrelevant for this particular phonetic feature, as is, apparently, a man's education. Easterners of whatever religion simply differ slightly from westerners. Other detailed phonetic differences that have little to do with affiliation to particular groups also set off speakers of one region from others. Many of these phonetic peculiarities reflect the characteristics of the regional or village dialects of the area, and they seem to be carried over from these more familiar forms of speech into the local varieties of the standard language as local speakers adapt the standard to their own habits.

Punjabi-Hindi Bilingualism

So far, I have written only of conditions within the Hindi-Urdu area, and, however diverse those dialects may be, all are felt in some way to be affiliated as members of a single language. Yet people also switch back and forth between different languages, borrowing forms from one language into another, just as they do from one dialect to another. A striking example is provided by Punjabi, a language which is spoken both in India's most northwestern regions and in parts of adjacent west Pakistan. Like Hindi, Punjabi is an Indo-Aryan language, and, indeed, the two languages share many features. But Punjabi has different written conventions than either Hindi or Urdu, and unlike Urdu its geographical center is clearly distinct from Hindi. Migration of speakers has brought the two languages into contact, however, so that they have influenced each other considerably. In particular, many speakers of Punjabi have moved to Delhi, where the majority of people speak Hindi. This move does not necessarily change a man's linguistic environment very radically, since even before moving, a Punjabi is likely to have occasionally encountered shopkeepers or officials who used Hindi. Varieties of Hindi are widely used as trade media in the Punjab bazaars, and even Hindi and Urdu literary forms are well known. Moreover, even after moving, a Punjabi is likely to continue to associate with others from his home district and to continue speaking Punjabi. But now he is likely to encounter Hindi speakers somewhat more often than before, so his own chances to use Hindi increase, and the numbers of bilingual among Punjabi speakers is certain to be higher than at home, so it is easier to incorporate Hindi borrowings even into one's predominantly Punjabi speech.

The differences between the two languages are largely grammatical, and in particular, morphophonemic differences are quite sharp. The greatest part of the lexicon is common to both languages, or at least it differs only by regular and readily recognizable phonological rules. (One can regard the deep structure of the two languages as almost identical and see the differences as occurring as a result of different rules leading to the surface structure.) The similarities help to make it easy for Punjabi speakers to borrow Hindi forms, and many who live in Delhi do so with no apparent misgivings. In fact, both because of similarity of structure and because of widespread bilingualism, borrowing is so easy that Punjabi becomes almost indefinitely merged with Hindi, not only in lexicon but in all its grammatical and morphophonemic features. All sorts of gradations between the two languages are used, and in the end it is but a limited set of specific items that are used as criteria by which Punjabi is kept distinct. For instance, in place of Hindi *kyaa*, 'what?,' speakers cling to Punjabi *kii*. If a person wants to show that he is speaking Punjabi rather than Hindi, all he need do is to make a few rather simple lexical substitutions such as *kii* for *kyaa*.

One must ask whether such a speech form is best referred to as Hindi or as Punjabi. Linguistically, it is certainly closer to Hindi, but the speakers call it Punjabi, and it is connected to more standard forms of Punjabi by an unbroken chain of increasingly Punjabi-like styles. It is sometimes charged that this barely Punjabi speech represents an imperfect attempt by Punjabis to speak Hindi, but this charge is hardly reasonable, since anyone who can approach Hindi so closely could surely drop the last few distinguishing markers of Punjabi. The markers must instead be seen as an attempt to cling to something special. They are signs that the speaker means to be speaking another "language" however slightly it may differ from Hindi.

These Indian examples are meant to show how people at all levels of society can demonstrate their affiliation to various social groups by their choice among alternative forms of their language. Choices are made within the narrow range available to the castes within a single village, and also within the wider range that divides regional dialect from the national standard, educated Hindu speech from that of an educated Muslim, or even Hindi-Urdu from Punjabi. But wherever a choice is made it marks the speaker as belonging to a particular caste, village, region, or religion. To some degree, speakers learn to switch from style to style, from dialect to dialect, or even from language to language. The more diverse a man's experience, the more styles he may be able to use himself, and indeed skillful use of diverse styles may be a characteristic needed for leadership or high social position in a nation like India. The ability to switch styles or languages may allow men to overcome to some degree the limitations of their own narrow backgrounds, but no man can ever learn all of the available forms of speech and so everyone is in some ways limited. Language turns out to be a subtle index of social affiliation, an index from which no speaker can completely escape.

9 *Black English*

Origins of Diversity

An American who first hears of caste dialects and of the stylistic switching that is so common in India is likely to react with dismay if not outright horror. Polydialectism seems a poor basis upon which to build a unified nation, and the variability of language along caste lines seems downright undemocratic. Yet many of these same phenomena can be found in America too, and indeed, once we recognize how easy it is for linguistic cues to come to symbolize sociological or situational differences, it should be surprising if American social class divisions were not reflected in the way we use language. In particular, we ought to look at our sharpest sociological cleavage—the division between blacks and whites—and ask whether it is not marked by linguistic variables.

Most white Americans probably believe that they could distinguish Negro speakers from white even while blindfolded. Some may imagine that whatever linguistic differences they perceive are simply the result of underlying racial differences. They may suppose that Negro mouths are built differently from white mouths or that Negroes are simply incapable of such clear and accurate articulation as whites. Such racial notions can easily be disproved, for when northern whites are asked to judge taped samples of speech they often mistake a southern white for a Negro, but conversely they will identify the voice of the rather rare Negro who grows up in an otherwise white northern community as belonging to a white speaker. It is unquestionably the experience of the speaker, particularly his experience in early childhood, that determines how he will speak, not his race.

It is easy to dispose of this racist explanation for Negro-white differences, but a contrary linguistic myth is also current among many Americans today that is more difficult to deal with. A good many well-meaning

117

Americans would like to maintain a sort of dogmatic faith that Negro and white speech is in all essentials identical. Many white Americans, who feel deeply that discrimination is wicked and who insist that Negroes be offered all the same opportunities as whites, are eager to deny any difference at all between the two groups, for they are afraid any admission of cultural differences would provide a rationalization for discrimination. But the fear of offending egalitarian ideals should not stand in the way of an investigation of dialectical variability, and when such an investigation is made, it is abundantly clear that most Negroes in the United States today do have features in their speech that separate them from their white neighbors. Indeed, when we remember the history of black Americans and understand the conditions of segregation in which they have lived and continue to live in both the north and the south, it would be startling if important differences were not found. Unfortunately, serious studies of dialects used by Negroes have begun only very recently.

The first and most obvious generalization to make about the English of many Negroes is that it shows abundant characteristics of the southern United States. Throughout the South, where most Negroes once lived, their speech has probably approached in considerable degree the varieties of English spoken by their white neighbors. They need not have spoken identically to these whites, and indeed the segregated conditions of their lives would almost force us to guess that important linguistic differences would separate the speech of the two groups.

In recent decades, as southern Negroes have surged into northern cities, they have brought along their varieties of southern speech. Since they have largely been forced to live in segregated ghettos, often shut off even more completely from association with whites than in their southern homes, their dialects have been perpetuated and passed on to their northern-born children. What had been geographically distinctive features have been converted into ethnic features. Most northern urban Negroes, for instance, fail to distinguish /i/ from /e/ before /n/, so that words like *pin* and *pen* become homonyms. This is characteristic of most southern speech, both black and white, but in a northern city like New York it is hardly found except among Negroes. Most whites do distinguish those two sounds, but only the rare Negro who grows up in a predominantly white neighborhood learns to do so. As a result a New Yorker could guess the race of a fellow New Yorker with a good chance of being correct simply by hearing him pronounce these two words. Many other southern features, besides the collapse of the *i/e* contrast, have no doubt become generalized as ethnic features in the north. Certainly the totality of features is so pervasive that more often than not northern urban Americans can distinguish Negroes from whites simply by hearing them talk.

Not all the special characteristics of northern urban Negro speech are simply southern, however. The ghettos create their own social climate and evoke their unique linguistic signals. The ghettos, after all, draw upon many southern areas, so the migrants do not arrive with a single uniform dialect. Features that have originated from one southern area can be generalized and accepted by other speakers, while other southern features are dropped as people adjust to their new surroundings. As a result, the recent migrant from the South is clearly marked off from older residents by his purer southern traits, and as the years pass, a new and unique dialect, a synthesis of southern and northern forms with some added local innovations, becomes characteristic of many urban Negroes. Instead of a geographically based dialect we can only speak of one that is ethnically based.

It even seems that in some northern cities the speech of Negroes and whites has been becoming more distinct in recent decades. Southern Negroes have been moving north in such large numbers that their speech has tended to swamp out the more northern dialects of their northern Negro predecessors. In Washington, D.C., immigration of whites from the north has tended to shift white dialects in the opposite direction. In some northern cities the differences between black and white speech have now become so clearly marked that radio stations which carry programs and advertising directed toward a Negro audience sometimes use announcers who have recognizably Negro characteristics in their speech. Perhaps this should be no more surprising than the use of Spanish for programs directed to Puerto Ricans in New York or of Navaho for some programs in the Southwest, but the use of Negro English dialects does constitute an almost unique exception to the bland uniformity of most broadcast English in the United States.

A common southern background and a common reaction to ghetto life in the north can account for many of the differences between Negro and white dialects. But it is also worth noting that a number of striking linguistic features, which are not found in either southern or northern white dialects, seem to be common among Negroes in all northern urban areas. Not all the features that tend to set off the kind of English used wherever Negroes are concentrated in large numbers are simply southern. It may be that the seemingly unique character of black English can only be understood as deriving from a long separate history from white English. It may even be that the English of some black Americans still shows the influence of the time when slaves were first imported into this country or even a few traces of their African origin.

When slaves were brought to the Americas, men and women of diverse linguistic background were thrown together with relatively little chance to learn the English of their masters, but with no way of communicating with one another except by means of some approximation to English. The situation would seem to have been ideal for the development of a pidgin language based upon English, and then for its subsequent creolization in the generation that grew up in America knowing no other language but learning to speak by imitating the imperfect English of their parents. A pidgin is a contact language, native to no one, and generally used in a limited range of situations. It may be simple in structure and may show varied influences from the diverse languages of those who use it. When children grow up basing their speech upon such a pidgin, they can be expected to elaborate it and adapt it to all the varied situations of life. But having been filtered through the distortions of the contact period, this newly developed creole, while a full and flexible medium of communication in its own right, can be expected to differ quite markedly from the original language upon which its ancestral pidgin had been based.

A few New World Negro populations continue to speak forms of English that are so divergent as to be recognized as creoles. The only true creole to survive in the United States today is the so-called Gullah dialect spoken along the coast of South Carolina, but others are found in the West Indies and in Surinam on the north coast of South America. It is remarkable that all these creoles seem to resemble each other to some degree, and a few of their features are even reflected in the less deviant English spoken by many Negroes in the United States.

Hints about the characteristics of the English spoken by Negroes over the past two and a half centuries can be found in fragments of dialogue that have periodically appeared in print and purport to reflect the speech of Negroes. It is not uncommon in such dialogue for *me* to be used even as the subject or possessive form of the first person pronoun. A copula is often missing from sentences in which standard English would always have a form of the verb *be*, though *be* itself sometimes appears where it would not be used in standard English. Some words also suggest an avoidance of final consonants or of complex final clusters, either by dropping or simplifying the consonants or by adding vowels at the end, thus shifting the former final consonant into a prevocalic position. These various features appear, among other places, in the dialogue attributed to a Virginia Negro in the play "The Fall of British Tyranny" written by John Leacock of Philadelphia in 1776. A conversation between a certain "kidnapper and the Negro Cudjo" goes as follows,

Kidnapper	What part did you come from?
Cudjo	Disse brack man, disse one, disse one, disse one, came from Hamton, disse one, disse one, come from Nawfok, me come from Nawfok too.
Kidnapper	Very well, what was your master's name?
Cudjo	Me massa name Cunney Tomsee.

Kidnapper	Colonel Thompson—eigh?
Cudjo	Eas, massa, Cunney Tomsee.
Kidnapper	Well then I'll make you a major—and what's your name?
Cudjo	Me massa cawra me Cudjo.[1]

Similar features appeared in dialogues attributed to Negroes, supposedly coming from the West Indies and Surinam. But, in English-speaking areas of the New World, Negro dialects were never taken seriously enough to be systematically described. We can only infer their characteristics from scattered literary sources. Surinam, however, was ruled by Holland, and here Dutch immigrants had to do their best to communicate with Negroes who spoke an English-based creole. To assist the Dutchmen, grammars of this creole were printed as early as the late 18th century, and these suggest features of the language found all the way north to the United States.

The English spoken by Negroes in the United States today is certainly not a close replica of an 18th century creole, but at least a few details of present day Negro American English may be attributable to an earlier period of pidginization and creolization, followed by persistent modifying influences from standard English. As I will point out, the attrition of final consonants is an important feature of the speech of many Negroes in the United States, and the copula is often missing where it would occur in standard English. One cannot help asking if all forms of New World Negro English might not have a common origin and if centuries of segregation might not have allowed common features to be perpetuated down to the present time. It has even been argued that Negro dialects can be traced all the way to the slave ports of west Africa, where African and European speakers first had to devise makeshift forms of communication. The pidgin English established in these ports would have been carried everywhere in the New World where Africans used English. In subsequent centuries the language would only slowly be modified in proportion to the contact between blacks and speakers of more standard English.

We should even be willing to wonder whether traces of African languages might not have managed to survive the centuries. Certainly African lexical items live on in the more extreme creoles such as Gullah. More tentatively it is tempting to ask if the attrition of final consonants and simplification of final clusters that is so characteristic of much of Negro English is not a distant reflection of the influence of west African languages, for these often have few final consonants. Conceivably this feature of west

[1]Quoted by William A. Stewart in "Sociolinguistic Factors in the History of American Negro Dialects," *Florida FL Reporter* (Spring 1967), p. 24.

African languages has even reached out to affect white speakers as well as their Negro neighbors, for in spite of the great status differences dividing blacks from whites in this country, some influences can have gone in both directions. It may not be mere coincidence that certain final consonant clusters are more often simplified in southern white dialects than in those of the north. The *t* of northern pronunciations of the final clusters *-pt* and *-ft* is omitted by some southern white speakers, for instance, with the result that *slept* becomes *slep*, *stopped* becomes homonymous with *stop* (unless the *t* is reintroduced by analogy with other past tense forms) *left* becomes *lef*, and *loft* becomes *lof*.

Just how important the influence of African languages is in the speech of either Negroes or whites in the United States today must remain an open question until far more has been learned both about the various dialects spoken today and about their antecedents. But it does at least seem clear that many features widely distributed among Negroes today can only be understood as a result of their long and special history.

A Stigmatized Dialect

The diverse patterns of English would be no more than linguistic curiosities if they were accepted as the social and cultural equivalent of standard patterns. Americans tend to be relatively tolerant of most regional dialects, but Negro speech patterns have been closely associated with their inferior social position and, like the dialectical specialties of lower-class whites, their patterns have become stigmatized. Many people look upon them not simply as divergent but as inferior. This is true not only of whites. Those Negroes who have themselves struggled for an education and fought to acquire the linguistic symbols associated with education may have little patience with the language of the lower class. Indeed, it is sometimes educated Negro teachers, themselves managing very well with standard English patterns, who most strongly resist any suggestion that the special characteristics of their black student's dialects deserve respect or attention. It may be difficult for some of them to accept the notion that the speech they have worked so hard to suppress is anything but just plain wrong.

To dismiss his speech as simply incorrect or inferior burdens the Negro child who grows up in a northern ghetto with a nearly insuperable problem. To speak naturally with his parents and to compete with his contemporaries on the street, he simply must learn their variety of English. Indeed, if in some miraculous way, he could learn standard English, he would be nothing but an impertinent prig to use it with his parents, and surely his contemporaries would rapidly tease it out of him. The language the child first learns is a rich and flexible medium in its own terms, and it can be used effectively in most of the situations he encounters in daily life. No wonder teachers have only meager success when they try to persuade him to abandon his own easy language in favor of an unnatural—almost foreign—medium. Inevitably, many students simply reject their education and all it stands for.

Years of classroom drilling, exposure to movies and radio, and the brute necessities of trying to get a job do eventually have their effect. While few Negroes from the ghetto fully achieve the middle-class goal of their teachers, many learn to go part way, and many northern Negroes are accomplished dialect switchers. They move toward middle-class standards where that seems to be called for, but they relax into more natural patterns when speaking with their families or close friends, or whenever pretensions would be out of place. They act a bit like speakers in those situations that have been called diglossia. Like Swiss Germans, Negro children first learn a dialect suitable for their home and their close friends. Only in school, if at all, do they learn the standard dialect, which then becomes appropriate for certain kinds of educated discourse, for writing, or for communicating with people outside their own group. Yet in German-speaking Switzerland the two dialects are more clearly recognized as distinct. Each is admired in its own sphere and each can be clearly referred to by its own name. No Swiss, whatever his education, is unwilling to use Swiss German in his home or with close friends. Every Swiss is proud of his dialect, proud of its very distinctiveness from standard German, and no one in Switzerland simply stigmatizes the Swiss dialects as inferior and debased. Although a Swiss switches back and forth as the occasion demands, he is generally clear about his choice, speaking full Swiss German when that is called for but approximating standard German quite closely at other times. He is not likely to glide indecisively between them.

Northern urban Negro dialects are more recent, in more rapid flux, and more consistently despised by speakers of standard English. This has made it difficult for Negroes to develop the pride in their own dialect that the Swiss have in theirs, and most speakers probably slide along more of a continuum than do the Swiss. At one end of the continuum is a speech style close to the standard language and this is the style toward which formal education aims. Students of Negro speech in Washington, D.C., have called this the "acrolect" and have contrasted it with the "basilect" that lies at the opposite and most humble extreme. Ghetto children first hear and speak the basilect, and many Negroes in Washington seem to take it for granted that this is the natural way for small children to talk, just as Javanese expect their children to learn the lowest level of speech first. As children grow older, they learn new or alternative forms and develop more or less skill in switching toward the acrolect.

Consciously or unconsciously, many Negroes learn to slide back and forth along this continuum of styles, though individual speakers vary greatly in the range through which they can switch. The most recent southern migrant, the most severely segregated, the man with the least formal education, may not be able to get far from the basilect. The long-term northern resident, the educated member of the middle class who has daily contact with white speakers of standard English, may use the acrolect easily but be unable to get all the way to the basilect; but many speakers shift over a considerable range. The fluidity of this shifting makes it extremely difficult to make a serious investigation of Negro speech patterns. The middle-class investigator, particularly if he is white, may have great trouble eliciting realistic examples of the more relaxed Negro styles, since the very formality of the investigation encourages informants (whether consciously or not) to shift as far toward the acrolect as they can manage. Where Negroes have adjusted to prejudice and discrimination by accommodating outwardly to the whims of whites, they may be ready to support white stereotypes by guessing at the information the investigator wants and then providing it. They may deliberately conceal the characteristics of their in-group language. Partly for these reasons, though even more through sheer neglect, we have had tragically little reliable knowledge of the speech of lower-class Negroes. By the late 1960s, however, as part of an increasing concern over the fate of segregated Negro children in our educational system, investigations in several cities had finally begun. It is at last possible to sketch a few of the major differences between standard middle-class English and the speech of many urban Negroes. There can be no doubt that the differences extend to every part of language, phonological, grammatical, lexical, and semantic.

Phonological Contrast

One set of features that distinguishes the speech of many Negroes is the obscuring of certain phonological contrasts found in standard English, spoken in the northern United States. In final position standard /θ/ often merges with /f/, and standard /ð/ merges with /v/. As a result, words like *Ruth* and *death*, which northern white speakers virtually always pronounce with final interdental fricatives, are often pronounced by Negroes with labiodental fricatives so that they become homonymous with *roof* and *deaf.*

The standard vowels /ay/ and /aw/ as in *find* and *found* may lose their diphthongal qualities and merge with /a/ of *fond,* and all three of these words become homonyms. A number of other vowels may fall together when preceding /l/ or /r/, so that pairs like *boil* and *ball, beer* and *bear, poor* and *pour,* are often homonyms. In all these cases, as in the loss of contrast between, the vowels in *pin* and *pen,* many Negroes simply have a few more sets of homonyms in their speech than do most northern whites. Perhaps it is some compensation that a good many southern Negroes do make a distinction between the vowels in *four* and *for*, or *hoarse* and *horse*, which most northern whites confound, though even this distinction tends to be lost by northern migrants.

The existence of these extra homonyms in the speech of Negro children presents them with a few special reading problems, though these should not be insuperable. All English speakers have many homonyms in their speech, and in learning to read English everyone must learn to associate different orthographic sequences with identically pronounced but semantically distinct words. This is one of the barriers we all must overcome in becoming literate. For the most part, a Negro child simply has a somewhat different and larger set of homonyms to cope with. They will give him serious problems only if his teacher fails to understand that these words *are* homonyms in the child's natural speech.

If a student sees the word *death* and reads [def] he is correctly interpreting the written symbols into his natural pronunciation, and he deserves to be congratulated. If his teacher insists on correcting him and telling him to say [deθ], she is pronouncing a sequence of sounds that is quite literally foreign to the child, and he may even have trouble hearing the difference between his own and his teacher's versions. Unwittingly, the teacher is correcting the child's pronunciation instead of his reading skills. The child can only conclude that reading is a mysterious and capricious art. If he has enough experiences of this sort he is all too likely to give up and remain essentially illiterate all his life. It is clearly of the utmost importance for anyone who is teaching such children to understand their system of homonyms and to distinguish cases of nonstandard pronunciations from real reading problems.

In other ways Negro speech often differs more dramatically from that of whites, ways that may pose even more serious barriers to literacy. The most important of these seem to involve the loss of final consonants and the simplification of final clusters. Several related developments are involved in this simplification, and they deserve to be considered individually.

-*r*   In many Negro dialects, (as in some white dialects, of course, both in the north and south) post vocalic and preconsonantal -*r* tends to be lost. As in some white dialects, this can result in the falling together of such words as *guard* and *god*, *sore* and *saw*, *fort* and *fought*. Negro speech, however, may go even further than other *r*-less dialects by also losing the intervocalic *r*'s that are preserved in most white dialects, certainly in those of the North. For instance, most New Yorkers in a relaxed mood pronounce *four* without *r* constriction when it occurs finally or before a consonant, as in *fourteen* or *four boys*. But they generally do have *r* constriction when the same word occurs before a vowel as in *four o'clock*. This gives a white New York child some hint about the orthography he must learn, and it must help to rationalize the spelling of the word for him, even in those positions where he would not actually pronounce the *r*. To many Negroes, however, these -*r*'s are absent under all conditions. They may say [fɔ'ɔklak] with as little *r* constriction as they use in [fɔtiyn]. Even an intervocalic *r* occurring in the middle of the word may be omitted, a pronunciation that has been reflected in dialect spellings such as "inte'ested." The name *Carol* may be pronounced identically to *Cal*, and *Paris* and *terrace* become honomymous with *pass* and *test*. A Negro child who first learns this *r*-less dialect has no clue in his own speech about why these words should be spelled with an -*r*, and so he has one extra hurdle to cross if he is to learn to read and write.

-*l*   Although English *l* is phonetically rather like *r* being similar in its distribution within the syllable and even in its effect upon preceding vowels, it is less often completely lost than -*r*. In most English dialects *l* may be replaced, when preceding a consonant, by a back unrounded glide which amounts to little more than a modification of the preceding vowel, as in the rapid pronunciation of *ball game*. But the complete loss of post vocalic *l* and merger of words spelled with *l* with others that are not are largely Negro phenomena. It is not uncommon for Negroes to fail to make a distinction between such words as *toll* and *toe; tool* and *too; help* and *hep; all* and *awe; fault* and *fought*.

Simplification of Final Clusters.   Final clusters may be simplified by losing one of the elements in the cluster. The most common simplification is the loss of the final /t/ or /d/ from such clusters as -*st*, -*ft*, -*nt*, -*nd*, -*ld*, -*zd*, -*md*. Individual speakers vary in the degree and regularity with which these are simplified, and most Americans, both white and black, sometimes simplify them in certain positions (particularly before consonants) or in certain styles of speech, but the tendency toward simplification is more pronounced in the speech of some Negroes. For many Negroes *past* and *pass; meant, mend* and *men; wind* and *wine; hold* and *hole* have become homonyms. Cluster simplification can even be combined with loss of -*l* so that such words as *told, toll* and *toe* may all become homonyms. Clusters with final -*s* or -*z* such as -*ks*, -*mz*, -*lz*, -*dz*, -*ts* are somewhat less frequently simplified, and these give rise to more complex situations for sometimes it is the first element of the cluster, sometimes the second, that is lost. It is at least possible, however, that the loss of final -*s* or -*z* will reduce such words as *six* and *sick* to homonyms.

It is often difficult to be sure whether the simplified final cluster that we hear really reflects the underlying form of the word as the speaker knows it, or whether we hear only the surface manifestation of a more complex underlying form. One particular case is instructive however: the word *test* seems to be pronounced without the final *t* by many Negroes. Words ending in /t/ in

English regularly take an additional /s/ to show the plural, but words ending in /s/ are pluralized by /-iz/. For some Negro speakers the plural of *test* is [tesiz] and the plural of *ghost* is [gosiz]. This seems to demonstrate conclusively that for these speakers, *test*, *ghost*, and many other words completely lack any trace of the *t* of our orthography or of the standard pronunciation.

Other Final Consonants   Final *-r*, *-l* and clusters ending in *-t*, *-d*, *-s* and *-z* are those most frequently reduced, but a few Negroes go even further. Final *-t* may be realized as a glottal stop (as in many white dialects), or it may completely disappear. Final *-d* may be devoiced or disappear. Less often *-k* and *-g* may suffer the same fate. Final *-m* and *-n* may be weakened although they usually leave a residue behind in the form of a nasalized vowel. At its most extreme, this reduction in final consonants can go so far that a few individuals seem predominantly to use open syllables, initial consonants followed by a vowel with hardly any final consonants at all. But even for speakers with less extreme reduction, the final parts of words carry a considerably lighter informational load than for speakers of standard English.

Loss of Suffixes

Even moderate consonant reduction may give speakers rather serious problems in learning the standard language, for it happens that it is the tongue-tip consonants /r,l,t,d,s,z/ that are most often lost. These carry a great semantic burden in standard spoken English, since they are used to form the suffixes. Not only are the plural, possessive, past, and third person singular of the verb shown by one or another of these tongue-tip consonants, but so are most of the colloquial contractions that speakers of the standard use orally, though they write them infrequently. Standard speakers most often indicate the future by a suffixed *-ll*, as in *I'll go, you'll go, where'll he go?* , and so on. The colloquial contractions of the copula generally consist of *-r*, *-z*, or *-s: you're a boy, he's a boy, we're boys, they're boys, the book's good.* If a regular phonological rule leads to the loss of these final consonants, then the grammatical constructions would also be in danger of disappearing. This would imply a series of important ways in which the English of some Negroes would deviate from that of most whites. At least some grammatical changes like these seem to have occurred, although the details appear to be very complex, and are so far only partially understood.

That grammatical change has not been simply the automatic consequence of phonological change is shown by the varying treatment of the plural and of the third person singular marker, which, of course, are phonologically identical in standard English. If loss of suffixes were nothing but a simple result of regular phonological change, then we would expect the plural -*s* and the third person singular -*s* to have suffered exactly the same fate. In fact, the plural marker is usually as well preserved as any suffix, and it shows little if any tendency to be lost. By contrast, in the speech of many Negroes, the third person singular verb suffix is completely absent. These speakers simply lack this suffix, under all conditions, even in cases in which the usual phonological rule for the loss of -*s* would not apply. The easiest way to view this situation in historical perspective is to imagine that both suffixes were first lost under the same conditions, particularly when occurring after other consonants where to have retained them would have resulted in an unpronounceable cluster. When either suffix was added to a root, ending in a vowel, it should have been more readily pronounceable. Upon the identical results of this regular phonological rule, divergent analogical processes could than have brought divergent consequences. If the third person singular marker (which, after all, carries a rather meager semantic load) could be skipped in some positions, it might be skipped elsewhere and so dropped by analogy even from verbs that posed no phonological problem. The plural marker carries a far more significant semantic load, and here, perhaps, the plural signs that survived phonological reduction could serve as a model by which plurals could be analogically reintroduced even onto nouns where a difficult consonant cluster would result. The actual historical processes, by which the plural survived but the third person singular was lost, were no doubt a good deal more complex than this simple scheme would suggest, but the results seem understandable only in terms of both phonological and analogical change.

Other suffixes have suffered varied and complex fates. Contracted forms of the copula often fail to be realized in Negro speech, so instead of *you're tired* or *they're tired*, some Negroes say *you tired* and *they tired*. This much conforms to the regular phonological loss of final -*r*, but when *he's tired* appears as *he tired*, an analogical extension of the missing copula is likely to be involved since loss of final /-z/ when it is not part of a cluster is unusual. Absence of the copula is frequently cited as a characteristic of Negro speech, and this seems to suggest a rather fundamental altering of the organization of tenses. One form of the copula seems not to be lost, however, for the '*m* of *I'm* seems to survive, perhaps because /-m/ has much less tendency for phonological reduction, even than /-z/.

Some possessive pronouns can become identical to the personal pronouns: *your* and *you* may become homonyms as may *their* and *they*. The school child who reads *your brother* as *you bruvver* is actually doing a skillful job of translating the written form into his dialect. Teachers ought to be equally skilled so as to reward rather than to punish such evidence of learning. The noun possessive written '*s* is frequently omitted, even in words ending in a vowel. The possessive forms of some pronouns do survive: *my*, *our*, *his*, *her*, usually remain distinct, and since nobody says *I book* by anology with the common *they book* and *you book*, the possessive cannot be said to be completely lost even if it is far less frequent than in standard English.

With cluster simplification, the past forms of the verb often became identical to the present forms. *Walked* becomes homonymous with *walk*, *pass* with *passed*, *drag* with *dragged*, and similarly for a great many verbs. Nevertheless, the past tense is preserved by irregular verbs, for the loss of the past-present distinction has not been carried by analogy so as to eliminate such distinctions as *tell* from *told*. The irregular verbs of course, are extremely common in ordinary conversation so the past tense is well preserved in colloquial Negro speech, but the regular verbs are still common enough to reduce the amount of information conveyed by the past tense markers.

The phonological loss of final *-l* is related to a frequent loss of the contracted form of the future. This, of course, does not mean that Negroes are unable to convey notions of future time. Expressions with *going to* are common, for instance, but beyond this, the full and uncontracted form of *will* (perhaps pronounced without a final *-l*) is available and regularly used. A Negro child may be able to say *I go* with an implication of future time, and to be more emphatic, he can say *I will go* or *I wi' go*, but he may never use *I'll go*. For such a child, a reader that uses what appears to a speaker of standard English as the slightly stilted construction "I will go" may be considerably easier to read than a book which uses "I'll go."

Grammatical Change

It is clear that some dialects spoken by Negroes have come to contrast with the dialects of most whites in many ways: the loss of phonological contrast particularly at the ends of words, the weakening of suffixes, and the analogical extension of the resulting patterns. Similar changes are known to have occurred in many languages. They represent the kinds of processes which have been active in every family of languages whose history is at all well known. It is proper, therefore, to view these dialects as exhibiting entirely normal and understandable historical developments from an earlier form of the language, a form that standard English continues to approximate a bit more closely. Like many historical developments in language, it is possible to look upon some of these modifications of the Negro dialects as though they involved a degree of simplification in the language, but if historical changes could only bring increasing simplicity, then sooner or later languages would simplify themselves out of existence. There must be countervailing mechanisms that reintroduce complexity.

Recognizing the apparent simplification of some aspects of the Negro dialects, it is tempting to ask whether there are balancing ways in which those same dialects have become more complex than standard English.

It is impossible to give any confident answer to this question, partly because Negro dialects have been so imperfectly studied but even more because we have such meager means of measuring complexity. Still, one cannot help wondering whether the near disappearance of the possessive '*s* is not compensated for by other devices, if by nothing else but a more consistent use of the possessive with *of*. When the past and future tenses are partially lost and when the copula construction is weakened, one must wonder if other tenses have not appeared to take their place. One set of contrasting constructions that has been recognized as common among Negroes but which is missing from white dialects, is represented by the contrast between *he busy* which means 'he is busy at the moment' and *he be busy* which means 'he is habitually busy.' The use of *be* allows the easy expression of a contrast between momentary and habitual action that can be introduced only by rather cumbersome circumlocutions in standard English. Here is one place where the speech of many blacks has a useful resource surpassing the speech of whites.

Many other constructions, typical of Negro speech, suggest other tenses not found in the standard dialect: *he done told me; it don't all be her fault; I been seen it; I ain't like it; I been washing the car* (which is not simply a reduced form of the standard 'I have been washing the car'); *he be sleeping.* Such sentences surely utilize rules exceeding the limits of standard English. Unquestionably the rules governing them are as orderly and rigid as those of the standard, but they are just as surely different in important ways. From the viewpoint of the standard language, it may look as though these dialects lack certain familiar mechanisms. From the complementary viewpoint of the dialects, other mechanisms seem to be lacking in the standard. Certainly standard rules are not rich enough to generate the examples cited here.

Ghetto Education

The language of many Negro children of the northern ghettos is divergent enough from standard English to present educators with a terrible dilemma. Everyone agrees that these children deserve an education that is at least as rich as that of the children in the white suburbs. Negro children ought to be able to take pride in their own background and should not be burdened with shame for cultural differences that are not of their making, and which are inferior only in the sense that people with power happen to have different patterns. If black children are to compete successfully with their white suburban contemporaries in the practical if unjust world of the present day United States, they may have to learn the standard language. But if in learning it, they are forced to reject their own native dialect and to accept the dominant society's view that their native language habits are simply inferior, the experience may do them more psychic harm than social good.

Some would argue that Negroes are no worse off today than the generations of children of European immigrants who entered English-speaking schools knowing nothing but Italian, Greek, or Yiddish. These children too were faced with a strange language, which they had to learn to speak and to read. For some, their education may have been traumatic, but many succeeded, and they or their children have been progressively assimilating into the mainstream of American life. Why, it may be asked, are Negroes any worse off? There are at least two reasons.

First, the economic opportunities for a man with a poor knowledge of standard English have declined. Automation has been progressively eliminating unskilled jobs. More than ever before, a man needs an education. But even more than this, the child of the European immigrant spoke a language that both he and his teacher regarded as a real language. It had a literature, it had its own dictionaries, and it had a writing system all its own. These children were not accused of speaking an inferior variety of English; they spoke something entirely different, and their teachers knew they had to start at the beginning with them. It is easy to be deluded into imagining that Negro children simply speak careless English, to conclude that their language patterns are the result of their own laziness, or stupidity, or cussedness. Some of their teachers never realize that they face a situation with similarities to instruction in a foreign language. Even the child may hardly grasp the truth that his own dialect has its own patterns and structure, and he may all too easily accept his teachers' judgment that he is incapable of learning the "proper" way of speaking. In a just world it would seem fairer to ask others to accept Negro speech as a respectable dialect, one that is as valuable and flexible as any other, than to demand that Negroes, already burdened with problems enough, should have to struggle to learn a different dialect. But such a laudable ideal is probably too remote a dream to be taken seriously.

The problems of ghetto education might be clarified if its various objectives were clearly distinguished. The first goal of language teaching is surely to teach children to read, but it is a depressing truth that thousands of Negro children sit through years of school without ever becoming effectively literate. One important reason for their failure is surely the divergence of the language they bring to school from the language of their teachers and from the language reflected in their textbooks. But whatever the defects of the English spelling system, it has at least one virtue: it does not idiosyncratically favor a single English dialect. Northerners, southerners, Americans, and

Englishmen read the same written forms, but each pronounces what he reads in his own way. Our written conventions are not identical to any single spoken dialect, so everyone must learn to translate between the written word and his own native speech habits. To the extent that spoken dialects differ, children come to the task of gaining literacy from various vantage points, and it might seem that the task of the Negro child is not much different from that of other children who have also first learned a particular spoken dialect. The Negro child, however, is likely to be seriously handicapped in two ways. First, his spoken dialect is likely to be even further from the written form than is that of most white children, and inevitably this causes him more difficulty when learning to read. Even more important, his teacher may fail to appreciate the children's special dialect. The teachers of most white children speak dialects enough like that of their students to make their learning problems immediately understandable. A teacher readily understands and sympathizes with a northern middle-class child who has trouble remembering when to write *four* and when to write *for*. She does not balk at her students easy conversion of the written *hit you* into the spoken colloquial [hičuw]. She will probably not be upset when her students uses '*em* when speaking naturally instead of *them*. The same teacher may be utterly mystified by a Negro student's apparent inability to know when to write *toe*, *toll*, and *told*, or by the apparent capriciousness with which he interprets the past tense, the third person singular, or the possessive suffix. The task of teaching ghetto children to read should benefit greatly from an understanding of what spoken Negro dialects are really like and from reading programs that are specifically designed for speakers of this dialect. One would hope that such a program could avoid stigmatizing the children's own dialect while opening the literate world to them.

Such a reading program will not teach these children standard pronounciation or to speak with standard grammar. That is really a quite separate task, and perhaps it is one that should wait until children are older and until they themselves feel it to be necessary. To try to teach the standard dialect to segregated slum children who have no chance to practice it in their home or on the street, seems to have little more promise of success than the teaching of foreign languages in monolingual America. An older child who has already learned to read and who, from watching television and visiting the movies, has acquired a passive understanding of the standard dialect, may also have both more motivation and more opportunity to escape the restrictions of the ghetto. The prospects may be better for helping him to add active control of the standard to his linguistic repertory, particularly if the curriculum could take realistic account of the language patterns the students start with. What is needed is an instructional program that borrows a few techniques from methods of foreign language instruction and no more than in a foreign language course, need such instruction carry with it the implication that the students' own native language is inferior.

In recent years many of those who have been concerned with education in the ghettoes have come to feel that their realistic goal should be to encourage bidialecticalism, to capitalize upon the skill in dialect switching that many Negroes already have, and to develop ways by which they can learn to do it systematically and well. It is not only arrogant but no doubt utterly useless to ask them to stop speaking with their friends and families in the natural way that they have learned first. They can learn the appropriate time and place for the intimate language and the appropriate time and place for the standard, but they should not have to reject either. The first step in developing such an attitude in students, however, is probably to persuade the thousands of teachers of Negroes that the native dialects of their students have an irreplacable value to them. These dialects deserve respect and understanding for what they are, not blind and uncompromising opposition.

10 Verse and Linguistic Games

Introduction

We exhibit our place in society and we convey our feeling of formality and intimacy by linguistic variables that are grammatically optional and that also leave referential meaning unchanged. If we can say that options left by grammar can be used to convey referential meaning, we can also say that options left by reference can in their turn be used to convey a sense of the situation. Even the variables depending upon formality and social role may be quite rigidly patterned, for it may be a serious breach of etiquette to use informal language where formal language is expected, or the reverse, and everyone is expected to follow some rules of linguistic courtesy. Nevertheless, even after grammar, reference, and situational variables are all taken into account, there still remain options open to speakers. These allow us to use language expressively and to demonstrate something of our individuality and of our own personal style.

On some occasions we can even manipulate our language quite deliberately. We may do this in frivolity or in styles that we take more seriously as art, but in either case the results may be quite different from more mundane language. This manipulation of language, whether in play or in art, often shows more individual variability, and it demands more individual innovation than do the more codified variables by which we express meaning, status, or situation. For this reason we face something of a paradox when we try to analyze the playful and aesthetic use of language. To the extent that we admire innovation and the expression of individual linguistic skills, we have to expect the forms to be less consistent and to show fewer regular patterns than the more prosaic language usually dealt with by linguists. Nevertheless, even our expressions of individual skill are done in a systematic way. We do not admire all random deviation from

134

standard usage but only certain limited types of deviation. When exhibiting linguistic skills, a speaker must follow patterns that others can grasp, patterns that they can recognize as particularly admirable.

In this and the following chapters I will consider a few examples of what might be called linguistic virtuosity, ways in which we more or less deliberately manipulate our language so as to achieve some particularly admired effect. Some linguistic manipulation begins in early childhood. While these earliest forms come to seem banal and uninteresting by the time we reach adulthood, they are followed by other more subtle genres, some of which are mastered only by the most skillful and highly trained adults. However, even the ways in which children distort their language should be of interest to the linguist. I will begin by describing two linguistic patterns that Americans, like speakers of other languages, consider to be the special domain of children—pig latins and simple metrical verse.

Pig Latins

At some time during childhood, most American children learn to use "pig latin." Instead of *he will give it to me*, a child will learn to say *iyhey ilwey ivgey itey uwtey iymay*. This distorted form, of course, is accomplished by a simple phonological transformation. Children teach the pattern to one another by some such instruction as this: "take the first sound of each word and put it on the end and then add *a*." This rule is reasonably accurate though a linguist might want to refine it by observing that it is the entire prevocalic segment of the word that is moved, whether that is a simple initial consonant or a complex cluster. It is not entirely clear just exactly what a word is, although children seem able to learn pig latin without worrying very much about where word boundaries should go. Other secret languages are used by some American children, though perhaps none is quite so widespread as pig latin. The so-called "op" language would change the same sentence into *hapiy wapil gapiv apit tapuw mapiy*. Here one simply inserts /ap/ immediately before the vowel of each syllable.

The phonological transformations required to produce such languages are simple enough for young children to learn but still difficult enough to keep the distorted forms from being easily understood. Indeed they would be useless if instruction, or at least some experience, were not needed to make them understandable. One who is uninitiated into the secret of pig latin or op soon finds the message becoming obscured by gibberish. Inevitably these secret languages can be used only during a rather limited period of childhood, the time when some children have mastered them while others remain ignorant. Once everybody has learned it, a pig latin loses its usefulness, but for a time the children who can use one have an advantage over their less skilled contemporaries.

It seems likely that children throughout the world use similar phonological tricks to obscure their speech. Since they are characteristically childish phenomena, pig latins are often ignored by adults and certainly by linguists, but the devices used are not without linguistic interest, and a few examples will show how similar the devices of various languages are. In Japanese "He will give it to me" can be expressed normally as:

> Anohito-wa sore-o watashi-ni kureru-deshoo
> that person   it   me   to   give will

and a disguised form of the same sentence is Akanokohikitoko-waka sokoreke-oko wakatakashikiniki kukurekeruku-deke shoko oko.

Here each vowel of the normal form must be followed by a syllable consisting of /k/ and a vowel echoing the normal one. In Taiwanese, the same meaning, in normal form and in two disguised varieties is the following:

> /í bé hō gūa/
> he will give me
> /āyí ābé āhō āgūa/
> /ía béá hōā gūaā/

In the first of the disguised Taiwanese forms, /ā/ is simply inserted before each syllable. In the second, /a/ follows each syllable, but the tone of the added /a/ repeats the tone of the preceding syllable.

In Cairo Arabic the corresponding sentence in normal and disguised form is:

> /huwa ha jedihali/
> he will give-it-me
> /hutinuwa ha jedihatinali/

Here, /tinV/ is inserted before the final syllable of each polysyllabic word, but the second vowel of the insertion echoes the preceding normal vowel. Finally, in Benkulu, a Malayo-Polynesian language of Sumatra, the same meaning can be expressed as:

> /dikasikan no ke sayo/
> was give he to me
> /didakasisakika nina kika sayiya/

Here, /iCa/ is substituted for the vowel and final consonant of final syllables and also of some, but not all, syllables appearing earlier in the word. The added consonant echoes the preceding normal consonant. This Benkulu form differs from the other examples in that it alone results in the loss of some phonological material. Many of the original vowels and the final consonant of the first word are lost in the disguised form. Apparently enough remains to allow initiated Benkulu speakers to understand such sentences.

The details of these secret styles vary, but even without pretending to sample the world's languages or to explore the full range of techniques by which children disguise their speech, a number of similarities appear. In all these examples some phonological material is added. This lengthens the time needed to make a statement, but it adds no new information since the rules by which the phonological transformation is accomplished are entirely mechanical. The added noises simply serve to confuse the uninitiated eavesdropper. The order of phonological material is occasionally changed as in English pig latin, and in the Benkulu example some sounds are lost.

The ways by which children can learn to manipulate their normal phonology when they produce pig latins must depend upon quite general phonological principles. Since many of the phonological manipulations of pig latins must be defined in terms of syllables, the syllable might be assumed to be an important universal phonological feature of language. It might also be rewarding to investigate the criteria, whether syntactic or phonological, by which language is broken up into longer word-like units in some disguised styles and to examine the degree to which the resulting units correspond to conventional orthographic devisions of written languages. It seems unlikely that the word boundaries recognized by speakers of pig latin always correspond precisely to those of English orthography. I have heard *underey andstay* for "understand." Although usage is surely not consistent, it could turn out that the divisions children use in speaking pig latin would throw some light on the phonological or syntactical units of our language.

English Nursery Rhymes

Another way in which very young children learn to manipulate their language is in the formation of simple verse. It seems likely that children throughout the world recite nursery rhymes, which follow rather uniform patterns of rhythm and rhyme. A description of some features of English children's verse will illustrate these patterns.

The overwhelming majority of English nursery rhymes have sixteen beats divided into four lines of four beats each. Each beat is typically (but with an important exception to be noted later) marked by a stressed syllable, and the beats are spaced evenly in time from their neighbors (exactly like the stressed notes of western music which introduce each measure). The rhythm of a nursery rhyme can thus be called isochronic (with stresses equally spaced in time) and can easily be recited to the accompaniment of a metronome. It is this regularly recurring stress that distinguishes simple metrical verse from prose. Thus, in the following examples, any fluent speaker of English will stress the syllables marked with the numbers, and he will space these stressed syllables evenly in time, even if, as may be the case with the third example, he is unfamiliar with the particular poem.

1   2   3   4
Humpty Dumpty sat on a wall,
5   6   7   8
Humpty Dumpty had a great fall.
9   10   11   12
All the king's horses and all the king's men,
13   14   15   16
Couldn't put Humpty together again.

1   2   3   4
Ride a cock-horse to Banbury Cross,
5   6   7   8
To see a fine lady upon a white horse;
9   10   11   12
Rings on her fingers and bells on her toes,
13   14   15   16
She shall have music wherever she goes.

1   2   3   4
Two little monkeys jumping on a bed,
5   6   7   8
One fell off and bumped his head.
9   10   11   12
Mommy called the doctor and the doctor said,

13   14   15   16
"Had no business jumping on the bed."

The number of weak or unstressed syllables between adjacent beats is variable and is apparently irrelevant to the larger rhythmical pattern. Anything from no to three unstressed syllables can occur between any two adjacent beats, and the number of unstressed syllables does not affect the isochronism of the major beats. This can be easily verified by reading the examples given here or by experimenting with other verses. When two or three weak syllables come between beats, they are simply said more rapidly, so that the next beat is reached at the same moment it would have been reached had there been no intervening syllables at all. There is a limit, however, and the unpleasant quality of the line

5   6   7   8
She had so many children she didn't know what to do.

seems to be due to the excessive number of weak syllables falling between the last two beats. Three successive weak syllables are allowed, but this example suggests that four are too many. The irregularity of the number of unstressed syllables means that any attempt to analyze English nursery rhymes into feet such as iambs, trochees, or spondees, with regularly recurring numbers of strong and weak syllables, is doomed to failure. Metrical feet probably have no relevance whatever for simple English verse.

The four-beat line has one important variation: the fourth beat may be filled by a rest instead of by a stressed syllable. The pause that constitutes the rest is essential to the rhythm, and it serves to maintain the sequence of four beats even in a line with only three stressed syllables. Rests are ignored by our conventional writing system (only musical notation indicates them explicitly), but they are as obligatory in simple verse as in music. The commonest pattern in our nursery rhymes is for the last beat of the second and fourth lines (that is, beat 8 and 16) to be rests, while all other beats are filled by stressed syllables:

$$
\begin{array}{cccc}
1 & 2 & 3 & 4
\end{array}
$$

Old King Cole was a merry old soul,

$$
\begin{array}{cccc}
& 5 & & 6 & 7 \ \ 8
\end{array}
$$

And a merry old soul was he; R

$$
\begin{array}{cccc}
9 & 10 & 11 & 12
\end{array}
$$

He called for his pipe and he called for his bowl,

$$
\begin{array}{cccc}
13 & 14 & 15 \ \ 16
\end{array}
$$

And he called for his fiddlers three. R.

To verify the obligatory nature of the rests, the reader need only attempt to recite "Old King Cole" without them. It is mechanically possible to do so but it is clearly wrong. Dozens of nursery rhymes have this pattern. They are sometimes said to have alternating four-beat and three-beat lines, but to describe them that way is to forget the obligatory rest and obscure the fundamental similarity of these verses to those in which every line has its full complement of four occupied beats.

Other distributions of rests are less common, but "Hickory Dickory Dock" has rests at positions 4, 8, and 16, only the third line being complete. A few other distributions of rests are occasionally found:

$$
\begin{array}{cccc}
1 & 2 & 3 & 4
\end{array}
$$

Hickory, dickory, dock, R.

$$
\begin{array}{cccc}
& 5 & 6 & 7 & 8
\end{array}
$$

The mouse ran up the clock. R.

$$
\begin{array}{cccc}
9 & 10 & 11 & 12
\end{array}
$$

The clock struck one, the mouse ran down

$$
\begin{array}{cccc}
13 & 14 & 15 \ \ 16
\end{array}
$$

Hickory, dickory, dock. R.

We have a few couplets (for instance, Old Mother Goose), a few six-line verses (for instance, the rhythmic recitation of the alphabet followed by

"Happy happy we shall be . . . ," and so on), and even more rarely we have verses with a degenerate final line. In "This little pig went to market" the fifth toe seems to be more than the four-line Mother Goose pattern can cope with. The fifth line, "This little pig cried wee-wee-wee-wee all the way home," simply cannot be given regular rhythm.

Rhymes are adapted to this pattern of lines and rests and they help to reinforce it. In a verse with no rests, the syllable at beat 4 usually rhymes with that at beat 8, while the syllable at beat 12 rhymes with that at 16. When rests occur at beats 8 and 16 it is usual for the syllables immediately preceding the rests (beats 7 and 15) to rhyme. The verses already given offer a number of examples.

Internal rhymes within the first line are quite common. Here the syllable at beat 2 rhymes with that at beat 4:

1   2   3   4
Hey diddle diddle, the cat in the fiddle . . .
1   2   3   4
Jack Sprat could eat no fat . . .
1   2   3   4
Little Jack Horner sat in a corner . . .

Almost as common are internal rhymes in the third line by which the syllables at beats 10 and 12 are paired, as in the third lines of "Little Bo-Peep," and "Little Jack Horner":

9   10   11   12
. . . Leave them alone, and they'll come home . . .
9   10   11   12
. . . He stuck in his thumb, and pulled out a plum . . .

Limericks combine several of the features already mentioned. They have rests at the last beat of every line except the third (as does "Hickory, dickory, dock"); they have an internal rhyme in the third line (as does "Little Bo-Peep"); and like many nursery rhymes they also rhyme beat 7 to beat 15. Limericks also rhyme beat 3 to beat 7 (and indirectly to 15), a pattern that is not so common in nursery rhymes, though it is not unknown.

1   2   3   4
There was an old dame of Nantucket R.
5   6   7   8
Who kept all her cash in a bucket R.
9   10   11   12
Her daughter named Nan ran away with a man
13   14   15   16
And as for the bucket, Nantucket. R.

Of course it is conventional to write a limerick with five lines. What I have written as the single third line is usually split into the short third and fourth orthographic lines, but this orthographic convention is no more relevant to our habits of oral recitation than is our English spelling to phonological analysis. Our writing habits should not obscure the basic similarity of the limerick to other simple forms of English verse.

Jump-rope games, counting games, and clapping games are all widely, perhaps universally, played by children. All demonstrate clear examples of the same metrical pattern, and they depend in a particularly clear way upon the beat. In "Eeny-Meany-Miney-Mo," the one who is reciting points to a new child at each beat and pays no attention to the total number of syllables. One jumps to the beat in a jump-rope game and claps to the beat in a clapping game. Once we recognize these four-beat lines and their collection into four-line verses, they turn up in a far wider variety of popular verse than just nursery rhymes. Virtually all popular songs and advertising jingles fit this pattern, as do the ephemeral but easily grasped poems that appear in our comic strips or as contributions to our popular magazines.

This metrical pattern is closely related to the rhythm of music, and one may feel tempted to ask whether the rhythm of poetry is anything *except* music. The beats are related to the stressed positions or "down beats" of musical measures. It seems quite unnecessary to recognize any particular position in simple poetry as marking the end of one measure or the beginning of the next, but like the beats of simple poetry the measures in folk songs and popular music often cluster into groups of four. Four of these clusters frequently make a verse, although other multiples of four measures are not unusual. In spite of such manifest similarities, however, one cannot dismiss the rhythm of simple poetry as nothing but the penetration of music into language. One might just as well argue that the rhythm of music is merely a matter of the imposition of poetry upon melody. The more reasonable attitude would seem to be that we have general rules of rhythm that are neither exclusively musical nor exclusively poetic. These rules stand equally behind both music and spoken verse, and require adaptations in both melody and language.

The pervasiveness of this metrical pattern ought to make us ask to what extent it is uniquely English and to what extent generally human. To explore this question we can examine popular verse in languages as remote as possible from English and see whether comparable patterns exist.

Children's Verse in Other Languages

In many ways the Chinese tradition of children's verse is like our own. Similar topics appear in the poems and like ours they contain a certain amount of sheer nonsense. Also, like most English nursery rhymes, the

Chinese verses can either be sung with a melody or recited without one. Division into lines can be easily accomplished on the basis of both grammatical divisions and rhymes, for, as in English, rhymes come predominantly though not exclusively at the end of the line.

The first Chinese example given here is similar to many English verses. It falls naturally into four lines of four beats each. Rhymed syllables are italicized. Note that the number of syllables between the beats is irregular, varying from none to two.[1]

1 2 3 4 Syău hár, syău *hár* shāngjǐng *tár*	Little child, little child climbs the well platform
5 6 7 8 Shwāile ge gēntóu, jyănle ge *chyér*	Falls head over heels, picks up a coin
9 10 11 12 Yòu dǎ tsù, yòu măi *yèr*	And vinegar, and buys salt
13 14 15 16 Yòu chyŭ syífù, yòu gwò *nyĕr*	And gets married and lives out his years

Chinese also allows rests on the last beat of the line as in the following example:

1 2 3 4 Yí, èr, sān, sż, *wŭ*, R	One, two, three, four, five,
5 6 7 8 Jǐn, mòu, shwĕi, hwŏ, *tŭ*, R	Gold, wood, water, fire, earth
9 10 11 12 Yàndz lăi gwò chyáu, R,	Cross the bridge
13 14 15 16 Gēr gā yǐ chǐ *shŭ*. R.	(Noise of flying birds), let us count together

These first two Chinese verses fit precisely the same pattern that accommodates English, and examples could easily be multiplied. As in English, each line has four beats, but the last beat of each line may be filled by a rest.

[1]The verses are transcribed in so-called "Yale Romanization" which has been used in numerous textbooks produced by the Institute of Far Eastern Languages at Yale. In this transcription, each vowel or pair of adjacent vowels signals a syllable, but "ts," "dz," and "sz" may also count as separate syllables. When "r" has an accent—that is, a tone mark—it must be considered as a vowel. The four main tones of Peking Chinese are marked in this transcription as -, ´, ˇ, ` , respectively, while—the fifth "tone" the so-called "toneless" syllables are left unmarked.

The number of weak syllables between beats is irregular, though perhaps not quite so variable as in English.

However, some Chinese examples do deviate from English patterns. A few verses have irregular first lines, as though it takes a while for the verse to settle down to its meter. In the next example the first line has six beats instead of the more usual four, but thereafter it immediately reverts to the four-beat rhythm.

★   ★   1   2   3

yau, yau, yì yáu *yáu* dàu wàipwó   Rock, rock, rock to grand-
      4   mother's bridge
   chyáu

5   6   7   8

wàipwó *jyàu* wǒ syǎu bǎu*bǎu:*   Grandmother calls me lit-
                               tle "baubau"

9   10   11   12

táng yi*bāu*, gwǒ yí*bāu*,   Package of candy, package
                             of fruit,

13   14 15   16

chī̆de wǒ dòur gǔ gāu*gau!*.   I ate until my stomach was
                             big and full.

Chinese also appears to be somewhat less rigid than English in the number of lines per verse, though four lines is still most common.

It is worth noting that the beats in Chinese nursery rhymes are not marked by any particular pattern of tones. Unlike some more sophisticated varieties of Chinese poetry, any tone may occur in any position in children's verse. The beat seems to be imposed by higher level intonational patterns that correlate closely with syntax but have little to do with segmental phonology.

Chinese rhymes operate much like those of English. They generally occur at the end of the lines, most often between adjacent lines, but occasionally the second and fourth beats of the same line are made to rhyme just as they are in English. Rhymed syllables must have identical "finals" (vowels and final consonants, if any), but the tones need not be identical. Unlike English, where some sort of rhyme seems to be obligatory, a few Chinese verses lack them entirely.

Chinese differs from English in being less variable in the number of weak syllables between beats. It is more variable in the number of beats per line, in the numbers of lines per verse, and probably in its rhyming patterns, but these differences operate within a remarkably similar framework.

Examples from one other language, Benkulu, a Malayo-Polynesian language of Sumatra, will show a few variations on a similar basic pattern. The first Benkulu example raises no problem. Each line has three beats occupied by a slightly stressed syllable, and a fourth beat is occupied by a rest. The lines begin with a surprisingly large number of weak syllables. The fourth line has four weak syllables before its first beat, more successive weak syllables than occur in any position in either English or Chinese. These weak syllables are said very rapidly however and by no means crowd out the preceding rest. (Each vowel, or the sequence "ai" indicates a separate syllable.)

$\overset{1}{}$ $\overset{2}{}$ $\overset{3}{}$ $\overset{4}{}$ Anak ikan dimakan ik*an*. R	The baby fish is eaten by a fish
$\overset{5}{}$ $\overset{6}{}$ $\overset{7}{}$ $\overset{8}{}$ Anak tenggiri didalam la-*ut*. R	The baby mackerel is inside the ocean
$\overset{9}{}$ $\overset{10}{}$ $\overset{11}{}$ $\overset{12}{}$ Sanak buk*an* sudara buk*an*. R	Someone not a kinsman, not a sibling
$\overset{13}{}$ $\overset{14}{}$ $\overset{15}{}$ $\overset{16}{}$ Kareno budi mako tesangk*ut*. R	Has entangled you by a favor.

The next two examples appear to be more complex. "Pak-pak pisang" is a clapping game in which an adult sits with a small child alternately slapping his knees with his left and right hand, until the very last beat when he tickles the child. I emphasize the slapping by marking the points where the slaps occur with "l" and "r"—these beats being isochronic. One slap occurs at a rest. "Lenggang" was at one time a rather popular song in part of Indonesia. I first transcribed these verses with the rests marked as in the earlier English and Chinese examples, but, because of the irregularity of the lines, I mark the beats with stars (in "Lenggang") or simply with "l" and "r" rather than with numbers.

l r l Pak-pak pisang	Slapping sound; banana
r l r l r Pisangku belum masak R	My banana is not yet ripe
l r l Masak sebid*ji*	One is ripe
r l r ★ Diurung bari ba*ri*	In the middle of the thorny bush
★ ★ ★ ★ Lenggang lenggang kang*kung* R	Sway like a (certain kind of) plant

    ★   ★ ★ ★
Kangkung ditengah sa*wah*. R   Plant in the middle of a rice field

 ★ ★   ★
Nasib tidak un*tung*   (My) fate is unfortunate

  ★   ★   ★ ★ ★
Punja kawan separti dia. R.   Having a friend like him

At first inspection these verses seem to break the now familiar pattern, since the number of beats in each line is variable. The first verse has lines of 3, 5, 3, and 4 beats, while the second has lines of 4, 4, 3, and 5 beats. A little ingenuity, however, is enough to rearrange the lines and allow four beats to re-emerge consistently. One need only suppose that the rests occur at the beginning of the lines instead of at the end. A rest formerly written at the end of the verse must now be considered to come at the very beginning instead. One may wonder how he could ever recognize a rest that comes either at the very end of a verse or at its very beginning, but if, as in some of these cases, the song has more than one verse, the answer is simple—a rest must be left between adjacent verses. Of course this does not tell whether the rest is at the end of one verse or at the beginning of the next, and only a consideration of the general patterning of the poem can solve that problem. If the last two examples are rewritten so that rests come at the beginning, we have:

       l   r   l
R Pak-pak pisang
  r   l   r   l
Pisangku belum masak
  r   l   r   l
R Masak sebid*ji*
  r l   r ★
Diurung bari ba*ri*.

  1   2   3   4
R Lenggang lenggang kang*kung*
  5   6   7   8
R Kangkung ditengah sa*wah*.
  9   10   11   12
R Nasib tidak un*tung*
  13   14   15 16
Punja awan seperti di*a*.

Rearrangement of the rests may look like sleight of hand, but it brings some incidental advantages. Rhymes become lined up, so that they appear in the same position of successive lines. In the case of the slapping game, the left and right slaps appear in the same positions in each line. It is worth noting that in "Lenggang," the only two lines not separated by a rest are the third and fourth, the same lines run together without a rest in a limerick. In both cases the absence of a rest would seem to signal the approach of the end.

To recognize rests at the beginning of lines gives Benkulu one striking difference from either English or Chinese, but other than the peculiarity of its rests, Benkulu seems to fit much the same pattern as the other two languages. So far as can be judged from the limited examples, Benkulu is completely rigid in having four lines to the verse, and if rests are placed at the beginning, all lines have four beats. Benkulu appears to be as varied as English in the number of weak syllables between the beats. In its many weak syllables before the first nonrest beat of the line, it is very different from Chinese and goes even further than English.

Not only English, Chinese, and Benkulu, but most, perhaps all other languages as well, also have four-beat lines and sixteen-beat verses. In English, this pattern is by no means confined to children's verse, and it should not be expected to be confined to children's verse elsewhere, but one would suppose that any verse children can learn and appreciate must be simple, and it is easier to elicit children's verse than the less predictable genres of adult metrical language. But English has limericks, Spanish has metrical riddles, and other languages may well have other types of verse that fit the same pattern.

If these patterns should prove to be universal, they must depend upon our common humanity. We may simply be the kind of animal that is predestined not only to speak but also, on certain occasions, to force our language into a recurrent pattern of beats and lines. If all people use similar patterns, then cross-linguistic comparisons of the sort I have made between English, Chinese, and Benkulu should not be quite as difficult as might first be imagined. For the simplest form of verse, at least, the similarities are so great that comparisons are easy. If we knew more about enough languages, it should be possible to describe the general panhuman features of simple verse, the features within which our human nature limits us. To these general rules each language could be expected to add its own special restrictions, rules that limit the broader human capacity to the narrower channels of a particular cultural and linguistic tradition.

Adult Verse

More sophisticated poetic forms may follow quite different rules than nursery rhymes, and the rules are almost inevitably more difficult to learn. It is the ease with which we can master certain rhythmic and rhyming rules that makes them suitable for children's verse, but after enough repetition, their very simplicity makes the patterns seem banal. If patterns are to interest adults, they must deviate from and be more complex than the patterns of simple verse.

It seems plausible to suppose that the special characteristics of any distinctive style should be expressible by means of rules that somehow show how that style deviates from others. Some rules, governing children's verse, have been given in the last section. To the extent that we are capable of recognizing examples of language as representative of distinctive styles, it should be reasonable to try to formulate explicit rules that account for them. In some respects, for instance, poetic styles may display more rigid rules than ordinary prose. Perhaps all poetry has tighter phonological restrictions than prose, but in some poetry at least a few ordinary syntactical rules seem to be loosened. The linguistic description of special styles, therefore, should consist of formulating the various ways, whether phonological, lexical, or syntactical, in which new rules are added or the usual rules are loosened, tightened, or omitted.

The minimum definition of metrical language is that its phonological material must be deliberately arranged into some more or less strictly measured pattern, so that it will be distinguished from ordinary conversation or written prose. Nursery rhymes and many other poetic forms are distinguished by the regular timing of certain elements, but in some more sophisticated types of poetry the number of syllables in a line seems to be a more crucial variable than the time period required to complete one line. Thus, in the narrowest definition of iambic pentameter, each line is expected to have ten syllables divided among five iambic feet. Each foot is supposed to have one weak syllable followed by one strong or stressed syllable. The character of each syllable should be appropriate to its linear position within the line. It is true that many lines of so-called iambic pentameter deviate from this rather idealized pattern. Nevertheless, the number of syllables in lines recognized as iambic pentameter is rarely less than nine, or more than twelve, far narrower limits than are acceptable in nursery rhymes. On the other hand, the timing requirement in iambic pentameter is a good deal looser than in children's verse, and, for the most part, lines are not expected to require identical times for completion as do those in nursery rhymes. The two forms share a regular division of phonological material into some sort of lines, often with rhymes at their ends. Both have rules governing the relationship between stress and syllabicity, but the manner in which these relationships are achieved is different.

It has always been realized that the definition of iambic pentameter lines as consisting of five simple iambs is far too rigid. Too many respected iambic pentameter lines deviate in one way or another from this pattern. To account for these lines, certain kinds of deviation have sometimes been recognized as permissible but it has by no means been clear why some deviations seem to result in acceptable lines, while other superficially plausible deviations do not. Recently Morris Halle and Samuel Jay Keyser have suggested some rather novel rules that appear to cover the various kinds of permissible "iambic pentameter" lines in a satisfactory way. In these rules syllable position is a crucial variable, but, unlike the rules I have given for nursery rhymes, timing is not taken into account.

Halle and Keyser suggest an abstract pattern lying behind all iambic pentameter lines, which they describe as having ten positions that may be followed by one or two optional extrametrical syllables at the end. The odd-numbered positions are weak, the even positions, strong. So far this description resembles the standard definition of iambic pentameter, but Halle and Keyser argue that the more abstract positions have to be kept analytically distinct from the more directly observable syllables. Syllables can be mapped onto the positions only by the following rules. (1) Most commonly, each position is occupied by a single syllable. But, when two vowels are separated by no more than a single consonant, it is possible for the two syllables formed around these vowels to squeeze into the same position. (2) On the other hand, the very first position in the line (which is a weak position) may have no syllable at all. (3) The most complex part of Halle and Keyser's description (but an essential part if permitted lines are to be distinguished from impermissible lines) is the following: Syllables carrying more stress than those immediately preceding or following within the same syntactic construction are called stress maxima, and these stress maxima can only occur at even-numbered (that is, strong) positions. Not every strong position need be filled by a stress maximum, however, and the definition of stress maximum implies that the tenth position in a line cannot have a stress maximum unless the line has at least one extra metrical syllable following its tenth position. These rules dispense with the old concept of "foot" but they introduce a new and equally abstract concept of "position."

The rules, of course, will cover the simplest type of iambic pentameter lines such as the following in which each even-numbered or strong position that is filled by a stress maximum is marked by ´.

Much háve I trávelled ín the réalms of gold (Keats).

The rules will also cover a number of less stereotyped lines, however. The syllable occupying the tenth position cannot be a stress maximum, unless, it is followed by a less-stressed extra metrical syllable, and it need not be stressed at all. In the following example the strong position which is not filled by a stressed syllable nor, of course, a stress maximum is indicated by "x".

x

No líght, but ráther dárkness vísible. (Milton)

Other even-numbered positions may also lack stress maxima even though their syllables are stressed, and odd-numbered positions can have stressed syllables so long as they are not stress maxima. Thus in the following line (from Shakespeare's 73rd Sonnet) the second and eighth positions are strong and have stressed syllables, but these do not constitute stress maxima, because they are not more heavily stressed than adjacent syllables. At the same time, positions one and nine, weak positions, are *also* filled by stressed syllables, but again they are not stress maxima because of equal stress in adjacent syllables. (Stress maxima are again marked with ´. Strong positions lacking stress maxima are marked by "n" and stressed syllables *not* at strong positions and not stress maxima are marked "s".)

> s   n   n   s   n
> Bare, ruined chóirs where láte the sweet birds sang.

It is possible for many successive syllables to be stressed, none of which will be a maximum:

> s   n   s   n   s   n
> Rocks, caves, lakes, fens, bogs, dens, and shádes of death. (Milton)

It is also possible for the first position to be unactualized, to be occupied by no syllable at all, and in this case the first syllable of the line will occupy the second position.

> n
> Twenty bóokes clád in blák or reed. (Chaucer)

Even if the first position should have a stronger syllable than the second, it cannot be a stress maxima since it is not preceded by a weaker syllable. ("s" again shows a weak position under stress, and "x" an unstressed strong position.)

> s   x
> Silent upón a péak in Dárien (Keats)

Finally, when two syllables have but a single intervening consonant, it is possible for both to be squeezed into the same position.

> Yet déarly I lóve you and wóuld be lóved fain. (Donne)

It is clear that the patterns of English iambic pentameter rest upon quite different principles than do those of our nursery rhymes. Yet the apparent ability of many English speakers (probably all English speakers in the case of nursery rhymes) to distinguish proper from improper lines suggests that both patterns should be expressible by some sort of orderly rules. In both poetic forms the syllable is a significant unit, but in nursery rhymes it is the timing of accented syllables and in iambic pentameter it is their lineal position in the line that seems to be most crucial. It turns out that some classical Chinese poetry differs from Chinese nursery rhymes in a parallel way.

According to the description of John Lotz, this classical Chinese poetry was written under strict rules governing the number of syllables in each line and the characteristics of syllables occupying particular lineal positions. Stress seems not to have played an important role, but, unlike the case of Chinese nursery rhymes, tones were highly significant. The tones were grouped into two different classes. One of these classes may originally have included all even tones, whether high or low, and the other all changing tones, including complex rising and falling tones, although it is difficult to be certain of this, since the tones of the modern dialects have changed enough to obscure the earlier patterns. At any rate there were a number of different verse patterns, but typically certain positions of each line had to be filled by a syllable with a tone of the appropriate class. Other positions could be freely filled by syllables with any tone. The tone classes of adjacent lines sometimes mirrored each other, and the final syllables of the lines sometimes had to rhyme. In the following schematic forms of some typical verse patterns, 1 and 2 represent the two tone classes, and are written in positions where a syllable of that class is required; r is written in positions where the syllables must rhyme with one another; "." represents a free position, in which any syllable may occur:

. 1 . 2 r   . 1 . 2 . 1 r
. 2 . 1 r   . 2 . 1 . 2 r
. 2 . 1 r   . 2 . 1 . 2 r
. 1 . 2 r   . 1 . 2 . 1 r

Every language surely has a number of special styles that deviate in various ways from normal prose. The rules defining these styles can influence all aspects of phonology. Rhythm, stress, alliteration, and rhyme can all be used to distinguish special styles from casual speech. The special styles can set off some events as particularly dignified, others as particularly frivolous. Some styles, like pig latins and nursery rhymes, are so simple that we all learn them as children. Others are more subtle, and a few are so complex that many speakers never master them. This allows these most difficult styles to be used not merely to distinguish one sort of event from another but also to distinguish one sort of speaker from another. Those speakers who can display superior skills can set themselves apart from the less capable majority. This possibility leads to a new topic, the investigation of individual differences in linguistic skill.

11 *Linguistic Virtuosity*

Individual Linguistic Skills

Speakers of all languages in all parts of the world credit some of their fellows with superior linguistic skills, and those so recognized are often paid a special respect. The simplest of the poetic forms considered in the last chapter can be known and used by everyone in a linguistic community, but even simple poetry gives some people a chance to display their talent. English speakers, for instance, grant a modest respect to the man who can create a clever new limerick or other simple poem. Even the man who can remember and recite large numbers of poems learned from others is granted similar respect. We show even greater regard for those with sufficient linguistic talent to produce more sophisticated poetry, and, of course, we recognize many other linguistic skills as worthy of our admiration. The types of linguistic skills set off as specially admired differ from society to society, but with noteworthy regularity *some* linguistic skills are looked upon with admiration. Rewards are given to those who can demonstrate these skills. I will consider a few rather diverse examples.

Glossolalia In a few tribal societies and in some fundamentalist Christian churches, the ability to "speak in tongues" is much admired. Some men, often while in a state of trance, can produce sequences of vocal noises that do not add up to the normal linguistic behavior of the community. The speaker may not be able to offer a meaningful interpretation of what he says, and afterwards, he may not even be able to remember what he did. However, to other members of the community in which this glossolalia occurs, these utterances are looked upon as almost magically important, and they are often imagined to belong to a language unknown to anyone present.

The forms of glossolalic utterances are extremely variable. The noises

151

produced seem to vary all the way from a series of gurgles and grunts to deviant forms of a normal language. Members of the community sometimes interpret the simplest noises to be the language of animals or of animal spirits, which speak through the mouth of a medium. Slightly more elaborate noises, coming a bit closer to normal speech, may consist of repetitious sequences of syllables, often with simpler phonological form than the native language, but still interpretable in terms of its phonological resources. These performances are often presumed by members of the community to be in a foreign language, and it may be supposed that the speaker has acquired the ability to speak this language through some supernatural means. In some cases, a spirit or god is believed to speak through the medium of a person in a trance, and of course the spirit will use his own language, even if the medium cannot ordinarily speak it.

Though members of the community sometimes believe they are hearing a real language, they may admit ignorance of what the language is. Sometimes, however, the utterances are explicitly attributed to one particular foreign language. It is often claimed that the man who produces the noises is quite incapable of speaking the language except under such conditions as a ceremonially induced trance. It is difficult to assess these claims to foreignness. In some cases, a man who is skilled in glossolalia may have had enough experience with the foreign language to learn a few fragments. He might be able only to imitate its sounds, or he might repeat words or phrases without actually understanding them. Occasionally, when in a trance, a man might be able to produce quite long utterances that he would find impossible in his normal waking state. In many cases, however, there can be little question that the attribution of glossolalic noises to a foreign language comes not from any objective similarity with any known language but from the faith of believers. They find their faith confirmed by believing that they have actually produced or heard a language of which they know nothing.

If members of the community regard the language as foreign and as unknown to anyone present, they may make no attempt to interpret its meaning. Sometimes, however, a priest, or other communicant may claim to understand another's glossolalia, and he will "interpret" for the congregation's benefit. The interpretor has less need to go into a trance than the original speaker, and interpretation may be regarded as a rather mechanical skill, even if it is limited to specially qualified individuals. Of course, unless the glossolalic performance conforms closely to a real language, the interpreter must somehow supply the meanings himself, and he is probably quite free to supply whatever meanings he finds appropriate. Interpretation of glossolalia may allow a shaman to discover the will of the spirits or to decide upon the appropriate cure for a disease.

To the disinterested observer, the sounds of glossolalia may seem like gibberish. And it is difficult to make generalizations about any internal form or structure that glossolalic utterances may have. No doubt they are extremely variable, but what is important here is not to provide a linguistic description of the patterns found in glossolalia but to point out that the participants in these communities often look upon the utterances as though they constitute a language. They actively seek the ability to "speak in tongues"; they admire those who achieve the ability; and they recognize different degrees of skill.

Multilingualism in New Guinea   Another example of admired and rewarded linguistic skill comes from New Guinea. Richard Salisbury has described an area that seems not to be atypical, where translation occurs far more often than practical understanding and communication demand. The ability to speak two or more languages and to translate between them is a skill that is cultivated and rewarded. Salisbury worked in a village where a dialect known as Komuku was spoken. Komuku belongs to the so-called Siane group of languages, and in the immediate neighborhood of Salisbury's village another Siane dialect, this one known as Ramfau, was spoken, but the villages in one direction used an entirely different language, Dene. By usual linguistic criteria the Dene and Siane groups of languages are utterly unrelated, so that Salisbury's village lay beside a linguistic border that is about as sharp as any that can be found in New Guinea.

This linguistic boundary, however, did not correspond to a cultural boundary, for neighboring villages dealt with one another in similar fashion, whatever language they used. They held intervillage ceremonies, men had friendships in neighboring villages, they exchanged wives, and they waged war, all without linguistic discrimination. No enduring political ties united villages into larger chiefdoms or federations, and so no political boundaries could reinforce the linguistic boundary between Siane and Dene.

In fact, not even the linguistic boundary was quite as sharp as it first appeared, since many people could speak more than their own village dialect and language. Of course, when wives moved across the Siane-Dene border at marriage, they brought their own language with them, though after a few years they would gradually switch to the local language. Women gained no particular prestige by speaking a different language, so they could speak whatever was most convenient and effective. Many men could also speak languages other than that of their own village, and some could understand languages that they could not speak. Since women regularly married outside their natal village, and since men often visited back and forth, multilingual conversations were frequent. Each participant in a conversation might speak the language that came most easily to him, but he would be able to understand the languages used by others.

On formal and ceremonial occasions, speakers would deliberately use more than a single language. When people from two or more communities gathered at a ceremony, every public address was immediately followed by a translation. Besides the local language, others were sometimes heard. Missionaries had penetrated the area who used the coastal language called Kate. This was not natively spoken in the area where Salisbury worked, and so religious ceremonies had to include regular translation between Kate and the local languages. Representatives of the administration would use pidgin English, and it too would be immediately translated. More striking perhaps than this constant translation was that certain Siane men would use Dene, ostensibly a "foreign" language, when speaking publicly even in their own village. One man in Salisbury's village almost always used Dene in public, though he did not mind speaking Siane in private. His use of Dene encouraged translation in the village context, when it would not really have been necessary if communication were the only goal, for he could easily have used Siane. The head man of the village would speak to Salisbury in the Komuku dialect of Siane, which Salisbury understood, but he would insist that it be translated into pidgin before allowing Salisbury to respond. Salisbury would give his answer in Siane, but this would then have to be repeated and "translated" into a more embellished and elaborated form of the same dialect. These people, then, performed as good deal of gratuitous translation, and it was the repetition and translation itself that emphasized the significance of a discourse. Translation was deliberately used to set off a particular situation as public and important. This made bilingualism and the ability to translate useful skills for any man aspiring to leadership. So important was multilingualism that villagers actively cultivated new languages. Laborers who returned from the coast with some knowledge of pidgin English organized lessons to pass their skill on to others. A servant who came with Salisbury and who spoke still another language was used as a source from which to gain still further linguistic versatility.

Not everyone had equal facility in speaking varied languages, but it seems that those who had high status generally had the greater abilities. Perhaps this was partly because those with high status had more chance to display their skills for they had to rise more often on public occasions when oratory and translation were called for. But to some degree, bilingualism and multilingualism seem to have been a prerequisite of high status. The acquisition and display of linguistic skills were used to achieve and confirm high status in this part of New Guinea.

Walbiri upside down talk   The Walbiri are natives of central Australia, and Kenneth Hale has described a peculiar type of secret language known as *tʸiliwiri*, which Walbiri men use at the time of certain rituals. Boys first encounter *tʸiliwiri* when they are about 13, after their first initiation. At first they are unable to understand it. Its principles are never abstractly explained, but boys must infer them by listening to older men speak. Unlike pig latins, which attain their secrecy by distorting the phonology, *tʸiliwiri* distorts the meaning. Its most general principle is that all nouns, verbs, and pronouns are replaced by their semantic opposites. The phonology follows regular Walbiri conventions, and the grammatical markers are left intact, so the structure of the sentences is not obscured, but there is wholesale substitution of nouns and verbs. The youth who has not yet inferred the principles by which the language is derived from normal Walbiri may fail to realize that a sentence like 'that one is small' should be interpreted as 'this one is big' or that 'another is standing on the sky' must be understood as 'I am sitting on the ground.'

For words such as 'big,' 'small,' 'hot,' 'cold,' and so forth, the principle seems easy enough to apply, but only a few words in any language have transparent opposites. Nevertheless, the Walbiri are able to find opposites for all of the words of the major form classes of their language, and they even describe *tʸiliwiri* as turning ordinary Wabliri upside down. The most interesting aspect of the language is to see how the Walbiri settle upon opposites for concepts that do not have real polar antonyms.

Terms for plants and animals can hardly be described as having real opposites, and the Walbiri solution is to exchange the names of the most closely related species. Two terms are substituted for each other when they stand for animals that are differentiated by only a single characteristic. Thus the terms *wawiri* and *kanʸala*, which refer to two different kinds of kangaroos, can be substituted for one another as can *wakulʸari* and *yulkaminʸi*, two kinds of wallabys. If one is to learn to distort his language by replacing every noun with another noun, it is hard to imagine a more effective principle for plant and animal terms than the Walbiri one. As a matter of fact, we even recognize real polar opposites by a similar principle, for terms like 'hot' and 'cold' are very close in meaning, being differentiated by just one feature.

Kinship terms are also switched with as closely similar terms as possible. Walbiri kinship terms are differentiated by criteria such as sex, relative age, and kin-group membership, and it might be possible to move across any one of these dimensions of contrast or even some combination of them in finding an opposite. Indeed, the most opposite term of all might be supposed to be the term that is most differentiated from the intended meaning, contrasting with it on every possible semantic dimensions. The Walbiri, however, choose to concentrate upon the single principle of relative age and generation. Terms for 'older brother' and 'younger brother' are substituted for each other as are terms for 'older sister' and 'younger sister' and the terms for 'father' and 'son.'

Synonymous and even partially synonymous terms may be replaced by the same opposite term when speaking *tʸiliwiri*. The Walbiri words for 'hole' and for 'creek bed' are both replaced in *tʸiliwiri* by the word that ordinarily means 'even ground.' 'Before' and 'after' are both replaced by 'now.' The general context will usually be sufficient to resolve any resulting ambiguity. In some respects, however, the *tʸiliwiri* version may actually be somewhat less ambiguous than the normal Walbiri. The term ŋ*alapi* can mean either son or daughter in normal Walbiri and is, therefore, ambiguous as to sex. Since terms for the older generation in normal Walbiri are not ambiguous in this way, the *tʸiliwiri* substitutes for ŋalapi are *kidana* 'father,' when a male is to be spoken of, but *pimidi* 'mother,' if one intends the sense of 'daughter.' In cases like this, *tʸiliwiri* is less ambiguous than the normal Walbiri from which it is derived.

The way in which Walbiri makes substitutions can sometimes clarify the structure of a term's meaning. Thus *ṛampaku* can mean either 'weak' or 'light in weight.' *Wakuṭuḍu* means 'strong' and *pirtʸiḍi* means 'heavy', these two terms being opposites of *ṛampaku* in its different senses. When the normal Walbiri would have *ṛampaku* in the sense of 'weak,' the *tʸiliwiri* substitute is *wakuṭuḍu,* but when *ṛampaku* would be used in the sense of 'light' the *tʸiliwiri* is *pirtʸiḍi.* Clearly it is semantic features that govern the substitution of terms rather than mechanical rules based upon arbitrary pairing of morphemes.

A few substitutions are dependent upon particular concepts of Walbiri culture. The terms for 'fire' and 'water' are exchanged, reflecting the pairing of these terms in much Walbiri mythology. *Tʸiliwiri* also makes use of a number of idiosyncratic pairs that must simply be learned. However, in spite of all these complexities, a skilled speaker of *tʸiliwiri* can speak as rapidly as when he speaks normal Walbiri, and beyond its ritual associations Walbiri men take great pride and pleasure in their ability to produce skillful *tʸiliwiri*

Street talk   Urban Negro children are sometimes imagined to be so verbally deprived as to be almost tongue-tied, but any serious examination of the language of Negro youths when speaking with their contemporaries in the streets, suggests that admiration of fluent and innovative speech is as marked among them as among any other group. In a remarkable study, based partly upon observations in Chicago and partly upon an examination of literary sources, Thomas Kochman has described some of the terms used by Negro youths for various expressive forms of language.

Rapping for instance, describes a distinctively fluent and lively way of talking, one that is always highly personal in style. It can be a way of creating a favorable impression when first meeting a person, though it can also become rather competitive and lead to a lively repartee. *Rapping* to a woman implies a colorful way of propositioning her, but otherwise it is simply a lively way of projecting personality when style is more important than the information exchanged.

Shucking (or one of a number of synonyms such as *jiving*) is the kind of language used when facing authority, particularly white authority. *Shucking* describes a kind of speech that hides the speaker's true feelings of indignation or pride, masking them behind an apparent innocence and deference. *Shucking*, therefore, describes the role of shuffling ignorance that whites have forced upon Negroes, and it can cover not only speech and intonation but the gestures and facial expressions by which one feigns repentance and evokes the sympathy of those in power. Naturally, the more militant black leaders now look upon *shucking* with little favor. The term *shucking* can also describe a style of speaking to other Negroes who are not in a position of authority. Here it refers to attempts to create a false impression and can include anything from an outright lie to a more subtly misleading variety of discourse.

Running it down is used for straightforward communicative speech, where the purpose is to convey information, narrate events, give an explanation, or offer advice rather than to display personaltiy in some particular way. *Gripping*, apparently a fairly new term, refers to the speech and facial expression that go with a partial loss of face and even some fear. In a street code that emphasizes being fearless and tough and "keeping one's cool," *gripping* can hardly be much admired, but it is not as bad as *copping a plea*, which amounts to complete surrender to superior force and a pleading for mercy.

Signifying refers to teasing or taunting speech. It may include some boasting, and it may be used to goad another into an aggressive act. *Signifying* can arouse feelings of embarrassment, shame, or futility, but it may help to stir up a little excitement in an otherwise dull day. *Sounding* is an even more direct verbal insult, and the term refers specifically to the insults that are hurled back and forth in a rather stylized game also known as *Playing the Dozens*. *Sounding* refers most specifically to the initial remarks that test whether or not another person is willing to play the game. The game of *Dozens* involves competitive slurs upon one's opponent and upon his family, and it is often encouraged by *signifying* of onlookers.

The recognition of these distinct modes of speech suggests that verbal skills are by no means neglected in the street culture. It even seems that the ability to use words is as highly valued as physical strength. Perhaps, it is even more highly regarded, for a youth may resort to fighting only when he feels he can no longer hold up his reputation by verbal means alone. Violence may be an admission of verbal defeat. Language is used in the ghetto streets for self-assertion, competition, and when trying to manipulate others. Kochman concludes, "by blending style and verbal power, through 'rapping,' 'sounding,' and 'running it down' the Negro in the ghetto establishes his personality; through 'shucking,' 'gripping,' and 'copping a plea' he shows his respect for power; through 'jiving' and 'signifying' he stirs up excitement. With all of the above, he hopes to manipulate and control people and situations to give himself a winning edge."

It is these same Negro youths whom educators sometimes imagine to be verbally stunted and so inarticulate as to be incapable of expressing themselves clearly in the classroom. No doubt the educator would be just as inarticulate were he to try playing the *Dozens*. Each may be fluent in his own sphere, and each may equally admire verbal skills. Sadly, educators have rarely been successful in capitalizing upon the verbal skills their pupils display on the street. They often succeed only in persuading them that the classroom requires skills not easily acquired by the ghetto youth. Schools have not done well in teaching these skills.

Oratory   In countless societies around the world, the able orator has been a much admired figure. Especially in nonliterate societies, the orator, who can command the attention of his audience and persuade them to his point of view, may be able to assume leadership over his fellows. Samoans have a special category of chiefs whose particular role is oratory. The orators serve as a sort of mental storehouse for the traditions of the society, for they are the custodians of its knowledge. They manipulate words, and they lead people in practical daily affairs. Titles to the various Samoan posts, including the posts of orators, come partly by inheritance, but this is left flexible enough to permit some freedom of choice among those equally qualified by heredity. This makes it possible to fit the titles to men with ability. Outstanding individuals can then be drawn into the traditional system of leadership.

The main responsibility of the orators is in ceremonial affairs. Traditionally they are specialists in etiquette. They must be able to recite long histories of the communities, given in an elaborate allegorical language. Orators also provide the ceremonial preliminaries to speech-making in councils. But orators are also leaders in practical affairs. They participate in negotiations and use their adroit ability with language to guide meetings. Fluent speech is much admired in Samoa, and as among many other peoples it tends to go with positions of leadership.

Verbal Skills and Intelligence

The examples given in the last section are meant to suggest that all people recognize variable linguistic skills and that the rewards of leadership tend to be conferred upon those who have these skills. The particular skills that are admired and rewarded may vary from society to society—multilingualism and the ability to translate in parts of New Guinea, production of glossolalia in some religious communities, oratory in Somoa and *rapping* and *signifying* among ghetto Negroes. But verbal skills of some sort are honored everywhere. If all these people so consistently admire linguistic skills and assign leadership to those who exhibit these skills, it would be surprising if middle-class and academic American society were an exception. Of course it is not an exception, for even our standard intelligence tests by which we channel our children and youths into various careers, use scores for verbal aptitude as one of their most important components. The use of these tests seems to rest upon the assumption that individuals do vary in verbal skills, and that these skills are somehow related to whatever it is that we call intelligence. Of course everyone realizes that test scores are influenced by the individual's experiences and the best we can hope for is to measure the effect of a man's experience upon his native ability. If people with roughly equivalent experience perform unequally on a verbal aptitude test, that would seem to confirm the belief that some sort of native inborn capacity influences test results.

American tests of verbal aptitude often rely especially upon knowledge of vocabulary. Perhaps this is partly because vocabulary is relatively easy to test by multiple choice questions and machine-scored answer sheets, but it must also be admitted that quite apart from intelligence tests, vocabulary size is widely felt by Americans to be peculiarly important. Our schools are not alone in trying to expand vocabulary, for our popular magazines help them out with columns on "how to increase your word power" or "this week's ten words." A big vocabulary is widely regarded as a good thing.

Those who design intelligence tests like to believe that systematic efforts to increase one's vocabulary by memorizing lists of words will not render their tests invalid, but one who is not committed to vocabulary tests may occasionally wonder if they do not really measure a student's willingness to accept the cultural values of those who tell him that it is good to have a large vocabulary. Perhaps the tests are primarily a measure of docility.

Yet this charge would surely be too extreme, for the variability in measured vocabulary is too marked to be dismissed completely. We probably will have to admit that some people have a special aptitude for remembering words. It is the belief of our test-makers—and of the college admissions officers and employers who use the test results—that an aptitude for learning and remembering words is somehow related to other desirable abilities such as doing well in school or succeeding in a profession. Americans do not make chiefs of those who can orate or translate with skill, but the rewards for verbal dexterity are no less real in the United States than in Samoa or New Guinea.

Even if we agree that the aptitude for learning words has something to do with skills that are important to society, it is obvious that tests of verbal aptitude can only discriminate among people with rather similar linguistic experiences. Our tests, of course, are designed for native speakers of

English, and it is useless to give them to Italians or Chinese. It ought to be equally obvious that the tests will fail for those who grow up speaking a sharply different dialect than the one upon which the test has been based. If the test is not language independent, it will not be dialect independent either. A Negro child, who is fluent in his own dialect and who has a rich and varied vocabulary of that dialect, might do badly on a standard intelligence test, simply because the test asked for a different set of vocabulary items than the child ever had the chance to learn.

Testers seem to agree that bilingual children do less well on their tests of verbal aptitude than monolingual English speakers. The low scores of bilinguals are surely due in part to the low status to which society relegates them. Most bilingual children in America have been the sons and daughters of immigrants with a relatively low socio-economic position. As they struggled to be accepted in the United States, they all too frequently were made to feel ashamed of their foreign background. If their special background was ridiculed, bilingual children could easily have become inhibited, not only in their use of their parents' language, but in their use of English as well. This could cause failure on verbal tests, though the failure would be due to general sociological conditions and not simply to bilingualism alone. Without trying to minimize the sociological factor in the poor performance of bilinguals, however, some more purely linguistic factors may also be at work. It should not be entirely outlandish to wonder whether the human brain might have some sort of finite capacity. The anatomy and physiology of our brain must set limits upon how much knowledge it can absorb. One might speculate that a child who learns two languages will not learn quite so much of either as he might have by concentrating on one. One hardly need imagine any subtle or mysterious process of interference between the two languages. Perhaps the child of immigrant Italian parents who learns 2000 words of Italian can simply be expected to know 2000 fewer words of English than his monolingual classmates. If he knows even 1000 fewer, he can hardly be expected to do as well as monolinguals on many tests of verbal aptitude. It has sometimes been concluded from the poor performance of bilinguals that it is a mistake to teach a child two languages. It would seem more reasonable to conclude that standard verbal intelligence tests are badly biased in favor of monolinguals. Of course, as long as colleges base their admissions on tests scores, it may be strategically unwise to let a child waste too much of his mental capacity on a language in which he will not be tested. This concentration will only allow him to do well on "intelligence tests"; it will not make him more intelligent.

Nevertheless, as we minimize the factor of diverse linguistic backgrounds and as we narrow our consideration to a reasonably homogeneous population with comparable linguistic experience, individuals still vary appreciably in their test results. Children from the same family do not all do equally well on such tests, and identical twins are likely to be more similar than other siblings. It is difficult not to conclude that there is a component of genetically inherited verbal skill reflected on tests. Moreover, the results of verbal aptitude tests do seem to correlate rather well with scores on some other kinds of tests and with grades in school. Whether we like it or not, verbal test scores do, with some reliability, predict success in school or college. The assumption of the testers must be that however imperfect they are, the tests still reflect some sort of native ability that is at least partially independent of experience. We do suppose that a big vocabulary is an indication of more generalized abilities.

If vocabulary size were related in some simple way to inherited intelligence, one might suppose that the relationship would be found in all cultures, not just in our own. If the range of human intelligence is shown by the range of vocabulary size, every language should show similar vocabulary variability, reflecting individual differences among its speakers. Unfortunately, for most languages we have little evidence about vocabulary variability. Vocabulary is difficult to study, for an investigator must have an extraordinarily extensive knowledge of another language to be able to judge the kinds of subtle skills that are measured by our own vocabulary tests.

An attempt was once made in Burma to construct aptitude tests that would help screen applicants to Rangoon University. The psychologist who was helping to design these tests found it impossible to discriminate among students on the basis of their vocabulary. He concluded that all Burmese knew about the same range of words. Everyone did equally well. A linguist's first reaction to this might be that the test-maker simply failed to find the right words, but perhaps this would be too hasty a conclusion. Perhaps some linguistic communities do have a more homogenous vocabulary than we do. Linguists tend to believe that all languages have roughly the same degree of complexity. Complexity is difficult to define or measure, but we suppose that the average complexity controlled by each individual is roughly the same, whatever his language. We do not have to argue that the total vocabulary of Samoan or Zulu is comparable in bulk to the contents of the unabridged English dictionary, but it is not so difficult to imagine that the vocabulary of the average Samoan or Zulu speaker might compare favorably to that of the average Englishman. If the unabridged vocabulary of English is larger, however, an English speaker with a great aptitude for learning words may have an opportunity to excel in this direction, while an equally talented Samoan or Zulu might not find the resources within his language to develop that particular talent. Perhaps the American cultural value placed on a large vocabulary is a bit unusual. On the other hand, it is not at all unusual to recognize *some* linguistic skill as admirable and as valuable enough to deserve a reward. With noteworthy regularity, some sort of verbal skills are admired, and although the particular skills vary, skills of some sort are often regarded as a prerequisite to positions of leadership or responsibility.

Perhaps we can see the particular American admiration for an enormous vocabulary as one example of a far more widespread belief that verbal skills of some sort are a sign of ability. American culture happens to concentrate upon vocabulary size; other cultures put their emphasis elsewhere. But some linguistic skills are always to be valued. Whatever general intelligence may be, it is closely enough related to a man's facility with his language to allow all people in their various ways to judge intelligence by linguistic criteria. We might even speculate that the emphasis Americans place upon vocabulary size limits our other linguistic skills. Could the poor American record for learning foreign languages be partly blamed upon too many of us having exhausted our linguistic resources by expanding the range of our English? Conceivably, the person who does learn two or more languages may limit his potential for learning a vast English vocabulary. It is only our particular cultural emphasis that rewards the skills of bilingualism less than those of vocabulary size.

Some Americans, of course, do learn other linguistic skills. Many Negroes, for instance, are highly skilled dialect switchers and can move easily from a form that is close or identical to the standard to a form that is deviant in every respect. Though rarely recognized as such, this skill is much like bilingualism, but the skills of the expert dialect switcher are not measured on verbal aptitude tests or rewarded by college admissions officers. To the extent that his linguistic abilities have been invested in mastering two rather different dialects, a man may be handicapped by comparison with a man of equal native ability who has been able to concentrate all his talents upon elaborating a single dialect.

These comments have been nothing if not speculative, but we know far too little about the range of linguistic ability in societies other than our own to let us draw more firm conclusions. We do know that linguistic skills are widely recognized as a sign of some sort of talent. We know that those who are skillful are often given responsibility and assigned positions of leadership. If we believe that human intellectual activity and the human ability to cooperate in an orderly society is bound up with language, the use of linguistic skill as a measure of general ability may not be unreasonable. But if the particular linguistic skills to be rewarded are those most easily acquired by a limited middle-class segment of our society, we may perpetrate a tragic injustice upon those who happen to be born in a different class.

Elaborated and Restricted Codes

Several distinct factors may cause individuals to speak differently from one another, though it is often difficult to sort them out and choose among them when observing an example of linguistic variability. First, whenever we deal with a linguistic community that is at all heterogeneous, we certainly have to consider dialectical variability. Linguists have most often studied geographical dialects in which the linguistic variables are dependent upon the location where speakers live or grow up. But, as we have seen in Chapters 8 and 9, dialects that correlate with social class can also be recognized. Whether dependent upon geography or class, it is unfair to attribute any sort of special linguistic virtue to one dialect as compared to another. One may come to be recognized as a standard, but that is a sociological fact and is in no way a reflection of inherent superiority. Some of the differences between upper and lower-class speech are unquestionably merely a matter of dialectical differences and are linguistically no more important than the differences that separate British from American. We are ready to accept geographically defined dialects as having equivalent resources and flexibility, and the variables that separate social dialects must, at least in part, be of exactly the same type, whatever the popular connotation of these variables may be.

Second, we should at least leave open the possibility that there are individual differences in inherited native ability that differentially affect linguistic behavior. This is an idea that many Americans reject because their egalitarian ideals lead them to imagine that somehow we are all equally endowed. In the preceding sections, I have offered some tentative evidence for individual differences in linguistic ability. If ability is randomly distributed among all social classes, of course, one would expect to find as many outstandingly skillful speakers of lower-class dialects as of upper-class dialects. To allow the possibility of individual inherited differences does not rule out other factors as having a simultaneous effect. There need be no contradiction between inherited differences and differences based upon varying individual experiences. Both can act together. It may be difficult for an observer to sort the factors out, but the difference should not be difficult to maintain conceptually.

Neither the recognition of individual differences nor of class dialects gives any support to the belief that the speech of one class is less flexible or in any way inferior to the speech of another. Nevertheless, it has been argued with some vigor in recent years that we have a "culturally deprived" segment in our society that suffers special linguistic disabilities. A particularly forceful statement of this viewpoint has been given by the British psychologist Basil Bernstein, and in considering Bernstein's evidence it is worth keeping in mind this question: is there evidence for linguistic differences between individuals that are neither simply dialectical nor simply dependent upon varying inherited abilities? Simple dialectical differences do not represent different potentialities for expression or flexibility. Differences based upon native intelligence are not attributable to class background. Bernstein seems to claim that there is also a class-based variability in valuable linguistic skills. What is the nature of his argument?

Bernstein investigated the linguistic abilities of teen-aged boys in London. Some were regular students in a "public" school (that is, what an American would call a private school), and Bernstein regards them as middle class. The others, presumably of working-class origins, worked as messengers and attended only part-time classes. Their average age was sixteen, and they were divided into five groups, two of middle-class and three of working-class background. Bernstein tested the boys for verbal and nonverbal intelligence, and he managed to arrange the groups so that one middle-class group was closely matched to one working-class group in both verbal and nonverbal I.Q. as measured by standard tests. The other middle-class group measured somewhat higher on verbal I.Q., while the other two working-class groups measured a bit lower either on the verbal or nonverbal test scores. Bernstein felt that if the groups with similar I.Q.s performed differently at some task, while groups with different I.Q.s but similar class background performed similarly to each other, he would have demonstrated the effect of the divergent class background.

Each group of boys was separately assembled and asked to discuss the abolition of capital punishment. Bernstein recorded their conversation and, after cutting out the first five minutes, subjected the next 1800 words to various kinds of analysis. He felt that the three working-class groups were rather similar to each other whatever their I.Q. scores, as were the two middle-class groups. He did find a number of differences which distinguished the middle-class from the working-class boys, however.

Middle-class speakers used more complex verbal stems—more infinitives, auxiliaries, and considerably more passives—and they used a larger number of subordinate clauses than working-class boys. Several very common adverbs were used freely by both classes but middle-class boys also used a number of less common adverbs, which working-class boys rarely used. Middle-class boys also used a larger number of adjectives in proportion to the total number of words in the sample, and a higher proportion were relatively uncommon. The two classes used about the same proportion of prepositions, but the middle class used "of" more frequently. Middle-class speakers used uncommon conjunctions (other than "and," "so," "because," "also," "then," "like,") more often than the lower class. The middle class used personal pronouns *less* often in proportion to the total number of words spoken than the working-class, but, of the pronouns they did use, a higher proportion were "I," and they used the phrase "I think" more often than the working-class boys.

On the basis of these relatively measurable differences and perhaps also on the basis of more subjective impressions of his subjects' speech, Bernstein concludes that the working-class boys used short, grammatically simple sentences, often unfinished and having poor syntactical form. Working-class boys stressed the active as opposed to the passive voice. They used simple and repetitive conjunctions, and he believes that their limited variety of subordinate clauses made it difficult for them to break down the initial categories of the dominant subject. They were, he claims, unable to hold a formal subject through a speech sequence, and this brought difficulties in conveying information clearly. Their use of adjectives and adverbs was rigid and limited, and they used many statements where the reason and the conclusion were confounded. They used many phrases such as "wouldn't it?" "you see," "just fancy," which Bernstein interprets as reinforcing the idea of the preceding sentence.

More generally still, Bernstein says that "The working class child is sensitive to a form of language use quite distinct from the middle class child's usage." He gives the names "restricted code" and "elaborated code" to the two different forms and argues that these codes are alternative ways of speaking the language. Each is appropriate to some occasions, but the two codes are not equally available to everyone within the society. Middle-class speakers can use both, but working-class speakers are limited to the restricted code. The fundamental difference between them is that the restricted code is the more predictable. It allows the speaker relatively few alternative choices either in lexicon or in syntax. The elaborated code is relatively flexible and more capable of subtlety and precision, but it also requires a "higher level of verbal planning."[1]

The extreme form of the restricted code seems to be a stereotyped conversation such as the following, which Bernstein offers as typical of what might occur between a newly acquainted boy and girl at a London dance hall (1964:59):

> "Do you come here often?
> "Bit crowded-nit?"
> "S'nice floor?"
> "Band's alright/dead/with it."

Bernstein even argues that the restricted code may be so redundant and predictable that it requires special reliance upon the "extra-verbal channels" of gesture or intonation to clarify the speaker's intentions. Those who habitually use only the restricted code become particularly sensitive to such cues. Speech in the restricted code can have logical gaps, for some things can remain unstated when the participants in a conversation share mutual assumptions and understandings. The content of speech in the restricted code is likely to be "concrete, narrative and descriptive, rather than analy-

[1]Basil Bernstein, "Elaborated and Restricted Codes: Their Social Origins and Some Consequences," *in* John J. Gumperz and Dell Hymes, eds., *The Ethnography of Communication.* Special Publication of the American Anthropologist, Vol., 66, Part 2, No. 6. (Menasha, Wisconsin, 1964), p. 56. Page references in the following paragraphs are for quotations taken from the same article.

tical or abstract" (1964:62). The elaborated code is "quantitatively and qualitatively different." An "extensive range of syntactic alternatives" is available within the code so the probability of any particular alternative being used is relatively low (1964:63). The forms of the elaborated code are relatively unpredictable, and the procedures needed for speaking it "promote a relatively higher level of structural organization and vocabulary selection than in the case of a restricted code" (1964:64).

Bernstein is surely right when he argues that we all vary from time to time between relatively stereotyped speech and more expressive or unpredictable speech. The startling aspect of Bernstein's argument is not that each person's speech is variable, but that our experiences, particularly those we have as children, affect our relative ability in the two codes. Even the patterns of child socialization typically found among lower- and middle-class families evoke different abilities to use the codes. Middle-class children are said to have a wide range of social experience so that they have every opportunity to learn both codes. By contrast, working-class children are said to have a more limited range of experience both within their family and outside of it, and they may never learn to speak *except* with the restricted code. If used consistently enough, this restricted code gives rise to "quite different intellectual and social procedures which may be only tenuously related to their purely psychological abilities" (1964:57). As a result, working-class children tend to fall ever further behind in school, since the restricted code equips them so badly for the kinds of intellectual challenges they face.

If Bernstein's conclusions could be substantiated, they would have profound implications for educational policy. They suggest that if we want to provide all children with equal opportunities, we will have to catch them very early so that we can give them enough enriched verbal experiences to let them rise above the restricted code to which their own family and social-class background would condemn them. Conclusions of this sort seem to have motivated recent efforts in the United States to offer enriched preschool and elementary school environments for children who come from so-called "culturally deprived" backgrounds. While the exact meaning of "cultural deprivation" is a bit obscure, it does seem to suggest that something can be missing from a child's early environment that, quite apart from any question of his native intelligence, can condemn him to educational disabilities. Perhaps Bernstein has put his finger on an important, and specifically verbal, component of cultural deprivation.

Before accepting Bernstein's argument, however, several serious difficulties have to be considered. Bernstein draws extreme conclusions from rather limited observations, and we should be cautious about too ready an acceptance of his pronouncements. At least we have to say that the confidence with which he draws a sharp contrast between the two different modes of speech seems quite unjustified. At most we have a number of rather subtle scales along which speech can fall, and Bernstein never justifies the claim he seems to make, that he has discovered two strikingly contrasting codes. Perhaps it would be fairer to speak of elaborated and restricted extremes of continuously variable speech.

There are, however, other problems. First, Bernstein never really justifies his use of "social class" to characterize the differences he finds. The boys whose speech he recorded differed, to be sure, in their educational background, and they were at different educational levels at the time they were tested. One cannot help wondering if the differences observed by Bernstein might not be interpreted quite simply as the result of their differing education. Better schools may have taught the so-called middle-class boys to perform well on the kind of task with which Bernstein presented them. Such an obvious explanation goes counter to Bernstein's objectives, however, since he is concerned with finding a *cause* for educational failure. He would like to find a variable, such as a deficiency in linguistic ability, that would explain the school failure of lower-class youths, but it is not easy to be sure whether verbal deficiencies are really the cause of educational failure or whether instead educational deficiencies were the cause of verbal failure. In particular, the task which Bernstein set his subjects, a discussion of the abolition of capital punishment, would seem to be a far more familiar one for better educated or middle-class boys than for others. Perhaps Bernstein would have found fewer verbal differences had he posed a different sort of problem, or sampled verbal behavior in some other way. At any rate, Bernstein has not effectively ruled out the possibility that he is measuring the *effect* of educational deficiencies rather than their cause.

Beyond these difficulties, there is also a question of whether Bernstein has adequately ruled out dialectical and individual differences as an explanation for his experimental results. Clearly he believes the differences he finds are more than simply dialectical, since he believes that they bear upon the ability to speak logically and clearly. On the other hand, he also believes his varied results depend upon experience rather than upon native intelligence. But has he really ruled out either dialect differences or differences in individual verbal aptitude? To take care of individual differences he relies without apparent misgivings upon the results of I.Q. tests. He never entertains the possibility that his so-called "working class" subjects may have dropped out of school because they lacked some aptitude not shown on standard I.Q. tests, but which could have caused difficulty in school and also have shown up upon exposure to Bernstein's problem. If individual aptitudes do have any bearing upon the results of his tests, then the contribution of social-class background to the differences he finds is correspondingly reduced. Bernstein may be right in dismissing individual differences, but his evidence is somewhat meager.

Finally, Bernstein never entertains the possibility that straightforward dialect differences might separate middle- and working-class London speech. A linguist would expect social classes in a city as big and complex as London to have divergent features in their speech, but he need not attribute relative superiority or inferiority to these features. Of course, the upper class is likely to stigmatize lower-class speech, but this is a sociological rather than a linguistic phenomenon. We should certainly expect that some of the differences dividing social class dialects to be as qualitatively irrelevant as the differences between two geographical dialects or two languages. Linguists have even tended to assume, though with little solid justification, that all languages have broadly equivalent complexity and flexibility and that all can be equally adapted to all purposes. What is true for different languages ought to be true of dialects. To the upper-class speaker, of course, the lower-class speaker may appear clumsy and awkward, particularly when he tries to meet upper-class expectations. But, if the upper-class speaker ever seriously tried to speak lower-class English, he might find just as many subtle complexities in that dialect as in his own, and his fumbling efforts might seem just as awkward to lower-class speakers. If the dialects of Bernstein's London youths diverged, one must ask how well Bernstein knew the dialect of the lower class. Could he have failed to understand some of the subtleties of their conversation, or could the situation in which he placed the boys have been so colored by middle-class expectations as to seriously inhibit the boys in their free use of language?

Bernstein clearly feels he has discovered linguistic differences that are neither the result of native ability nor of simple dialectical variation. Unlike differences based upon native ability, he attributed his differences to the experiences of the speakers. Unlike simple dialectual variation, Bernstein does believe his two codes show qualitative differences. One is more flexible than the other, more capable of communicating a wide variety of topics. This is the code that predisposes its speakers to educational success. One should probably remain skeptical of Bernstein's claims, until he has more successfully ruled out individual or simple dialectical variability, but the differences that Bernstein finds cannot be simply dismissed. If his experimental results can be confirmed, his facts need explanation. Bernstein's data do raise interesting questions. Educational policy should be sensitive to the factors responsible for the linguistic differences that distinguish individuals and social classes.

12 Borrowing and Linguistic Continuity

The Determinants of Borrowing

The perpetuation of human language depends upon our human propensity to imitate. No child can learn to speak without imitating the linguistic patterns of his elders and progressively incorporating these patterns into his own speech. It is this same propensity—even eagerness—to imitate that makes it possible for patterns of one language to be borrowed into another. Indeed, whenever two languages come into contact, words, less frequently sounds, and occasionally even some grammatical patterns manage to filter across from one language to the other. No process is more familiar to linguists.

For some purposes one can look upon borrowing as if it proceeded rather mechanically—linguistic habits seem to be generally contagious. But any subtle understanding of borrowing, and in particular an understanding of why some patterns are borrowed while others are not, requires an intimate knowledge of the conditions under which the two languages come into contact, and one must examine the role of the bilingual speaker who stands at the point of contact and who is finally the agent of borrowing. At least three important sociological variables affect the kind and intensity of borrowing: (1) the relative prestige of the languages that come into contact; (2) the relative number of speakers of the two languages; (3) whether or not a language is learned by adult speakers who carry fixed habits from their old language into the new one. Each of these three variables requires a brief comment.

When two languages meet, it often happens that one of them gains a dominant social position. The dominant language may be that of a conquering tribe or nation or it may be the language of an established majority among whom socially subordinate immigrants filter, but it seems difficult for

169

two languages to meet on genuinely equal terms. In Canada, for instance, no insistence upon the legal equivalence of French and English and no amount of abstract assertion that the two languages should, in principle, be equally acceptable can mask the fact that English is dominant. The comparative reluctance of English Canadians to learn French is both a sign of the dominant position of English and a factor in its perpetuation. French speakers learn English so frequently that in practical life few English speakers really need to learn French. The French Canadians with whom they deal have almost always learned enough English to allow them to communicate, and the situations in which an English speaker usually meets his French compatriots are unlikely to give him much chance to practice what little French he knows. The difficulty of learning French as a second language in Canada has been compounded by the fact that teachers of French have generally aimed at standard Parisian French. Though sometimes admired by French Canadians, Parisian is quite different from the Canadian dialects, and it lacks a number of influences from English that Canadian dialects have undergone. This means that Parisian is not only more remote from the practical needs of English speakers but probably more difficult for them to learn.

The French Canadian who wishes to learn English faces a far different situation. He knows that whenever he leaves his own community, he will have to deal with fellow citizens who speak little or no French. If he wishes to rise in education, in government, or in business, he will almost certainly have to learn English. Even to practice separatist politics effectively, he may have to learn the language of his opponents. So long as English remains the language of communication between the two groups, practical considerations will force French speakers to learn English but will leave most English speakers free to avoid the struggle with French. Reciprocally, so long as speakers continue to make these choices, English will remain the dominant language. It is a difficult circle to break. French Canadians may feel that others discriminate against them because of their language, and this belief can help to inspire separatist political sentiments. But short of a major political upheaval, it is difficult to imagine any drastic change in the situation.

When more than two languages come into close contact, they may fall into a hierarchy of dominance. In the Shan States of eastern Burma, more people speak Shan, a dialect of Thai, than any other language. But scattered about the Shan States are many smaller tribes whose members speak one of a dozen or more tribal languages, all of which are utterly different from Shan. Speakers of these tribal languages often learn Shan, since it is used more widely than their own language and allows them to communicate not only with the Shans but with members of the other small tribes. Shans, on the other hand, rarely bother to learn the tribal languages. Both Shans and speakers of the tribal languages occasionally learn Burmese, the language of the nation's majority, spoken by many government officials posted to the Shan States. Few Burmese, on the other hand, ever learn Shan, let alone one of the tribal languages. The hierarchy of languages does not even end with Burmese, for any man who receives much education, whether tribal, Shan, or Burmese, will certainly have to learn some English, for this is still used in many spheres of government, and it remains an important symbol of education. Rarely does a native speaker of English learn Burmese, Shan, or a tribal language. The hierarchy of dominance in the Shan States is clear: English, Burmese, Shan, and finally tribal. Nothing intrinsic in the structure of one language makes it superior to another, but the relative social positions of the speakers of varied languages seem almost always to give one language a dominant position.

Since two languages rarely meet on equal terms, the two languages can be expected to undergo different influences. While many other variables can complicate the situation, the subordinate language is the one more likely to be influenced. Native speakers of the dominant language may resist the incorporation of features that are derived from what they may regard as an inferior source. Even without this prejudice, the higher proportion of monolinguals ordinarily found among the dominant group makes the incorporation of foreign items more risky, since borrowings may not be understood. If bilingualism is common, as it often is among speakers of a subordinate language, then borrowing can be relatively free since foreign items have a good chance of being understood. If they are used often enough, any initial connotations of foreignness will gradually wear off. When speaking among themselves, bilinguals can incorporate foreign patterns almost without limit.

One factor that complicates this simple picture of the influence of the dominant language is the relative number of speakers of the two languages. If the dominant language is spoken only by a small minority of the population, its position is much less inviolate than when its dominance is supported by its widespread use. One need only compare the English spoken by the British during their rule in India with the English spoken in America. Although American and British English have drawn apart in many ways, few of the special characteristics of American can be attributed to the influences of other languages. Of course, both the indigenous American Indian languages and the later immigrant languages have been in a clearly subordinate position with respect to English. More than this, the number of their speakers has been so small that except for a few scattered lexical items for objects of foreign origin, such as *canoe*, *tomato*, *papoose*, or *pizza*, American English has hardly been touched by these languages.

By comparison, the English used in India, even by foreigners who are but temporary residents of the country, is filled with Indian expressions. Immersed in a new country, surrounded by foreign languages and unfamiliar objects, it is easy for an English speaker to accept new terms for the new objects. The washerman quickly becomes the *dhobi*, the taylor the *durzi*, and a European man soon becomes reconciled to answering to the title *Sahib*. If he is not prejudiced by its colonial connotations, he may wear a sensible pith helmet and call it a *topee*, and if he is willing to compromise with the climate by wearing sandals he is likely to call them *chapals*. When he ventures to eat native foods, he calls some of them by their native names, and if he gets involved in finance, he soon learns that a *lak* is 100,000 rupees and that a *crore* is 10,000,000. These borrowed words, to be sure, hardly touch the core of his language, for he adapts them phonologically and grammatically to his own habits; they are simply new words for new things. But if the visitor has children, they may learn to speak English with an Indian lilt. Many an Englishman has sent his children back home to school in England, in part to make sure they would acquire a proper English accent and not grow up carrying in their speech an indelible badge of their colonial upbringing.

Besides social dominance and relative number of speakers, a third important variable bears upon the intensity and variety of borrowing. English is widely used in India not only by native speakers of English but also by native speakers of the indigenous languages, and it is among the latter that the most far-reaching changes can be seen. When a man tries to speak a language to which he is not native, the opportunities for his first language to influence his second are almost limitless. If enough people learn to use a second language, many foreign features can become stabilized and serve as the basis of a new linguistic tradition.

When Indians learn English, they carry many habits from their native languages into their acquired English, not only lexical habits but phonological and even grammatical habits as well. Of course most Indians learn their English from other Indians—each man does not independently make the same innovations. The cumulative effect of hundreds and thousands of Indians painfully acquiring the same foreign language has been to create a new set of linguistic traditions, traditions that deviate in many ways from British or American standards but nevertheless have great vitality. Innumerable varieties of English are spoken in India today, from pure Oxford to the broken phrases of struggling school boys. A remarkable number of these school boys eventually learn to speak fluent English, but very few ever learn enough to hide their Indian origin. Gradually a compromise between Oxford and Indian school-boy English has developed. This is a form of English incorporating many uniquely Indian features, but it may ultimately come to be accepted as an Indian spoken standard, just as Englishmen and Americans are each content with their own somewhat diverse spoken standards.

Perhaps the most obvious Indian departure from British standards and the one that is most difficult to escape is phonological. For instance, English /r/ generally becomes a flap when spoken by Indians, and /w/ is usually more labiodental than when on the lips of British or American speakers. Most English speakers make a contrast between apical /t/ and interdental /θ/. Indians usually shift these somewhat backwards and often articulate both as stops, so that the Indian contrast is between apico-dental and retroflex stops instead of between a fricative and a stop. In these respects and in many others the English used in India shows considerable phonological approximation to native Indian languages.

It might seem tempting to dismiss the Indian rendering of English sounds as nothing more than a foreign accent, but as these patterns become well established and get passed on from one generation to the next, they assume such stability and continuity that they can be seen more like new dialect forms than ephemeral foreignisms. One can even foresee the establishment of a type of Indian English that could be phonologically far more like Hindi (or some other Indian language) than like other dialects of English. Even the English of the substantial number of Indians learning it as their first language shows many of these special features, but an essential step in the development of Indian English, a step that distinguishes it from American English, has been its predominant use as a second rather than as a first language.

By comparison with some forms of the language, however, Indian English is but modestly altered from British standards. In parts of the world where people from heterogeneous linguistic backgrounds have been thrown into intermittent contact with Europeans, simplified contact languages have grown up. These are originally based on the European language that assumed a dominant position in the area but show even more penetrating influence from the indigenous languages than does Indian English. The linguistic processes giving rise to such contact languages are not different than those that have brought about Indian English, but they may be more extreme. If the results are dramatic enough, linguists have come to use the term "pidgin language" for the resulting form. Perhaps the most important pidgin in use today is Melanesian Pidgin English or "Neo Melanesian" as it is sometimes called, which is widely used in Australian New Guinea and the nearby islands. A very brief example will give some idea of just how drastically the language has changed from its ancestral English.

Bɪfor mi drim kɪlɪm wənfɛlə snek. wənfɛlə tɔk: "kɪčɪm spir." "mi no lajk; ɛm i-bɪgfɛlə tuməč." mi tɔkɪm papa: "mi lukɪm gudfɛlə spir. mi tɪŋk wənfɛlə snek stap lɔŋ diwaj." ɛm i-tɔk: "ju go lukim." mi luk, mi siŋawt bɔrata kəm kwɪk lukɪm snek. mi tufɛlə šutɪm, gɪvɪm lɔŋ kandari, bandarap. bandarap ɛm i-kukɪm.

Previously I dreamed that I killed a snake. One man said: "Get a spear." "I don't want to; it is very big." I said to my father: "I am looking for a good spear. I think there is a snake near a tree." He said "Go and look." I looked, and called my brother to come quick and look at the snake. The two of us shot it, and gave it to my mother's brother, Bandarap. Bandarap cooked it.[1]

Even in a passage as brief as this a number of typical Melanesian pidgin characteristics turn up and some of these are also typical of pidgins in other parts of the world. The phonology, as compared to standard English, is somewhat simplified. In this passage *brother* appears as *bɔrata*, the cluster having been split and the interdental fricative changed to a stop. Further examples would show extensive phonological adjustments, more or less in the direction of the lowest common denominator of the native languages of pidgin speakers. Grammar also seems to be simplified in some ways: *mi* and *em* serve as personal pronouns without distinction of case, and all the usual English suffixes seem to be lost. On the other hand, some new grammatical devices are in evidence: *-fɛlə* serves as a suffix which marks numbers and adjectives; *i-* is a third-person marker prefixed to the verb or to the first word of the predicate; *ım* is used as a suffix to mark a transitive verb, even though an object may follow as in *kıč ım spir* "get a spear." Many recognizably English words have shifted meanings: *tuməč*, "very"; *tɔk*, "say"; *siŋawt*, "call"; *kıč*, "get". Most of the words are clearly of English origin, however, for only *kandari* "mother's brother" and *diwaj* "tree" seem to be derived from other languages. A longer sample would show extensive influences of the Melanesian languages. Where English phonology is different from that of the Melanesian languages, it tends to be adjusted to accommodate Melanesian habits. Many of pidgin's special grammatical characteristics can be shown to have Melanesian parallels, and although this passage is largely formed with English words, a good many words from Melanesian and other languages are also used by pidgin speakers. Semantic shifts sometimes bring borrowed words into line with native habits. Many Melanesian languages, for instance, have separate "inclusive" (you and I) and "exclusive" (he and I, they and I) first person plural pronouns. Pidgin has developed an inclusive pronoun *jumi* "you and I" constructed of English forms but filling a Melanesian semantic slot.

Pidgin languages have arisen in response to urgent practical needs for communication between people of sharply divergent backgrounds. In recent centuries pidgins have typically arisen when Europeans first ventured into areas where they had no previous experience. One can imagine European merchants and sailors arriving in a remote spot where the natives were unfamiliar with any language known by Europeans. The visitors might try to use English, though they would be likely to restrict themselves to a limited

---

[1]From Robert A. Hall, Jr. *Melanesian Pidgin English Grammar, Texts, Vocabulary,* Special Publications of the Linguistic Society of America (Baltimore, 1953), p. 48

vocabulary and simplified sentences. The visitors might shout and they might curse, but the natives in their eagerness to communicate might attempt to imitate whatever they heard. Of course, their imitation would be imperfect, for they would bring all their own linguistic skills and semantic habits to the conversation. When the visitors heard these distortions they might make the condescending assumption that the natives were incapable of anything better than this broken speech, but even without imagining this, their own urgent need for communication would encourage them to use the limited vocabulary that the natives seemed to grasp, to alter word order if that seemed to help understanding, and even to adjust their pronunciation a bit. Their efforts surely helped them to meet their practical problems, but at the same time they would sharply limit the natives' opportunity to learn a more normal variety of the new language. The willingness of the foreigners to change their own speech restricts the natives to this new form. Gradually a new set of conventions grows up with some characteristics derived from both languages, which both natives and foreigners must then learn if they are to converse with one another.

So long as a pidgin language is used only as a means of contact between people of diverse linguistic backgrounds, it is likely to remain relatively simple. Its vocabulary will be limited, its grammar reduced, and its phonology will avoid the more difficult features of either language. Morover, since it is nobody's native language, everyone is likely to be tolerant of variability. This makes it far easier for both sides to learn than the full language of the other group, and it can serve as a sort of neutral meeting ground and provide a practical solution to the day's problems.

If the contact language begins to assume a more important role it will have to expand. Natives of various linguistic backgrounds may come to use the pidgin with each other as well as with foreigners, and if people with different native languages begin to intermarry, their children may grow up learning a variety of the pidgin as their own first language. In a community where this happens regulary, the language will have to be used for all topics and in all situations, and it would need to develop a re-expanded vocabulary. Given the human tendency to let language symbolize many social subtleties, other linguistic complexities might be rapidly introduced. The expanding vocabulary could be borrowed from the various native languages of the speakers or constructed by compounding terms already known. But however re-expansion occurs, the resulting language is likely to remain strikingly different from the colonial language on which it is ultimately based. When a pidgin expands in this way, it is known as a "creole," a full language that can be used for all ordinary daily purposes, a language that is perpetuated within a social group and learned in the normal way by children. But a creole shows an abrupt discontinuity with its antecedents at the point where the preceding pidgin was first formed. Melanesian Pidgin

English seems to be entering the stage of creolization, for an increasing number of Melanesians are now learning it as their first language.

In other parts of the world large populations speak older and more thoroughly established creoles. Gullah is a creolized form of English still spoken, largely by Negroes, on the islands off the Carolina coast. Creole French is still spoken in parts of Louisiana, and Haitians speak a somewhat different form of French creole. In Haiti the prestige of standard French has been so great as to lead some Haitians almost to deny the existence of a creole. Government business has been conducted in French; newspapers are published in French; and the members of the educated Haitian elite may be fluent in both standard French and in creole. But the speech of Haitians varies markedly. The type of creole spoken by ordinary peasant Haitians is so divergent from standard French that it seriously interferes with attempts to bring them education, since standard French is the language of the schools.

Pidgins and creoles constitute the most dramatic examples of abrupt changes introduced in one language by the influence of another. But even when systems from one language penetrate another more gradually, they may slowly but cumulatively bring far-reaching alterations. A few more illustrations of various kinds of borrowing will show how pervasive the process can be.

Lexical Borrowing

The most familiar type of borrowing is certainly lexical. English speakers like to think of their language as being relatively receptive to foreign words, and it is even part of our folklore that the majority of words in our dictionaries are actually derived from other languages. We can easily point to words of relatively recent foreign origin, and, indeed, by comparison with Germans or Frenchmen, English speakers are relatively untroubled by worries about maintaining the purity of their language. Yet English speakers may exaggerate the degree to which they still borrow new words, for by now most of the borrowed words in our dictionaries have been too thoroughly assimilated to be still considered foreign. The rate of borrowing into English today is far lower than when the Norman French ruled Britain, for at that time French words were incorporated in huge numbers. Today, the most productive area of lexical innovation in English is probably in scientific and technical terminology. These terms are often built from originally foreign roots, but many of the roots themselves have already been thoroughly naturalized into English. When new formations are constructed out of familiar parts, they hardly deserve to be called real borrowings. Other sources of modern lexical innovation—slang and advertising neologisms for instance—are usually built upon native roots.

For really impressive examples of active lexical borrowing today, we have to go to languages where the speakers are being subjected to massive cultural pressures from other people and where linguistic innovation is part of a more general outside influence. Once again, India can provide striking examples, and the Garo language probably shows as extreme lexical borrowing as can be found anywhere. The quarter million Garos are surrounded on three sides by speakers of Indic languages—Bengali and Assamese. Until about a hundred years ago, the Garos were relatively isolated from their neighbors, though even then they periodically visited markets at the base of their hilly district, and occasionally they sallied forth into the plains hoping to capture a few heads. They practiced a primitive form of agriculture, had little or no enduring political organization larger than their villages, and had neither the caste organization or Hinduism of their neighbors. In the 1860s, the Garos were abruptly incorporated into a larger world. Losing patience with the harrassing tactics of Garo headhunters, the British government of India sent in troops, set up a permanent government headquarters, and proceeded to stamp out intervillage feuding, establish law courts, build roads, and encourage schools and markets. Christian missionaries came to teach the Garos a new religion, and suddenly the ideas and the technology of both India and the West became available. Garos had already had enough contact with Indic languages to allow a good many words to seep into their own speech, but more and more Garos now began to learn both Bengali and English. They found it necessary to discuss many new ideas brought in by Europeans and Indians, and they readily incorporated the words that the foreigners used.

Hundreds of new crops, manufactured objects, religious and legal concepts, diseases (when diagnosed by western medical techniques), and the drugs used to treat them have come with their foreign labels. *Embi*, an aspirin compound named for the initials of the British pharmaceutical house May & Baker, is a popular medicine. The Garos call pineapple *anaros* (derived ultimately from Portuguese, more immediately from Bengali). Potatoes are called *alu* as in Bengali. Garos sometimes eat a pastry known as *biskut*. Some of these *biskut* are made in the shape of an "s" and are known as *esbiskut*. When a Garo drinks tea he calls it *cha*, the word used throughout most of Asia, and more rarely he drinks *kapi*. The beverages are flavored with *dut* (from the Bengali word for 'milk') and *chini* (Bengali for sugar) and are drunk from a *kap*. Metal or china cups have only recently taken the place of more indigenous bamboo containers. Garos have their own numbers, but for telling clock time they have adopted Bengali numbers, though they have modified them to suit their own tongues. Names of the months and days of the week are all derived from Bengali. Poinsettias are known as *krismas pul* from the time of year when they bloom and the Bengali word for 'flower.' A Garo lights his house with a *lem* that he fills with *kerosin*. He writes with a *pensil* or *pawnten* (from 'fountain pen') on *leka* (Bengali for 'paper') and reads from a *kitap* (Bengali for 'book,' ultimately of Arabic origin).

One of the institutions introduced by the new government was the court system, and the legal terminology now used by Garos is almost entirely derived from either English or Bengali, much of the latter deriving ultimately from Persian and Arabic. The court itself is the *kachari* (from Bengali); the presiding officer is the *hakim* (from Bengali); and when a case gets thrown out of court, the Garos say it is *disimisi* (from English). The chief government official in the district is known either as the *Disi* (from the initials of his English title, deputy commissioner) or as the *boro sep* (from the Bengali word for 'big,' 'important,' and the Garo rendition of *Sahib*).

A Garo can hardly speak without using recently borrowed terms. For the most part these are readily incorporated into the phonological and grammatical system of Garo, though it seems slightly awkward to attach verb suffixes to a borrowed verb. This can be avoided by using a dummy verb base (*ka-*), which is placed after borrowed verbs and can then have suffixes attached to it. Garos can then say the case was *disimisi kajok* (the case 'was dismissed') or *kam kagen* 'will work' (from Bengali *kam*, 'to work'). The *ka-* is a grammatical device used specifically to incorporate foreign verbs into the language, and it is very common form.

This list could be expanded almost without end, but no list could possibly convey the full impact of foreign languages upon the linguistic habits of Garos. It is no exaggeration to say that a Garo feels free to use any word of either Bengali or English origin that he believes will be understood. If he is talking about an unfamiliar subject, where a certain measure of exotic vocabulary can be expected, he may use a foreign word and explain its meaning, just as anyone does when explaining a subject to novices. In 1955, when early proposals for launching artificial satelites were being discussed, I was asked by some Garos to explain how they would work. I did my best, but found myself using the word *grebiti* when trying to explain why the satelites would circle the earth and not fly off into space. I had never before heard the Garo word *grebiti*, but I believe I used it correctly, and that a native Garo speaker would have used it in the same way. I took a word I had heard elsewhere, altered it phonologically to conform to Garo habits and, as part of my explanation of the phenomenon, did my best to explain the word's meaning. I was doing exactly as I would have had to do, had I been speaking to uneducated speakers of English (such as children) who had never before heard the word *gravity* and who needed to have it explained. The word was as readily acceptable in Garo as it would have been in English.

So great has borrowing been that it is difficult to define the limits of Garo vocabulary. In English we imagine that our lexical resources somehow include the entire contents of the unabridged dictionary. Of course, nobody knows all those words, but they are all there, ready to be used when needed. No one doubts that all those words are English, even if most of them are as unfamiliar to most speakers of English as is the word *grebiti* to a Garo. But when the word *grebiti* is needed in a Garo context, there is no more difficulty in using it than in using one of the less familiar items in the dictionary in an English context. In a perfectly real sense, then, the entire resources of the English dictionary are as available to a Garo speaker as they are to an English speaker. In one way, indeed, Garos have even richer resources than English speakers, since they can also draw upon the Bengali vocabulary and upon their more indigenous stock of terms as well. Of course, standards of education are low in the Garo hills, and many subjects commonly discussed by speakers of English are rarely approached by Garos. When a Garo learns enough to discuss automobile mechanics, Christian theology, or agronomy, he learns the new vocabulary of these topics in exactly the same way as does any English speaker when he first learns about a new subject.

It is utterly futile to try to draw limits around the "real" Garo vocabulary, to say that one list of words is Garo and another list foreign. For some languages, those with a lexicographic tradition or where speakers are more self-conscious about linguistic purity, it may seem possible to separate the native from the foreign. For Garo it is quite impossible, and in principle it is probably impossible for other languages as well. There is no clear way to decide when a word has ceased to be foreign and when it has become assimilated to a new language. One cannot, in other words, characterize a language by its lexicon.

While it is often impossible to say whether a particular *word* is truly Garo or not, one can almost always say whether a particular *sentence* is Garo, because the lexical items are arranged into Garo grammatical patterns. There has surely been continuity between the less influenced Garo of a century ago, and the heavily influenced modern language, for at no time in Garo history was there an abrupt change in the linguistic habits of the speakers such as happens in the development of pidgin or creole languages. In Garo there has only been progressive and continuous modification. Even if Garo speakers can now call upon the entire vocabulary of English, their language is still Garo and not English, for it uses Garo grammatical patterns, and it is the product of an unbroken development from an earlier form of the language.

Phonological Borrowing

Phonological borrowing is less easy to perceive than lexical borrowing, yet it also occurs. At least two mechanisms can lead the phonology of one language to affect that of another. The first and less radical is through the influence of borrowed words carrying some foreign characteristics with them. In an attempt to imitate French, a good many English speakers probably pronounce "fiancée" with a nasal vowel in the second syllable. If enough words with nasal vowels were borrowed from French and if enough speakers used these vowels consistently, it is not inconceivable that a distinction between oral and nasal vowels could be introduced into English. The vowel in "oil" and "noise" did originally become established as a newly distinct vowel in English through borrowings from French, though subsequent phonetic change in both languages has obscured the phonetic similarity of the borrowings to the original.

Perhaps it is a bit more likely for borrowings to bring changes in the distribution of sounds already found in the language than to introduce entirely new sounds. Words like *schnauzer*, *schnaps*, *schmaltz*, and *schlamiel* may gradually introduce an entirely new set of initial clusters into English, built out of already familiar parts. Borrowings can also break up old patterns of complementary distribution. In some varieties of modern Garo, and no doubt in all varieties of an earlier period, a flapped [r] is used only as syllable initial and a lateral [l] only as syllable final. It is natural to regard these two sounds as being in complementary distribution. In some dialects of modern Garo, however, many borrowed words preserve a foreign pronunciation with an initial lateral, and one must recognize a new initial contrast. Phonetically this new initial is much like the older final lateral, so no new phonetic element has come into the language, but the older complementary distribution has been destroyed.

Far more extensive phonological influence occurs when people learn a second language. Like Indians who learn English, they generally carry many of their old phonological habits into the new language. There is less complete continuity of linguistic tradition here than when words and their sounds are simply borrowed. Fairly abrupt changes can occur at the point where a language passes from native speakers to those who learn it as adults, but in the case of Indian English at least, the break with its antecedents is not so sharp that it deserves to be called a pidgin language. Indian English must be credited as being a dialect of English, showing continuity with other dialects because it is mutually understandable in spite of its divergent phonology.

Grammatical Borrowing

Grammar seems to be rather more resistant to borrowing than is either lexicon or phonology. It has often been confidently stated that even after a language has been subjected to heavy external influence and acquired a massive overlay of borrowings, it will still retain a grammatical core characteristic of its language family and demonstrating its true affiliation. But not even grammar is completely immune to borrowing, and under some circumstances grammar can even be borrowed quite separately from phonology or lexicon. John Okell has analyzed a striking case of grammatical borrowing in Burmese.

Burmese is a Tibeto-Burman language, but it has borrowed heavily from Pali which is Indo-European. In genetic origin the two languages are as diverse as any two languages can be, but geography and religion have brought them into intimate contact. Pali was an Indo-Aryan dialect used somewhat more recently than Sanskrit but closely related to it. Pali was spoken at about the time the Buddha preached, and its lasting importance has been due to its use as a sacred language by the southern school of Buddhism. The Pali canon, the most sacred of the southern Buddhist texts, was codified in Ceylon in about the fifth century A.D., and ever since that time it has remained the most fundamental document of southern Buddhism.

In Burma, this form of Buddhism became established as the most important religious element among the majority of the people. For almost a thousand years, the Pali scriptures have been studied by the Burmese people and cherished as their most sacred documents. For the Burmese, however, Pali was a difficult foreign language, and its mastery was not something to which every man could reasonably aspire. A few learned monks could indeed master Pali, and many boys had enough monastic schooling to know at least a few rudiments of the language, but for most people the original texts could hardly be directly understood. For them, a special kind of text was developed in which the Pali forms were written in the usual fashion, except that after each word or phrase a Burmese translation was inserted. These bilingual texts, called Nissaya Burmese, are known from at least as early as the 15th century, and since that time they have been produced in considerable quantity. The Burmese of these texts, of course, was by no means a close approximation to colloquial speech. The words inevitably followed the Pali order rather than that of Burmese. As the Nissaya style became established, certain particles came to be used in the Burmese portions of the texts as conventional equivalents for Pali particles of number, case, tense, and mood in spite of the fact that such particles are not generally found in colloquial Burmese at all, at least not in a form that corresponds at all closely to that of Pali. The result was that Nissaya Burmese came to duplicate Pali in the range of contexts in which a particular form was used, in word order, and even in much of the morpheme order, but the morphemes themselves were largely Burmese.

Nissaya was certainly an artificial and distorted form of Burmese, a form that a Burmese speaker could hardly understand without considerable training, but it would still have been far easier for him to learn than the original Pali, for he would be relieved of remembering most of the foreign lexicon. Some speakers probably used the Nissaya Burmese forms simply as a crutch to help them with the original Pali that lay beside it on the page, but others probably relied largely or exclusively upon the Nissaya Burmese itself.

Here is a linguistic system in which the grammar was Pali but the lexicon Burmese. It was artificial and deliberately contrived as a linguistic bridge between two languages, and if this were the end of the story, Nissaya Burmese would have no more importance than the scores of interlinear translations that have clarified texts in exotic languages for speakers of English. But Nissaya Burmese has had more importance than this, for the Pali texts were so sacred that some of the sacredness rubbed off on the Nissaya forms too. Burmese began to look upon Nissaya patterns as models of exalted linguistic usage.

Translations and adaptations of Pali texts were produced. Often these were virtually identical to the interpolated forms of Nissaya Burmese except that the original Pali was now omitted. Such texts were no longer meant primarily as a bridge to the Pali texts but were intended to be read in their own right. A famous example of such a work was a five volume translation of 550 Jataka tales, produced about 1800, which reads almost exactly like Nissaya Burmese, though it lacks the interpolated Pali original. Burmese readers had to make many linguistic adjustments to understand some of these texts, for their grammar remained almost pure Pali. Some translations, however, varied more or less in the direction of more colloquial Burmese. Some omitted plural particles, for instance, or particles marking genetive and nominative cases, which are more characteristic of Pali than of Burmese, but the prestige of Pali was so great that many Nissaya Burmese conventions were always used.

Even original Burmese writing then came to reflect some Pali or Nissaya standards. The closer the writing was to Pali, the more erudite or even "pure" it was taken to be. Although there has been considerable variation in the direction of the colloquial language, ordinary everyday speech has even come to be considered as somewhat debased. Today, Pali or Nissaya influence is still felt in Burmese writing, and modern newspapers and magazines continue to make use of many grammatical conventions originally derived from Pali.

Not even the dividing line between spoken and written Burmese has been impermeable. Pali conventions orginally entered Burmese through the medium of writing, but many of them began to leak over into spoken language as well. The most elegant forms of spoken Burmese, those used in oratory, in lectures, and today in radio news broadcasts, emulate to a greater or lesser extent the conventions of elegant written prose, and this implies the incorporation of Pali forms. Finally, Pali conventions have filtered from formal spoken styles to the more colloquial styles, so that every style of Burmese used today shows some degree of grammatical influence from Pali.

An unbroken continuum connects the most colloquial forms of spoken Burmese to straight Nissaya. Any degree of mixture of the two conventions seems to be possible. Some formal oratory is closer to the Nissaya end of the continuum than some written material that is intended for reading aloud. The result of Burma's linguistic history is that speakers now have an array of styles ranging from colloquial to formal, and many of the crucial variables distinguishing them are ultimately of Pali origin. When a Burmese stands up to use a microphone, or when he responds to a linguist's inquiries about his language, his speech tends to shift in a bookish direction. It seems that one cannot fully describe the linguistic habits of the Burmese without using two sets of grammatical rules, one just like the grammar of Pali, the other more characteristic of colloquial Burmese.

The effect of Pali grammar upon Burmese is so old and pervasive that it is difficult to be sure just how much of what we know as modern Burmese really antedates Pali influence. Pali came to Burma even before Burmese itself, and the earliest extensive Burmese writing already shows great Pali influence. One must ask, of course, whether the most extreme varieties of Nissaya are really varieties of Burmese or if they are really Pali. One might regard the deep structure of Nissaya as Pali and only the lexical substitutions of its surface structure to be Burmese. This would make Nissaya into a sort of Pali that had undergone overwhelming lexical influence from Burmese. On the other hand, Nissaya could be considered as Burmese that had received massive grammatical influence from Pali, and it seems difficult to decide between these alternatives on purely linguistic grounds. One consideration, however, suggests that Nissaya is better regarded as a kind of Burmese: it is connected by an unbroken chain of gradually varying styles to the most colloquial forms of Burmese. From bilingual Nissaya to monolingual texts in the same style to other texts and new compositions incorporating various proportions of Nissaya conventions, to high oratorical styles, and finally to ever more colloquial spoken styles, there is an unbroken continuity, a chain of gradually changing styles or dialects. From the Burmese forms in Nissaya texts to pure Pali, there is a gap that is nowhere bridged. However much of their grammar these two languages share, they remain two separate conventions and are not subject to the same kinds of mixture as are Nissaya and colloquial Burmese.

The influence of Pali upon Burmese is an extreme case of grammatical borrowing, but it is by no means unique. The Gothic Bible was virtually a word for word translation from Greek, preserving the word order and most of the grammar of Greek but using Germanic roots. Hebrew and Yiddish, having undergone centuries of coexistence have emerged to modern forms that have a close intertranslatability and that share much of their grammar. One can even see the penetrating influence of Latin and the Romance languages upon English in somewhat the same light.

In all these examples, written forms, and in particular, a sacred literature have helped to mediate between the languages. The written forms have also left records which allow us to disentangle their history. Of course, it is also possible for grammatical borrowing to occur without writing playing a major role, but the absence of written records may make it more difficult to trace the history of the borrowing. Along the border between the Aryan and Dravidian languages in India, the local dialects seem to have so thoroughly adjusted to one another that they hardly differ except in lexical content. As with Nissaya Burmese and Pali, their grammars seem virtually identical, though in this case the mutual influences must have come about through long years of contact between the two spoken languages. Adjustments have been made from both sides, and they have come through extensive oral bilingualism rather than through the prestige of a written form.

John Gumperz has examined the colloquial dialects of Marathi and Kannada in a village along the Maharastra-Mysore boundary in central India where these two languages come into direct contact. Marathi is an Indo-Aryan language, while Kannada is Dravidian. Historically these two languages go back to utterly different antecedents, but the Indo-Aryan and Dravidian languages have been in contact in India for several thousand years and have long influenced one another. Along the borders their mutual influence has been profound. In the village studied by Gumperz most speakers feel themselves to be bilingual, but the two village dialects share such a large part of their grammar that one can almost doubt whether they should count as separate languages. Consider, for example, the following sentence:

Kannada:	hog- i	wənd	kudri	turg	maR- i		aw	tənd
Grammatical Structure:	verb partic. stem suffix	adj.	noun	noun	verb stem	partic. suffix	pro- noun	verb past
Marathi:	ja- un	ek	ghoRa	cori	kar- un		tew	anla
Literal English:	go having	one	horse	theft	take having		he	brought
Idiomatic English:	Having gone and having stolen a horse he brought it back.							

All of the morphemes of the Kannada sentence are different from those of the Marathi sentence, but they are used according to identical grammatical principles. The sentences have identical constituent structures and their morphemes occur in the same order. The same kind of suffixes are attached to the same kind of bases. These sentences seem by no means to be atypical of village usage. In fact, one can plausibly suggest that these two languages (if indeed they *are* two languages) have the same grammar and differ only in the items filling the surface forms. One can translate from one language to the other simply by substituting one set of lexical items for another in the surface structure.

Both the Marathi and the Kannada used in this village differ from the more literary or educated styles of the same languages, but both can be shown to be related to the more standard forms according to the usual criteria by which linguists recognize genetic affiliation. Yet the village dialects have undergone such profound mutual grammatical influence as to almost obscure the boundaries between the two languages. Curiously, in this case, it is the lexicon that maintains the separation, and after considering the effect of Marathi and Kannada upon each other, one can hardly maintain that lexicon is always the easiest component of language to borrow or that the true genetic affiliation will necessarily be shown by the underlying grammar.

Linguistic Continuity

It seems that under ideal conditions, either grammar, lexicon, or phonology can be borrowed rather independently of one another or even transferred almost in their entirety from one language to another. The extreme examples of foreign influence must make us ask just where we wish to draw the limits of a language. We wonder how to decide whether a particular dialect is a variety of one language or of another. Somehow we feel that Indian English is a variety of English, that even with its massive lexical influence Garo is still Garo, that Nissaya Burmese is still Burmese, and that the modified forms of Marathi and Kannada are still dialects of those languages. But what is it that leads us to such conclusions?

The only characteristic that these heavily influenced styles or dialects share is what might be called their linguistic continuity with other forms of the language. The various forms of a language are connected to each other by a chain of mutually intelligible styles or dialects. We conventionally recognize a genetic relationship among languages by the demonstrable or presumed existence of such linguistic continuity. We say that English and German are genetically related because we suppose them to have been connected by a chain of mutually intelligible dialects stretching back over the last two or three thousand years. So long as borrowing does not destroy the links of mutual intelligibility, so long, in other words, as linguistic continuity is not interrupted, we can speak of related dialects and languages. It is linguistic continuity—either mutual intelligibility or a chain of step-wise mutually intelligible dialects and styles—that makes us certain that Indian English is indeed a variety of English, however much its phonology may approximate Indian languages. It is linguistic continuity that makes us certain that whatever lexical impact Garo has received, the resulting language is still Garo. Only in the same sense can we call Nissaya a form of Burmese rather than a form of Pali, and only in this sense are the mutually influenced dialects of Marathi and Kannada dialects of separate languages rather than divergent styles of the same language.

The most abrupt changes in the history of a language and perhaps the only occasions in which linguistic continuity might be doubted, occur in the formation of a pidgin language and its subsequent creolization. Melanesian Pidgin English as represented by the example given earlier in this chapter and the Neo-Melanesian creole derived from it are so unlike normal English that one may even question whether they should be called English at all. But if linguistic continuity can be taken as the criterion of genetic relationship, it is not irrelevant to remember how pidgin languages first arise, for pidgins and creoles have continuity backward in time with only a single language. They are by no means an equal mixture from various sources.

Neo-Melanesian has continuity back through pidgin to the English of the first traders and sailors. The first natives who talked with them must have been trying to imitate the sailors, trying, that is, to imitate English. At every step Melanesian influences have been felt, but nowhere was there an attempt to imitate Melanesian, and there has been no chain of mutually intelligible links tying the older Melanesian languages to Neo-Melanesian. From Englishman to native and back to Englishman, there was at least some degree of continuity and imitation, or at least this must be assumed if a pidgin language is to be assigned genetically to a language family.

There are more strictly linguistic criteria by which Neo-Melanesian and pidgin must be counted as varieties of English. In spite of their altered sound systems, it seems to be possible to relate the phonology of Neo-Melanesian and other English-based pidgins to the phonology of more usual English by means of the standard techniques of the comparative method. In other words, the development of sounds into pidgin languages can be seen as following the normal type of phonological rule. Moreover, the vocabulary of Neo-Melanesian is preponderantly English, just as that of Haitian creole is preponderantly French. It seems then that not even pidgin languages form an exception to the usual assumption linguists make, that each language can be traced back through one and only one line of antecedents.

The argument that Neo-Melanesian is a form of English and not a mixed language is one support for a widely accepted linguistic assumption: languages do not mix. Two or more separate languages, it is said, never converge to produce a single daughter language, though of course, one language may split up to produce separate daughters. However much one language may borrow from another, the argument runs, the result is never a truly mixed language, but simply a much modified form of one of them. But this assumption seems to be contradicted by two other widely accepted linguistic principles: (1) dialects *can* mix; (2) language differences and dialect differences are exactly the same type of phenomena, the one merely being a more extreme version of the other.

To say that dialects *can* mix is hardly subject to argument. In the extreme case a husband and his wife may speak somewhat divergent dialects, and their children may acquire some characteristics from each, so that it will be impossible to say which is predominant. However, this leaves us with an apparent contradiction between our assumption of the impossibility of language mixture and the theoretical identity of dialectical and language differences.

To count as genuinely mixed, a language would presumably have to be simultaneously tied by continuous chains of gradually diverging antecedents to two originally distinct languages. In the common situation where one language has borrowed heavily from another the resulting form certainly does not have such dual continuity. However much French has influenced English, it is quite impossible to imagine a continuous chain of mutually intelligible dialects that would lead from some sort of French down to modern English. As French forms were taken into English, they must always have been used in either the context of a French sentence with French grammar, or in a contrasting English context. The two can never have come close to mutual intelligibility.

Nevertheless, the examples of extensive borrowing suggest that no limitation in principle can be placed upon what can be borrowed. One cannot help wondering just how far borrowing could go, and whether in the most extreme imaginable conditions, a greatly modified language might not become mutually intelligible with a second language of independent origin. Could one language conceivably borrow enough of the phonology, lexicon, and grammar from a second language to become mutually intelligible with it? Dialectical Marathi and Kannada have already made such extensive mutual adjustment, that with continued lexical borrowing it would seem that the remaining differences might disappear. Already the only real difference between them seems to be in lexicon, and, of course, it is the lexicon that we imagine to be the easiest part of a language to borrow. Certainly these two languages need not change much more before the difference between them is no greater than that between the different styles of Javanese that were discussed in Chapter 7. Like dialectical Kannada and Marathi, the Javanese styles differ primarily in lexicon, though in this case they are reckoned as belonging to the same language.

Of course, it is not so easy to borrow the most common lexical items, and perhaps it is a strain upon our credulity to imagine that some items, such as grammatical markers, for instance, could ever be so completely borrowed as to obscure the distinction between two originally separate languages. Marathi and Kannada could exchange hundreds of words, and still the varying sets of grammatical markers could keep them distinct. This situation has been reached in the relationship between Hindi and some varieties of Punjabi as described in Chapter 8. The two languages have become indistinguishable, except for a few distinctive grammatical markers which a man clings to when he speaks Punjabi in a sort of demonstration that the language is after all not Hindi, however much it may sound like it. In this case the difference between Hindi and Punjabi has certainly been reduced to such an extent that linguistic continuity reaches out from the modified Punjabi in the direction of Hindi and in the somewhat different direction of more pure Punjabi dialects. In this case, of course, the languages that have become mixed were already closely related. Perhaps the fact that Punjabi and Hindi have been able to mix is an indication that their differences even at the beginning were merely dialectical. Since Marathi and Kannada are genetically unrelated, it would be far more startling for a mixed form to arise from their contact. Perhaps the chances of such a mixed form resulting from these two languages are so remote that we can dismiss the possibility from serious consideration. The point is that the more diverse two languages are to begin with, the more intimate must their association be in order for them to mutually affect each other, and the less likely they are ever to affect one another to the point where a single dialect can be seen as the offspring of both.

We must assume that languages differ from one another just as dialects do, only more so. One way of looking at this is to say that dialects are close enough that, given the right conditions, mixed forms are likely to arise; but languages are so different that mixed forms are unlikely. Where two dialects are close enough to start with mutual intelligibility, any dialect that results from a mixture of these two will have linguistic continuity with both of them. How distant two languages can be and still give rise to a mixed form should be an empirical question. Certainly, the more distant they are the more intensive the conditions for borrowing would have to be. Perhaps when languages are completely unrelated, the conditions necessary to produce a mixed language are so unlikely that the probability drops effectively to zero. Only if this is the case can we confidently draw the kinds of branching tree diagrams of linguistic relationship that have been traditional in linguistics.

13 *Language Diversification*

Introduction

If the borrowing of forms by one language or dialect from another were the only mechanism inducing languages to change, then languages could only grow more and more alike. The linguistic diversity so characteristic of our world could be expected gradually to fade. As languages drew continually upon each other's resources, the unique characteristics of each would be steadily minimized. Since our languages do remain so wonderfully heterogeneous, we must look for other processes that counteract the homogenizing effects of imitation and that reintroduce diversity. Linguistics has long studied borrowing, and the factors that favor and inhibit imitation are well understood. The factors encouraging linguistic diversification are not so clearly known, and most accounts of linguistic changes, not resulting from borrowing, are mere descriptions which make little attempt to explain why the changes take place.

We can start to understand the processes leading to diversification, once we realize that people do not always wish to speak exactly like others. Instead of always imitating, we often try, more or less deliberately, to make our speech distinct. As we try to distinguish our speech, new forms or new combinations of forms occasionally find their way into our language. The fact that all people seem to admire the man who can skillfully innovate suggests that, however important imitation may be to language, creativity is also sought after. Of course, for a man who wishes to be understood, the possibilities for creativity are limited. He can occasionally invent a new form; he can favor certain constructions over others; perhaps he can even alter his phonology slightly, but if he goes too far he will lose his ability to communicate. Our tolerance for linguistic innovation varies with the purpose of the message. In some kinds of poetry, our tolerance is very high, for here we place a premium upon experimentation. The reader or listener may be willing to spend long hours puzzling through a passage, for the sake of the joy the form brings. In other genres the limitations on innovation are much more strict, and, if rapid and efficient communication is deemed essential, the message must stay close to familiar forms. Except perhaps in some highly stylized rituals, some degree of novelty and some cleverness or stylistic skill is almost always valued. Novelty is sought after by speakers and writers and admired by readers and listeners.

If an innovation is to become more than a personal idiosyncrasy, others must imitate it and borrow it into their own language patterns. Even a new innovation depends upon borrowing if it is to become established. Few of us can claim to have made any significant innovation in our language that has been taken up by others and become established, but we have all helped the innovations of others to flourish. We are struck by a clever idiom, by a new and useful word, or even by a stylish pronunciation; and we readily adopt these innovations as our own. As they become established, their original value as clever innovations is inevitably lost, and if taken up too quickly and repeated too often, they may even grow so tedious as to be dubbed clichés and self-consciously rejected. Other innovations are always possible, however, and enough of them take firm hold to carry the language further and further from its antecedents. A language with a long written tradition may always have its purists, who bemoan the innovations they find vulgar and who champion the more archaic forms, but in the long run they seem utterly powerless to stay the course of change.

Lexical Innovation

Innovations, like borrowings, are most noticeable in the lexicon. Every social group, every profession, every sect, and every generation distinguishes itself in some degree by its choice of vocabulary. This is as true of thieves as it is of physicists, and indeed the argot of criminals and the jargon of the learned professions have much the same function, however different their characteristic forms may be.

The innovative resources of a language show with a special clarity in a criminal argot, and David W. Maurer has described the unique style of confidence men so skillfully that it can provide a valuable example. At least since Roman times, each professional criminal group has had some distinctive characteristics in its speech. The language of modern criminals in the United States differs from more standard speech largely in its special vocabulary. While criminals can speak normal English when they want to or need to, they can add the unique items of their argot when the occasion seems right. When speaking with one another, the language of criminals is often rich in slangy innovations, for the ability to use the argot fluently is the mark of a professional. In the case of confidence men, the skill required is so great that it takes several years to master. It is often imagined that criminal argots are used because the speakers need to converse in secret without letting uninitiated eavesdroppers understand, but to the very extent that the argot is difficult for noncriminals to understand, it is also highly distinctive. Even if it is not understood, its use could easily reveal the speakers' profession, were they to use it regularly in public. In fact, far from being used for secrecy, the argot is generally used only in private situations where secrecy is no consideration.

The argot conveys a sense of ingroup comradeship. It symbolizes and helps to support the mutual dependence of criminals. Criminals are, after all, in a peculiarly vulnerable position. They are part of the larger society, and indeed, they depend upon that society for their livelihood. Yet society's agents are also a constant danger, and a criminal can rely upon no one for aid except his fellow criminals, often only upon the members of his own criminal speciality. A common form of language, shared only with one's closest associates, helps to weld specialists into a reliable, mutually dependent group with its own sense of identity. Of course criminals, like the members of any other profession, also need technical terms to describe their own unique activities, but even more than with most professional jargons, the criminal argot serves not only to provide a specialized technical vocabulary but also to set the group off as a distinctive social unit.

Each criminal speciality has its own argot different in some respects from that of others. The members of the profession recognize the uniqueness of their argot and know it as something to be assumed or set aside at will. They take pride in being able to speak the argot fluently; they admire others in proportion to their skill; and they can even judge strangers by their ability to use it. Maurer describes the argot of confidence men so well that I can do no better than quote him:

> Of all criminals, confidence men probably have the most extensive and colorful argot. They not only number among their ranks some of the most brilliant of professional criminals, but the minds of confidence men have a peculiar nimbleness which makes them particularly adept at coining and using argot. They derive a pleasure which is genuinely creative from toying with language. They love to talk and they have markedly original minds, minds which are singularly agile and which see and express rather grotesque relationships in terms of the flickering vastly connotative metaphor which characterizes their argot.
>
> ... their proclivity for coining and using argot extends much beyond the necessary technical vocabulary. They like to express all life-situations in argot, to give their sense of humor free play, to revolt against conventional language. Thus they have a large stock of words and idioms for expressing

ideas connected with travel, love-making, the creature-comforts including food, drink, clothing, etc., recreation, money, people, the law, social relationships, etc. In fact, if con men find it necessary or convenient to discuss any topic for long, they will soon have an argot vocabulary pertaining to that particular subject. And one may rest assured that they will use good rich, roistering, ribald words which will radiate connotations for the initiate.[1]

The argot differs from the common language primarily in its lexicon. At least for confidence men, who are the intellectual elite of the underworld, neither the phonology or grammar of the argot seem to differ in any appreciable way from the forms used by noncriminals. As criminals switch back and forth from their argot to the language used when speaking with nonprofessionals, it is the lexicon rather than either grammar or phonology that changes.

What is true of a criminal argot is also true of the jargon of more legitimate professions. Every profession has some terminology of its own. Those within the profession may feel that their technical terms are needed to convey the special subject matter of their field. But when a linguist writes of "morphophonic alternation in the verb paradigm" or an anthropologist writes of the "structural implications of matrilateral cross-cousin marriage," they express, in part at least, their membership in a profession and their ability to use its language. To those on the inside, professional terminology may connote the comforting security of their familiar ingroup; to those on the outside it may seem an unneeded and pretentious use of mumbo-jumbo where perfectly adequate and simpler words would do as well. But whether needed or not, professional terminology does serve to differentiate language and to set the speech of one group apart from that of others. To that degree it is one force for stylistic divergence.

As befits ancient professions, law and medicine have particularly complex languages. Laymen may feel that their jargon is deliberately designed to to be so esoteric and obscure that it will exclude all but the initiated professional. Perhaps this charge is too extreme, but legal terminology is certainly meant to be distinct enough from colloquial speech to convey its serious import. If medical terminology has the magical function of making the healer's art seem just a bit awe inspiring and therefore persuasive, it also makes it more difficult for untrained people to masquerade as physicians or druggists.

Of course professional terminology is always subject to borrowing into nonprofessional styles. Terms from criminal argots, from medicine and law, the myriad new names for new chemical compounds, even occasional terms from anthropology or linguistics, sometimes find their way into wider use. Once a term escapes from its specialized origin, its value for distinguishing

[1]David W. Maurer, *The Big Con* (Bobbs-Merrill, Indianapolis; 1940), pp. 272–273.

professionals from laymen is lost. If, as it moves, a word develops less clear and precise connotations, then its function as a technical term may also be obscured. But men are always inventive enough to find still newer terms and so keep their own ingroup style distinct. Any regional, social, economic, or political group that wants its identity preserved can use special terms to mark themselves off as unique. So long as men feel the need to communicate across these social boundaries, there will be limits on how far the styles can diverge. Innovation will be balanced by mutual borrowing as long as the styles and dialects remain in contact. But it is easy to see that once communities no longer need or wish to communicate, and particularly if members of two communities want to demonstrate their mutual separation, then lexical innovation could rapidly pull the speech of the two communities apart into increasingly divergent styles, dialects, and languages.

Phonological Innovation

Convincing examples of phonological innovation are more difficult to find, but they may result from similar forces. The members of the more prestigious of two social groups may try, more or less self-consciously, to keep their pronunciation distinct. If those with lower status imitate them, a pursuit of the phonological elite could develop in which the lower-status individuals would continually try to imitate their social superiors while the upper class would continually move its pronunciation away from this encroachment. Imitation and renewed diversification continuing over a considerable length of time might explain some quite radical sound shifts that would otherwise have to be left as inexplicable diachronic trends.

William Labov has described one phonological innovation in unusually full detail, one which has occurred on the island of Martha's Vineyard in Massachusetts. Labov found that the islanders had quite varied pronunciations of the first elements of /ai/ and /au/ in such words as *right* and *house*. Although the sociological factors, which helped to fix a particular speaker's pronunciation, were complex, and the phonological details extremely subtle, they can be summarized as follows. People who lived in rural areas or were dependent upon fishing, those who resented and feared encroachment by the outside summer people, those who most stubbornly defended their own way of life and fought to maintain their own identity in the face of threats from the outside and a decaying economic base on the island, those, in short, who identified themselves strongly with a special and separate island tradition tended to use a more centralized position for these vowels than did less traditional speakers. Curiously, the speakers themselves did not seem to be aware of the phonetic variability of these particular vowels, although they were certainly conscious of a distinctive Vineyard dialect that served to set off islanders from mainlanders.

Synchronically, the variability in these vowels can be seen as distinguishing groups with varying social aspirations much as do some of the
variables considered in earlier chapters. But this variable also has a historical dimension. Most likely the older form of /ai/ used by early Martha's
Vineyard residents had a centralized first element, but the early form of /au/
probably did not. In the course of time, under influence from mainland
dialects, /ai/ tended to drop until its first element got down near the pronunciation of the first element of /au/. The low point was probably reached
during the late 1930s. Then, after World War II, as increasing pressures
from the outside were felt, /ai/ started to rise again, apparently in a partially
unconscious assertion of island loyalty. This was a time when older and
more rural islanders still preserved the distinctive form, and they could
serve as models for younger people to imitate.

By this time, however, /ai/ had come down so close to /au/ that the first
elements of the two diphthongs could be regarded as the same, and, when
/ai/ began to rise again, /au/ was pulled up with it. No older model suggested this change, but the internal structure of the dialect encouraged it.
Here then was a new sound change, one that was apparently motivated
even though unconsciously, by the social situation in which speakers found
themselves and by their desire to set themselves off as a separate group.

But if the islanders were not even aware of this particular variable, how,
one must ask, could it act as a signal with sociological significance? The
answer seems to be that the raising and centralization of /ai/ and /au/
is part of a more general "close-mouthed" style that taken as a whole *is*
socially recognized. Speakers who wish to demonstrate their uniqueness and
their differentiation from mainlanders use higher or closer variants. They
tend to raise /əer/ until it merges phonemically with /ɛr/, so that words
such as *Harry* and *hairy* become homonyms. They use /ɛ/ rather than /əe/
in such words as *have, had,* and *that;* and they use /ɪ/ rather than /ɛ/ in *forget,*
get, and *when.* The phonetic realization of many other phonemes is slightly
higher in this characteristically island dialect than in mainland speech.
Collectively, then, the close-mouthed dialect is recognized as symbolizing
adherence to island values and belongingness in the island community.
Such particular features of the dialect as the centralization of /au/ may not
themselves be recognized, but this new phonological change must nevertheless be seen as the result of sociological pressures, for it has come about
when some speakers wanted to signal their separation from others.

Phonological innovations can also occur when speakers of one dialect
try with less than perfect success, to imitate another dialect. In describing
the relation between the Brahman and non-Brahman dialects of Kannada,
William Bright has suggested that some rather startling changes may have
came about as the result of non-Brahman being unable to imitate Brahman
speech. In the Kannada speaking areas as in other parts of India, the Brah-

man dialects are innovating in some ways but probably conservative in others. Brahmans are more likely than their lower-caste neighbors to borrow forms from English or Sanskrit, and in this their speech is innovative, but Brahman literacy may encourage conservatism in some other areas of the language. It is the interaction between the Brahman and non-Brahman dialects, however, that is responsible for the most interesting changes. As an example, Bright gives the word for 'milk,' which in Old Kannada was *pal*. In medieval Kannada, this had changed (for unknown reasons) to *hāl*. The initial /h/ probably retained the voicelessness of its prototype at first, but in the modern Brahman pronunciation the word is *hālu*, and the initial has come to be at least partially voiced. This reduces to some degree the phonetic difference between the presence of the initial /h/ and its absence, though the phonemic contrast is certainly maintained by Brahmans. In the non-Brahman dialect, however, the word is pronounced *ālu*, with complete loss of the initial. This loss represents a more decisive change than any phonetic but subphonemic change of the initial, and this particular innovation is a distinctively non-Brahman one. It is possible that it arose through miss-imitation by the non-Brahmans of the more prestigeful Brahman dialect. Hearing the reduced contrast in the Brahman dialect, they may have supposed that it contained no initial at all and proceeded to pronounce the word in that way. Bright concludes "The upper class would now appear to originate sound change on the *phonetic* level; the lower class, imitating this inaccurately, produces change on the phonemic level."[2]

Linguistic Nationalism

The most far-reaching examples of linguistic innovation taking place today may be in the newly independent countries of Asia and Africa. There a reaction against all things colonial is often accompanied by a kind of linguistic nationalism and a desire to cleanse the native languages of all traces of borrowings coming from the colonial languages. The vast overlay of English borrowings that all Indians and Burmese use in their colloquial speech may still offend their national pride, and, particularly in writing, they find it disturbing to include too many English terms. As a result, active efforts have been made to substitute new native words, often built in India upon Sanskrit roots or in Burma upon Pali roots, for the familiar English technical vocabulary. In India and in Burma, commissions have been established to design and pass judgment upon the appropriate terms that every country now needs for science and technology, although in a fierce assertion not only of national but of regional independence, the champions

[2]William Bright, "Social Dialect and Language History," *Current Anthropology* 1 (1960), 425.

of the various languages of India have sometimes advocated a quite different set of terms for each language. If local patriotism is successful the languages of India may pull away not only from English but from each other as well, and mutually antagonistic regional feelings will come to be faithfully reflected in speech.

Irish and modern Hebrew surely offer the most dramatic recent examples in which distinctive linguistic patterns have come to symbolize cultural and political independence. In these two cases, languages that had been known only to a minority of the people (and in the case of Hebrew a language that was used principally in ritual) were resurrected as languages for daily use and as symbols of the people's political independence. The circumstances in which Israel has grown up have made Hebrew the more successful experiment. Early Jewish immigrants to Palestine may have known little Hebrew, but it was often the only language that both European and Middle Eastern Jews could use. The practical need to communicate reinforced the ideal of developing a national language. As later immigrants arrived representing a variety of linguistic backgrounds, they had only Hebrew to unite them, and the new national language that has developed is surely one of the most important symbols of Israeli independence.

The Irish experiment has not yet been so successful. By the time Ireland became independent, too many Irishmen used English too well for them to shift easily back to Irish. Without the migrations that have brought diverse people together in Israel, they had little practical incentive to change. Even in Ireland, however, the decline of Irish has at least been slowed if not reversed by the ideal of national independence.

Language in Equilibrium

The forces for change and the forces for stability act upon language to put it into a state of slightly unstable equilibrium. On the one hand, the practical need for communication keeps it from changing too rapidly or at random. We must speak in ways that allow our listeners to understand us, otherwise language would become useless for most, though not quite all, of the uses to which it is put. At the same time our aesthetic pleasure in innovation puts pressure upon language for change, for we prize new words, new expressions, sometimes even new sounds. We admire the man who can rise above the restrictions of his language, who can bend it in new ways and avoid too familiar clichés. But freshness is the most perishable of qualities, and so the search for ever new expressions inevitably pushes the language further and further from its origins.

Linguistic homogeneity like linguistic stability through time is encouraged by the requirement of intelligibility. Heterogeneity like change is encouraged by the value we place upon what is new and different. Though nationalist ideals may encourage diversity in some uses of language, the growth of world science and technology pushes some other aspects toward uniformity. For even where the words of science differ from one language to another, the area of a term's meaning is so parallel in all languages that foreign scientific and technical vocabulary is probably easier to master than the vocabulary of most other and more variable domains.

The forces that encourage stability and change are related to, though not quite identical with, other opposing forces acting upon language to encourage both simplicity and complexity. Many changes long examined by linguists can be understood as ridding language of complexities. Complex clusters become simplified, and inflections become regularized. One can almost begin to imagine that the history of a language is the history of ever more lazy people progressively abandoning the subtle complexities of their ancestors. But language that is too simple offends our taste, not so much because it is new and divergent, but because it is dull. We like our language to be complex, and, as fast as regularizing changes rid it of some complexities, we introduce others to keep the language interesting. Once it comes into general use, no creole retains the simplicity of its ancestral pigdin, and if advocates of an artificial international auxiliary language hope to keep their medium simple, they ought to make certain that it never comes into wide colloquial use. Today Americans admire a massive vocabulary, and at other times florid oratory and complex sentences have been the hallmark of a skillful speaker. Today we more often admire a crisp and rather parsimonious style. We tend to be amused by the elaborate flourishes of past generations, but we can still become bored with a repetitious sequence of similar sentences. We admire a writer's ability to vary his phraseology and so to avoid the monotony of too much simplicity. The opposing pressures for simplicity and complexity in language seem to balance each other fairly evenly, so that, as far as we can tell, all languages have roughly the same degree of complexity. The limits upon complexity and simplicity must be set by our common human linguistic capacities.

These forces for change and stability, for simplicity and complexity resolve themselves into language as we know it, always changing but always reflecting its antecedents. When we step back to look at the changes that have taken place over a long series of centuries, we see the major trends— the average outcome of a million adjustments by individual speakers—but in that long view we miss the many experiments that were tried and rejected. We miss the particular circumstances that favored one form over another at any particular moment in history. When we look at a language more closely at a single point in time, we see only the cross section of an ever changing system, but this cross section is never as homogenous as a rather rigid descriptive grammar can make it seem. When examined closely, it will be seen to have alternative expressions, styles, and dialects, which compete for the speaker's loyalty. It may be impossible to predict at any particular moment which of these styles is destined to win over its competitors in the next decades and centuries, but this linguistic variability is the stuff of which long-term linguistic changes are made. When we examine a speaker's choices in close enough detail, we find that many of them are made according to the relative prestige of particular styles at the moment. As one focuses upon linguistic change at shorter and shorter time periods, he comes finally to the point where factors in the social setting of the language must be taken into account.

Animals, Man, and Communication

Men have tried to distinguish themselves from the animals in many ways—as "featherless bipeds," as toolmakers, as the unique possessors of a soul—but perhaps it is our gift of language that most clearly sets us apart. Animals do communicate with one another. They cry, hoot, bleat, and coo, and to some degree these noises accomplish the same purposes as our language. They call infants, attract a mate, warn of danger, or cry in pain. Yet these animal noises are more like our human cries, screams, sighs, and grunts than they are like language. Language alone has an inherently meaningless set of sounds, which can be used to form a vast vocabulary; and language alone is productive of an infinite number of utterances and applicable to an infinite number of topics.

No animals speak in nature, and none can be taught to speak by man. Devoted researchers have tried to teach chimpanzees to say a few words, but after months of effort they will do little more than utter gruff noises, in a few situations where we might think a word would be appropriate. They never even come close to combining known forms into new combinations, a skill that is a crucial aspect of human speech and an ability that comes easily to every normal human child. The teeth, tongue, and larynx of a chimpanzee are adequate for speech, but his brain is not, and no amount of training can make up for this lack. All normal men on the other hand learn their first language with little direct instruction. Learn they must, but unlike the chimp they bring adequate equipment to the task.

In the several million years during which man has become differentiated from his fellow anthropoids, his brain has somehow developed a new and unique ability, an ability unknown elsewhere in the animal kingdom. Conceivably, it has been selection in favor of this ability that has brought much of man's unique development. It may even be that the expansion of the brain, a rather rapid development by usual evolutionary standards and a development that can be traced rather well through the record of fossil man, resulted from the progressive selection of ever more competent speakers. Once our barely human ancestors acquired the incipient beginnings of language, the individuals and the groups who were most skilled in speech must have had a considerable advantage when competing for limited resources. They could have cooperated more successfully, warned each other of dangers, and helped each other in time of need. Slowly but inexorably, the ever more skillful speakers would survive and pass on to their children their superior potential for speech. On the average, the better speakers probably had bigger brains, and perhaps this is why the human brain has doubled in size in the course of the last million or so years. It may even be fair to suggest that the unique character of the human brain and the trait that distinguishes it most clearly from other mammalian brains is its ability to produce language. It is hardly profitable to speculate on just how our brain accomplishes its task, but we cannot doubt that our ability to speak and the ways in which human vocal communication differs from that of our nearest nonhuman relatives rest squarely upon our biological organization.

Yet here lies a paradox, for our brains cannot produce speech without training: we must always learn our language. Any normal infant given a suitable opportunity can learn any language, and the languages we learn are certainly diverse. We can credit our biological capacity with our general linguistic abilities, but the varied details of a man's language depend upon his unique personal experiences. In the diversity of his behavior, man is again set apart from other animals, for man alone is capable of developing and perpetuating distinct traditions, or different "cultures," whether in language or in other aspects of his behavior. Other animals have but a limited capacity to learn varied forms of behavior, and virtually no ability to teach their juniors to follow them. Behavior varies from species to species, of course, and individual diversity in behavior among members of a single species is by no means negligible, but variation from band to band or from herd to herd appears to be a very minor matter.

It is here that man is strange. Surely the diversity in the behavior of various human groups, the diversity of tradition handed down to our children, is one of our most remarkable characteristics. In the past, these differences in tradition were sometimes attributed to the diverse biological or racial characteristics of the groups or believed to be dependant in some simplistic way upon the environment in which the group lived. Such explanations can no longer be taken seriously. Caught early enough, any child can learn any language and any culture. People with the same inherent capacities learn to eat different foods, to organize different sorts of families, to construct diverse political systems, and to speak Swahili, Mohawk, or English.

Our human potential for learning such varied behavior and for teaching our children to follow us in similar behavior must itself rest upon our uniquely human nature. It is easy to imagine that the pressures of natural selection might have produced an animal with a complex form of language that was still uniquely determined by the biological organization of the species. All members of such a species would speak exactly the same sort of language, or at least any minor variability would depend only upon the random genetic variability among the individuals. One member of such a species would not even have to be in contact with others in order to learn to talk. His speech could be a spontaneous and automatic concomitant of his biological organization, like the cries of animals or of babies, which need not be learned, though they are nonetheless used for communication. But evolution did not take this path, for each human child must learn some particular form of speech, just as he must learn some particular cultural patterns. So complex are the things he must learn, that every child, even in the most primitive of societies, must spend long years before he knows enough to behave as a responsible adult. No other species is so burdened.

The central facts of human language, then, are also the central facts of human culture: our ability to speak, like all our other human abilities, rests firmly upon our unique human inheritance. Even our peculiar ability to learn and then to perpetuate different traditions of language and culture is attributable ultimately to the kind of animal we are. The particular traditions of language or of culture that any one of us acquires result from our own individual experiences. Since language is learned so early and since it is central to so much of our other learning, it is even tempting to wonder if our ability to learn a language does not somehow lie at the core of our other human abilities. Conceivably our very ability to perpetuate varying traditions in all aspects of our culture rests in part, at least, upon our ability to perpetuate varying traditions in that most human of all our abilities, our ability to speak.

If language is so central to man, it is hardly surprising to find so much of human life mirrored in language. Not only do we give names to things, but our languages come to symbolize our social divisions, our particular position in our social organization, our attitudes, our personalities. In the perpetuation of language, in its borrowing, and in the way it changes, we see reflected the general properties of human culture. Linguists have learned much about the internal organization of language, but grammar and phonology, as they have been studied by linguists, represent only the beginning of the real complexity and importance of language. Language is so involved with the rest of our lives that it penetrates everything we do, and everything we do penetrates language. We can never hope to fully understand either language or other aspects of human behavior, without attention to both.

GLOSSARY

Allomorph: One of several variants of a morpheme, the choice among which is determined either by the phonological or by the syntactic environment. For example, the English plural can be said to have several different allomorphs: voiced /-z/ after most voiced consonants; voiceless /-s/ after vowels and most voiceless consonants; /-ren/ after child, and so on.

Analogy, analogical change: The extension of a pattern that occurs in one part of a language to another part where it did not formerly occur. For instance, the regular English plural might someday be extended to nouns that now have irregular forms. If *men* and *women* were replaced by *mans*, *womans*, we would say they had changed on the analogy of the more common regular pattern.

Apical: A speech sound involving the apex or tip of the tongue, such as the initial sounds of *top*, *day*, and so on.

Back: A feature of certain speech sounds, ordinarily vowels, in which the tongue is drawn relatively far back in the mouth—for example, the vowels of *foot* and *caught*.

Central: A characteristic of vowels in which the tongue is placed neither very far to the front nor very far to the back of the mouth, for instance, the vowel of *but* as pronounced in American English. Centralization is a process whereby a vowel moves toward the central part of the mouth from either the front or the back.

Class: A set of linguistic items, most often morphemes or words, which have some common characteristic. English verbs form a class because (among other things) verbs and only verbs are capable of taking such suffixes as *-ing*, the third person singular, and the past tense marker.

Close: A characteristic of a speech sound made with the jaw and mouth relatively far shut.

Cluster: A sequence of two or more consonants articulated without an intervening vowel.

Component, semantic: A feature of the meaning of a word or morpheme. Thus the pronoun *I* might be said to have two components of meaning—first person and singular. Each component contrasts with other components in its dimension of contrast. Thus, *I* contrasts with *we* along the dimension of number, because the meaning of *we* includes the component plurality. Singular and plural, therefore, are contrasting semantic components that can serve to differentiate such otherwise synonymous pairs as *I* and *we*.

Copula: A verb (such as the various forms of the verb *be* in English) that serves to tie together the subject and predicate of a sentence as in some way equivalent.

Deep structure: Within the framework of the transformational theory of linguistics, the deep structure refers to those aspects of a sentence that are provided for by the earlier rules of its generation. Thus, the first rules generate a deep structure, and this is seen as quite abstract and as rather closely related to the meaning. The later rules, in particular the transformations, then convert this underlying deep structure into the surface structure, which is more closely related to phonology and which is the physical sentence that we can hear and articulate.

Dental: Characteristic of a speech sound in which either the tongue or lower lip articulates against the upper teeth to partially or completely block the passage of air through the mouth.

Dialects: Varying forms of a language that are similar enough to be mutually intelligible. Linguists use the term with no implication that one dialect is inferior or marginal to another. Thus everyone speaks a dialect, not only those who use a nonstandard or nonliterary form of the language.

Diphthong: A complex vowel or a rapidly articulated sequence of vowels, during the course of which the tongue or lips move. Examples are the vowels in English, *bite, fate, boil.*

Dimension of semantic contrast: A semantic variable ranging over two or more components of meaning. Thus sex is a dimension of semantic contrast that includes the components male and female.

Family: A group of languages, all of which are presumed to have descended with changes and gradual diversification from the same ancestral language.

Final: The final part of a word or syllable. The term is usually used to refer to the consonant or consonants that follow the vowel. A final cluster is a sequence of two or more consonants following the vowel and terminating a word or syllable.

Form, formal: These terms have been used in two ways. On the one hand, form has been used to refer to the physical aspect of linguistic units, a sense in which it contrasts with meaning. On the other hand, a formal analysis is one that is presented in an explicit manner, with as little appeal as possible to intuition or to unstated assumptions. Thus one may attempt to give a "formal" analysis either to linguistic "form," or to "meaning."

Flap: A speech sound made with a very rapid flick of the tongue across the roof of the mouth, for instance, the Spanish "r."

Free variants: Varying forms of a linguistic unit that alternate randomly at least with respect to certain variables. The verb suffixes *-ing* and *-in* can be said to be free variants with respect to the grammar of English, since either can be used wherever the other can. They are *not* free variants with respect to the formality of the situation, however, but only with respect to the grammar.

Fricative: A speech sound in which the air stream is narrowed enough to produce some hissing or friction but not enough to cut it off completely—the initials of English *fit, vat, think, this.*

Glide: The changing portion of a complex vowel or diphthong. It is convenient for some purposes to analyze many English vowels into a simple vowel, followed by a glide. The vowel of *pipe* can be considered to consist of a simple vowel /a/, followed by a glide that carries the tongue upward and toward the front of the mouth. If the glide is represented by /y/, then the word pipe can be transcribed as /payp/.

Grammar: A term used in somewhat varying ways by linguists but used in this book for those aspects of a language that follow rules internal to the linguistic system. Grammar, therefore, is used to include both phonology and syntax, but it contrasts with semantics, which refers to the ways in which language is dependent upon and varies with nonlinguistic phenomena.

High: A characteristic of a speech sound, usually a vowel, in which the tongue is placed relatively high in the mouth, close to the roof. English high vowels include those in *fit, feet, put, boot.*

Indo-Aryan: A sub group of the Indo-European family of languages, which includes the languages related to or descended from Sanskrit. Examples are ancient Pali and the modern languages of north India such as Hindi, Urdu, Bengali, Assamese, Punjabi, Marathi, and so on.

Indo-European: A large family of languages which includes most of the languages of Europe as well as Indo-Aryan of India.

Initial: The first sound or sounds of a word or syllable, used particularly for the consonants occuring before the vowel.

Interdental: A speech sound in which the tip of the tongue is placed between the teeth. The initials of the English words *think* and *this* are interdental in most dialects, at least when carefully articulated.

Intervocalic: Occurring between two vowels.

Labial: A speech sound involving the lips. A bilabial sound (such as the initials of *pit, bit*) involves a closure of the two lips, while a labiodental (such as the initial of *fit, vat*) has articulation between the lower lip and the upper teeth.

Lateral: An "l" like sound in which the tip of the tongue articulates with the upper teeth or roof of the mouth while air is allowed to escape at the side.

Lexicon, lexical: Having to do with words. A lexicon is a list of the words of a language or of those units which require separate definition. Each lexical item (that is, each item in a lexicon) is characterized by (1) its characteristic pronunciation or in some instances a set of alternative pronunciations used in varied circumstances, (2) its grammatical role, for instance, some lexical items can be characterized as nouns, others as verbs, and so on, (3) its meaning.

Low: A characteristic of speech sounds, usually vowels, which are made with the tongue relatively far from the roof of the mouth, or with the mouth relatively wide open. The first vowel of *father* is a low vowel.

Marker: A term used by linguists to indicate characteristic features of a linguistic unit such as a word. In particular "marker" is often used when giving a semantic characterization of a word, and the term then has a meaning rather similar to that of component. Thus a semantic marker feminine may be said to characterize a term such as *woman* or *girl.*

Medial, medially: Occurring in the middle of a word. The term is used particularly for consonants that occur between two vowels.

Mid: A characteristic of speech sounds, usually vowels, neither very high nor very low. The tongue is placed somewhere in the middle range intermediate between its high and low positions—the vowel of English *red*.

Morpheme: A minimal unit of grammar. In a loose way, one may reach a first approximation to the meaning of morpheme by thinking of it as the smallest unit of language that has some sort of meaning. Thus a single word may include several morphemes. *Undoing* can be said to include three morphemes, *un-*, *do*, and *-ing*.

Morphophonemic: In a grammar that generates sentences by first providing for the syntax and for the organization of the morphemes into suitable sequences, the morphophonemic rules are those which convert this sequence of morphemes into a sequence of sounds. They provide the transition from syntax to the phonological component of the grammar.

Nasal: A speech sound, such as *m* or *n*, in which part or all of the air is allowed to escape through the nose.

Oral: A speech sound in which (unlike a nasal) all the air passes through the mouth.

Phoneme, phonemic: For some purposes it is convenient to analyse the sounds of a language or dialect into a set of mutually contrasting and distinctive units. Such contrasting units, each of which is different enough from all other sounds of the language to be capable of differentiating one word from another, are known as phonemes, and such an analysis is a phonemic analysis. One may gain a first approximation to the meaning of phoneme by imagining an ideal spelling system in which each letter would stand for a particular phoneme.

Phonetics: That aspect of the study of speech sounds that deals with the sounds themselves and the manner of their production rather than with their organization into the patterns of a particular language.

Phonology: The sounds of a language and their organization into patterns.

Postvocalic: A speech sound, usually a consonant, which occurs immediately after a vowel.

Referent: The object in the world outside of language to which a term refers.

Retroflex: A speech sound such as the English "r" in which the tip of the tongue is curled somewhat upward and back.

Rounded: A characteristic of vowels in which the lips are more or less pursed together into a circle, as in the vowels of English *caught, put*.

Rule: A more or less formal characterization of some observed process in a language. Linguists understand rules to be summaries or descriptions of observed features of the language and not injunctions to people about how they *should* speak. Rules are often formulated to account for patterns observed in a particular language, but linguists also speak of historical rules that describe the similarities and differences between related languages or show regularities by which a language has changed.

Semantic: This term has been used in many ways, but in this book it refers specifically to the manner in which linguistic phenomena are dependent upon, related to, or reflect, extralinguistic phenomena. Thus it contrasts with grammar, which refers to the internal organization of language.

Segmental phonology: Those features of the sound system of a language that can be described as sequential, occurring one after another. Segmental phonology, therefore, does not include intonational or stress patterns that extend over longer stretches of speech and occur simultaneously with other sounds.

Standard language: That particular dialect of a more or less heterogeneous language that is accepted by the majority of speakers as in some way suitable for wide communication, for formal or educated speech, or for writing.

Stop: A consonant, such as *p*, *b*, *t*, *d*, *k*, or *g*, that involves a complete (though often very brief) stoppage of the air stream through the mouth.

Stress: The loudness with which a speech sound is produced. A stressed syllable is pronounced somewhat more loudly than the surrounding unstressed syllables.

Subphonemic: A phonetic variable that is so minor it cannot be used to differentiate the pronunciation of separate words or morphemes in a particular language.

Surface structure: *See* Deep structure.

Tone: A phonological feature of some languages in which different pitches or different contours of pitches (high, low, rising, falling, and so on) are in contrast with one another. Different tones alone are sufficient to distinguish totally separate and unrelated words that are otherwise identical in sound.

Transformation: A type of grammatical rule that shows the relationship among certain sentences of a language or, more precisely, among the underlying structures of these sentences. Transformations help to convert these underlying structures into the less abstract surface structures of the sentences we can then say or hear.

Trill: A speech sound characterized by the fluttering of a speech organ, most often the tip of the tongue. This results in very rapid succession of closures and openings of the oral passage.

Unrounded: Characterized by the absence of lip rounding.

Voiced: A speech sound that involves the vibration of the vocal chords to produce a buzzing or humming sound. All the vowels and about half the consonants of English are voiced, including all the sounds in *Rover is a lazy dog*, but none of the consonants in *Chuck stopped at two*.

Voiceless: Characterized by the absence of voicing. Without vibration of the vocal chords.

BIBLIOGRAPHICAL NOTES

The literature dealing with one or another aspect of the field vaguely known as language and culture is scattered, disparate, and enormous. Fortunately, for those interested in pursuing these topics further a handy bibliographic tool is available in Dell Hymes, ed., *Language in Culture and Society: A Reader in Linguistics and Anthropology* (New York, Harper & Row, 1964), referred to below as "Hymes' reader." The book reprints a large selection of excellent articles on all aspects of language and culture, and also includes a series of massive and carefully indexed bibliographies. Since this book and its bibliographies are available, I can do no better than to refer the interested reader to it. In the following notes, I will confine my attention to the relatively limited selection of materials upon which I have drawn and to a few of the more general and important works that have appeared since the publication of Hymes' book.

Readers with little background in general linguistics may want to refer to some introductory works. Fortunately, several excellent introductions to general linguistics are now available, although it is not an easy subject to learn from a book. The following can be recommended. The first are relatively elementary, the latter, somewhat more difficult and technical: Dwight Bolinger, *Aspects of Language* (New York: Harcourt, Brace & World, 1968); Ronald W. Langacker, *Language and Its Structure* (New York: Harcourt, Brace & World; 1967); H. A. Gleason, *An Introduction to Descriptive Linguistics* (2d rev. ed.; New York: Holt, Rinehart and Winston, 1961); Charles F. Hockett, *A Course in Modern Linguistics* (New York: Macmillan, 1958); John Lyons, *Theoretical Linguistics* (London: Cambridge University Press, 1968).

Chapter 1

The general viewpoint expressed in this chapter has been widely current in anthropology for the last decade or two. I find it difficult to attribute it to any limited set of sources. Some of these ideas were well expressed in an article by Ward Goodenough, "Cultural Anthropology and Linguistics," in Paul L. Garvin, ed., *Report of the Seventh Annual Round Table Meeting on Linguistics and Language Study* (Washington, D.C.: Georgetown University Press, 1957), pp. 167–173.

I draw upon my own field work for most of the examples in this chapter, including those from Garo, which I worked on in the middle 1950s, and the Palaung pronouns, which I collected in Burma, in 1959–1960.

Chapter 2

The history of anthropological interest in kinship terminology is long and the bibliography enormous. G. P. Murdock, *Social Structure* (New York: Macmillan, 1949), summed up the work to that date and gave it new direction and impetus. Then in 1956, two articles appeared simultaneously that set the study of kinship terms on a new course: Ward Goodenough's "Componential Analysis and the Study of Meaning," *Language*, 32 (1956), 195–216 and Floyd Lounsbury's "Semantic Analysis of the Pawnee Kinship Usage," *Language*, 32 (1956), 158–194. The discussion in this chapter is closely dependent upon the ideas presented in these articles.

More specifically, the data on the Njamal is derived from an article by P. J. Epling, "A Note on Njamal Kin-Term Usage," *Man*, 61 (article 184, 1961), 152–159 though I have rearranged Epling's data somewhat, corrected a few obvious misprints, and edited out a few dubious kin-types. The analysis that I give for Njamal deviates from Epling's and follows that which I gave more fully in "A Structural Restatement of Njamal Kinship Terminology," *Man*, 62 (article 201, 1962), 122–124. The analysis of English kinship terminology is based upon that of Ward Goodenough, "Yankee Kinship Terminology: A Problem in Componential Analysis" in Eugene Hammell, ed., *Formal Semantic Analysis*, (Special Publication, *American Anthropologist*, Vol. 67, No. 5, Part 2, October 1965), 259–287. I have taken the liberty of altering Goodenough's symbolism and cutting out some of the more complex and technical aspects of his article, but I believe that my treatment stays close to his in spirit. David M. Schneider's article "American Kin Terms and Terms for Kinsmen" in the same volume, pp. 288–308, is a critique of Goodenough's analysis. Several of the other articles in the volume represent something of a climax in the anthropological interest in this type of kinship analysis.

Chapter 3

The materials discussed in this chapter are culled from many rather scattered sources. David DeCamp's succinct and elegant treatment of Jamaican terms for meals appeared in his review of Frederic G. Cassidy, *Jamaica Talk*, in *Language*, 39 (1963), 544. (Tables 3–1 and 3–2 are from the latter source, and are reprinted here by permission of the author and publisher.) Edward H. Bendix's analysis of English verbs is in *Componential Analysis of General Vocabulary: The Semantic Structure of a Set of Verbs in English, Hindi, and Japanese*, (Publication 41; Indian University Research Center in Anthropology, Folklore, and Linguistics, April 1966). (Table 3–3 is from the latter source and is reprinted here by permission of the author and publisher.)

Considerable literature has arisen dealing with taxonomies. Floyd Lounsbury gives a clear statement of the difference between a paradigm and a taxonomy in "The

Structural Analysis of Kinship Semantics," Horace G. Lunt, ed., *Proceedings of the Ninth International Congress of Linguists* (The Hague: Mouton, 1964), pp. 1073–1093. A more general and extensive discussion of taxonomies is given by Harold Conklin in his "Lexicographical Treatment of Folk Taxonomies" in Fred W. Householder and Sol Saporta, eds. *Problems in Lexicography*, (Bloomington, Ind.; Indiana University Press, 1962), pp. 119–141. Charles Frake's discussion of Subanun disease terms appeared as "The Diagnosis of Disease among the Subanun of Mindanao," *American Anthropologist*, 63 (1961), 113–132.

I raised what I felt were some problems of componential analysis in a rather flippant article entitled "Cognition and Componential Analysis: God's Truth or Hocus-pocus"? *American Anthropologist*, 66 (1964), 20–28. I now feel that the argument I developed in that article about the logically possible number of alternative analyses was somewhat overstated. I still believe the basic distinction, between a "hocus-pocus" analysis that simply provides a scheme that works to predict terms and a "God's truth" analysis that pretends to describe how people themselves use the terms, is an important one.

Formal semantics has managed to inspire among its practitioners a good deal of rather self-conscious examination as a new and exciting departure from older ethnography. Surveys of work in the field have been produced by William Sturtevant, "Studies in Ethnoscience," *American Anthropologist*, 2 (1964), 99–131 and by Benjamin N. Colby, "Ethnographic Semantics: A Preliminary Survey," *Current Anthropolgoy*, 7 (1966), 3–32. A valuable corrective to the tendency for the new ethnography to assume some aspects of a cult is Gerald Berreman, "Anemic and Emetic Analysis in Social Anthropology," *American Anthropologist*, 68 (1966), 346–54.

Chapter 4

The problems raised by literal and extended meanings have only been very tentatively approached by anthropologists, and then only from several not easily commensurable viewpoints. Brent Berlin and Paul Kay, *Basic Color Terms: Their Universality and Evolution* (Berkeley: University of California Press, in press), is the source for the radically revised view of color terminology presented in this chapter. Floyd Lounsbury's treatment of Crow and Omaha systems was given in his article "A Formal Account of Crow- and Omaha-Type Kinship Terminologies" in Ward Goodenough, ed., *Exploration in Cultural Anthropology* (New York: McGraw-Hill, 1963), pp. 351–387.

Chapter 5

Anomalous sentences have been widely used by linguists in the last decade to illustrate their varied points of view, though never, as far as I am aware, with quite the same goal as mine. I have given fuller accounts of Burmese numeral classifiers and of Burmese kinship terms in "How to Choose a Burmese Numeral Classifier" in Melford Spiro, ed., *Context and Meaning in Cultural Anthropology* (New York: The Free Press, 1965), pp. 243–264 and "Burmese Kinship Terminology" in E. A. Hammel, ed., *Formal Semantic Analysis*, pp. 106–117 (a work cited for Chapter 2).

Charles Fillmore's work on case grammar is less explicitly directed to semantic problems than the work of some of those linguists mentioned in the next chapter, but its implications for semantics are nevertheless important. See Fillmore's articles, including "A Proposal Concerning English Prepositions" in Francis P. Dinneen, ed., *Report of the Seventeenth Annual Round Table Meeting on Linguistics and Language Studies* (Washington, D.C.: Georgetown University Press, 1966), pp. 19–33; "The Case for Case" in Emmon Bach and Robert Harms, eds., *Proceedings of the Texas Symposium on Language Universals*, (New York: Holt, Rinehart and Winston, 1968), pp. 1–88; "The Grammar of HITTING and BREAKING" in *Working Papers in Linguistics No. 1* (Columbus, Ohio: Ohio State University Research Foundation, 1967), pp. 9–29.

Chapter 6

This chapter represents an attempt to draw together two very disparate lines of work—a limited amount of anthropological attention to relative product definitions in kinship and a much larger linguistic contribution to what has been called "semantics,"although limited largely to the relationship among linguistic entities.

Relative product definitions in kinship terminology were discussed by Anthony F. C. Wallace and John Atkins in "The Meaning of Kinship Terms," *American Anthropologist*, 62 (1960), 58–80. I gave a fuller account of Garo kinship terminology and argued in favor of verbal definitions in "Garo Kinship Terms and the Analysis of Meaning," *Ethnology*, 2 (1963), 70–85.

Linguists, always more ready to operate within language and thereby avoid reference to extralinguistic phenomena, have been more likely to approach the problem of verbal definitions, although this has sometimes come about rather indirectly. Semantics was embraced most closely by the generative grammarians in an important article by Jerrold J. Katz and Jerry A. Fodor, "The Structure of a Semantic Theory," *Language*, 39 (1963), 170–210 and developed more fully in *An Integrated Theory of Linguistic Descriptions* by Jerrold J. Katz and Paul M. Postal (Cambridge, Mass.; M.I.T. Press, 1964) and by Noam Chomsky in *Aspects of the Theory of Syntax* (Cambridge, Mass.: M.I.T. Press, 1965). Earlier, Robert Lees, in his monograph *The Grammar of English Nominalizations* (Bloomington, Ind.; Indiana University Press, 1960) had moved toward, if had not yet fully developed, the view that the meaning of a word or phrase might require a structure equivalent to the structure of an entire sentence, an idea expressed more fully in Uriel Weinreich's important article upon which I drew, "Explorations in Semantic Theory" in Thomas A. Sebeok, ed., *Current Trends in Linguistics*, Vol. III, Theoretical Foundations (The Hague and Paris: Mouton, 1966), pp. 395–477. Though showing great influence of the work of Chomsky, Weinreich takes sharp issue with the specific semantic suggestions of Katz and Fodor. See also Weinreich's earlier article "On the Semantic Structure of Language" in Joseph Greenberg, ed., *Universals of Language* (Cambridge, Mass.: M.I.T. Press, 1963), pp. 114–171. In "A Method of Semantic Description Illustrated for Dyirbal Verbs" in Danny D. Steinberg and Leon Jakobvits, eds., *Semantics: An Interdisciplinary Reader on Philosophy, Linguistics, Psychology, and Anthropology* (Urbana, Ill.: University of Illinois Press, in press), R. M. W. Dixon has distinguished between what he calls nuclear and non-nuclear words of a language in a way very similar to the distinction I draw between referentially and verbally defined terms.

For a somewhat different approach to the relationship between semantics and other aspects of language, the reader should be referred to the work of Sidney Lamb and his students, including Lamb's book *Outline of Stratificational Grammar*, (Washington, D.C.: Georgetown University Press, 1966) and his articles, "The Semantic Approach to Structural Semantics," in A. Kimball Romney and Roy G. D'Andrade, eds., *Transcultural Studies in Cognition* (Special Publication, *American Anthropologist*, Vol, 66, No. 2, Part 2; June 1964) pp. 57–78, and "Kinship Terminology and Linguistic Structure," in E. A. Hammel, ed., *Formal Semantic Analysis*, (Special Publication, *American Anthropologist*; Vol. 67, No. 5, Part 2, October 1965), pp. 37–64. A still different viewpoint that merges syntax even more completely into semantics was expressed by Wallace L. Chafe, "Language as Symbolism," *Language*, 43 (1967), 57–91. I first encountered the example of *left* and *right* in that delightful section of the *Scientific American* (May 1962), "Mathematical Games" by Martin Gardiner.

Chapter 7

The field of sociolinguistics has blossomed vigorously and suddenly in the last ten or fifteen years as witnessed by innumerable articles and several outstanding monographic studies. Linguists, anthropologists, sociologists, and psychologists have all had a share in this blossoming, and, although they have started from diverse backgrounds, they have managed to converge upon an interest in the way in which language reflects such variables as social class, status, and situation. Some idea of the scope of sociolinguistics can be seen from the articles in William Bright, ed., *Sociolinguistics: Proceedings of the UCLA Sociolinguistics Conference, 1964.* (The Hague: Mouton, 1966) and Stanley Lieberson, ed., *Explorations in Sociolinguistics*, (Bloomington, Ind.: Indiana University Research Center in Anthropology, Folklore, and Linguistics, 1966). Notable monographic treatments include William Labov's detailed *The Social Stratification of English in New York City*, (Washington, D.C.: Center for Applied Linguistics, 1966) and Joshua A. Fishman, *Language Loyalty in the United States* (The Hague: Mouton, 1966). See also the contributions of John J. Gumperz mentioned under chapter 8.

The specific materials presented in this chapter represent a somewhat random selection from this rapidly developing field. For the material on Javanese, I draw upon Clifford Geertz, *The Religion of Java* (Glencoe, Ill.; The Free Press, 1960), particularly his section of "Linguistic Etiquette," pp. 248–260, (Table 7–1 is adapted from the same source by permission of the author and The Macmillan Company.) and upon Hildreth Geertz, *Javanese Family* (New York: The Free Press, 1961). My treatment of address forms in American English is largely based upon the article by Roger W. Brown and Marguerite Ford, "Address in American English," *Journal of Abnormal and Social Psychology*, 62 (1961), 375–385 (reprinted in Hymes's reader), with a slight assist from David Schneider and George C. Homans, "Kinship Terminology and the American Kinship System," *American Anthropologist*, 57 (1955), 1194–1208.

Postvocalic *-r* being one of the most variable features of English has been examined by a number of linguists. Raven McDavid's article "Postvocalic *-r* in South

Carolina A Social Analysis" was published as long ago as 1948 in *American Speech* 23: 194–203 (reprinted in Hymes's reader), and, even if it were not beautifully written and not a subtle analysis, it would have to count as a pioneering work simply by virtue of its early date. More recently William Labov has treated postvocalic -*r* as part of his study of New York City English. Labov has reported this work in his book noted earlier and in his article "Phonological Correlates of Social Stratification" in John J. Gumperz and Dell Hymes, eds., *The Ethnography of Communications* (Special Publication, *American Anthropologist*, Vol. 66, No. 6, December 1964), pp. 164–176. See also L. Levine and H. J. Crockett, "Speech Variation in a Piedmont Community: Postvocalic r-" in Lieberson *Explorations in Sociolinguistics* (Bloomington, Ind.: Indiana University Press, 1967).

My discussion of -*ing* and -*in* is based entirely upon the acute observations of John L. Fischer as presented in his article "Social Influence in the Choice of a Linguistic Variant," *Word*, 14 (1958), 47–56 (Tables 7–2, 7–3, and 7–4 are reprinted from the same source by permission of the author). The term "diglossia" and the characterization of the situation to which it refers are due to Charles A. Ferguson, who discussed it in his article simply entitled "Diglossia," *Word*, 15 (1959), 325–340 (reprinted in Hymes's reader). My consideration of Paraguayan bilingualism depends entirely upon the work of Joan Rubin, as described in "Bilingualism in Paraguay," *Anthropological Linguistics*, Vol. 4., No. 1 (1962), 52–58.

The only part of this chapter for which I can claim any personal contribution is my brief mention of the multilingual situation in upper Burma, and even here my perception of the situation there has been very largely influenced, if not completely formed, by the description of Edmund R. Leach in his book *Political Systems of Highland Burma* (London: G. Bell & Sons, 1954).

Chapter 8

The materials reported in this chapter rest almost entirely upon the skillful investigations of John J. Gumperz, who for more than a decade has been reporting various aspects of sociolinguistics in India. His articles include the following: "Dialect Differences and Social Stratification in a North Indian Village," *American Anthropologist*, 60: (1958), 668–692; "Phonological Differences in Three Hindi Dialects," *Language*, 34 (1958), 212–224; "Speech Variation and the Study of Indian Civilization," *American Anthropologist*, 63 (1961), 976–988; "Hindi-Punjabi Code Switching in Delhi," *Proceedings of the Ninth International Congress of Linguistics*, (The Hague: Mouton, 1964) pp. 1115–1124; "Religion and Social Communication in North India," *Journal of Asian Studies*, 23 (1964). Together with Charles A. Ferguson, Gumperz has also edited *Linguistic Diversity in South Asia* (Bloomington, Ind.: Indiana University Press, 1960), which contains a number of articles dealing with Indian sociolinguistics, including John J. Gumperz and C. M. Niam, "Formal and Informal Standards in the Hindi Regional Language Area," pp. 92–118. Other linguists have begun to address themselves to similar questions. See for instance M. Shanmugam Pillai, "Caste Isoglosses in Kinship Terms" *Anthropological Linguistics*, Vol. 7, No. 3, Part 2 (1965), pp. 59–66 and Anoop Vhandra Chandola "Some linguistic influences of English on Hindi," *Anthropological Linguistics*, Vol. 5,

No. 2 (1963), pp. 9–13. Other articles on the language situation in India having to do with linguistic change as much as with social structure are mentioned in the notes to Chapters 12 and 13.

Chapter 9

Serious linguistic investigation of dialects used by Negro Americans is so recent that the results are still found primarily in scattered preliminary reports. Several groups are now actively engaged in research, however, and within a few years masses of data should at last be widely available. An early article by Raven I. McDavid Jr. and Virginia Glenn McDavid, "The Relationship of the Speech of American Negroes to the Speech of Whites," *American Speech*, 26 (February 1951), 3–17 was an attempt to see Negro dialects in a reasonable perspective. More recently McDavid and a number of his associates have been actively studying the general dialectical situation in Chicago including the place of Negro dialects there.

Linguists associated with the Center for Applied Linguistics in Washington, D.C., have been concerned with urban dialects for a number of years and this concern took formal shape in 1965 with the establishment under CAL auspices of the Urban Language Study. Materials coming from the work of CAL linguists include William A. Stewart, ed., *Non-Standard Speech and the Teaching of English* (Language Information Series 2, Washington, D.C.: Center for Applied Linguistics, 1964); a descriptive report on the urban language study by J. L. Dillard in the *Linguistic Reporter*, vol. 8, No. 5, (October 1966) and Bengt Loman, *Conversations in a Negro American Dialect* (Washington, D.C.: Center for Applied Linguistics, 1967). The most extreme argument I have seen for a stage of pidginization and creolization in the history of Negro dialects is in another article by William A. Stewart, "Sociolinguistic Factors in the History of American Negro Dialects," *The Florida Fl Reporter* (Spring 1967). The beginnings of some grammatical analysis appear in Marvin D. Loflin, "A Note on the Deep Structure of Non-standard English in Washington, D.C.," *Glossa*, 1 (1967), 26–31.

Some of the most subtle research on Negro dialects has been conducted in New York City by William Labov and his associates. These are reported in a preliminary way in Labov's, "Linguistic Research on Non-Standard English of Negro Children" in Anita Dorr, ed., *Problems and Practices in New York City Schools*, (New York: New York Society for the Experimental Study of Education, 1965); William Labov, Paul Cohen, and Clarence Robins, *A Preliminary Study of the Structure of English Used by Negro and Puerto Rican Speakers in New York City* (Cooperative Research Project No. 2091, New York: Columbia University, 1965); and William Labov, "Some Sources of Reading Problems for Negro Speakers of Non-Standard English," a dittoed report, prepared for the National Council of Teachers of English, Spring Institute on New Directions in Elementary English, March 1966. Labov, Stewart, Mc.David, and several other scholars have articles dealing with nonstandard American dialects and the problems they pose for our schools in Roger W. Shuy, ed., *Social Dialects and Language Learning* (Proceedings of the Bloomington, Indiana, Conference 1964, National Council of Teachers of English.)

Chapter 10

The miscellany reported in this chapter are but a small selection of a wide but poorly synthesized assortment of linguistically oriented studies of stylistics and verbal games. Pig Latins and kindred phenomena have probably struck most linguistics as a bit too frivolous to merit their serious attention, but two fine articles by Harold C. Conklin deserve mention: "Linguistic Play in its Cultural Context" *Language*, 35 (1959), 631–636 and "Tagalog Speech Disguise," *Language*, 32 (1956), 136–139. My own examples of non-English pig latins were all supplied by friends in the linguistics department of the University of Michigan, and my thanks go to Amran Halim, Ernest Abdel-Messih, and Yingchi Li. I offered a more extensive treatment of nursery rhymes in "The Metrics of Children's Verse: A Cross-Linguistic Study" *American Anthropologist*, 68 (1966), 1418–1441. In that article, I give numerous references to other treatments of children's verse and to the evidence for similar verse forms used by adults. My examples from Chinese were provided by Rose Li, then of the department of Far Eastern languages at the University of Michigan, and those from Benkulu by Amran Halim.

For my treatment of iambic pentameter, I depend upon the analysis found in two articles: Morris Halle and S. Jay Keyser, "Chaucer and the Study of Prosody," *College English*, 28 (December 1966), 187–219 and S. J. Keyser, "The Linguistic Basis of English Prosody" in David Ribel and Sanford Schane, eds., *Modern Studies in English*, (Englewood Cliffs, N.J.: Prentice Hall, 1969).

Several collections of articles have appeared in recent years that deal in one way or another with poetic and literary forms from a more or less linguistic perspective. Thomas A. Sebeok, ed., *Style in Language*, (Cambridge, Mass.: M.I.T. Press, 1960) includes among many interesting articles the one by John Lotz "Metric Typology" (pp. 135–148) in which he describes classical Chinese poetic forms. Another collection of articles is June Helm, ed., *Essays on the Verbal and Visual Arts*, (Proceedings of the 1966 Annual Spring Meeting of the American Ethnological Society, Seattle: University of Washington Press, 1967). An ambitious study of meter from a linguistic perspective has been made by Seymour Chatman, *A Theory of Meter* (The Hague: Mouton, 1965). The interested reader should also refer to a number of the articles reprinted in Hymes reader, particularly part VI, and to the bibliography that Hymes has provided in that book.

Chapter 11

The various examples of virtuoso linguistic performances assembled in this chapter come from a wide range of sources, my only contribution having been to gather them together in one place. Glossolalia has been described and discussed by L. Carlyle May in "Glossalalia and Related Phenomena," *American Anthropologist*, 58 (1956), 75–96. Richard Salisbury's observations on bilingualism in New Guinea appeared as "Notes on Bilingualism and Linguistic Change in New Guinea," *Anthropological Linguistics*, Vol. 4, No. 7 (1962), 1–13. Kenneth Hale has written on Walbiri upside down talk in "A Note on a Walbiri Tradition of Antonymy" in Danny D. Steinberg and Leon Jakobvits, eds., *Semantics: An Interdisciplinary Reader in Philosophy, Lin-*

guistics, Psychology, and Anthropology (Urbana, Ill.: University of Illinois Press, in press). Samoan orators are discussed by Felix M. and Marie M. Keesing in *Elite Communication in Samoa,* (Stanford: Stanford University Press, 1956). Thomas Kochman's vivid descriptions of the terms used by black youths to describe various verbal styles appear as "Rapping in the Black Ghetto" *Transaction* (February 1969), 26–34 and in fuller form as "Toward an Ethnography of Black American Speech Behavior," in Norman E. Whitten and John Szwed, eds., *Afro-American Anthropology* (New York: The Free Press, forthcoming).

The relationship between bilingualism and intelligence has been extensively, though not always intelligently discussed in the psychological and educational literature. Perhaps the best place for a linguist to turn for a summary of this work is still Uriel Weinreich, *Languages in Contact* (New York: Linguistic Circle of New York, 1953).

Over the past decade Basil Bernstein has produced a veritable barage of papers developing his ideas about elaborated and restricted codes. These tend to be somewhat repetitious, and I have relied particularly upon two: "Social Class, Linguistic Codes and Grammatical Elements," *Language and Speech,* 5 (1962), 221–240 which contains the fullest account I have been able to find of his experimental data; and "Elaborated and Restricted Codes: Their Social Origins and Some Consequences" in John J. Gumperz and Dell Hymes eds., *The Ethnography of Communication,* (Special Publication, *American Anthropologist,* Vol. 66, No. 6, Part 2, December 1964), pp. 55–69, which is a fairly recent and full statement of his views. This latter article also contains references to many of Bernstein's other papers.

Chapter 12

Borrowing is one of the oldest and most intensively studied topic in linguistics. I trust it will be obvious to linguists that the observations I make in this chapter are intended only to highlight a few special points and do not pretend to survey the entire field. Uriel Weinreich, *Languages in Contact* (New York: Linguistic Circle of New York, 1953) remains in my opinion the outstanding work, going beyond a description of simple borrowing to a sound linguistic and sociological perspective on the manner in which one language can influence another. Several of my examples in this chapter come from my own rather unsystematic observations in India (particularly in the Garo Hills of Assam) and later in Burma.

The example of Melanesian Pidgin English, or, as Robert A. Hall, Jr., now prefers to call it "Neomelanesian" is derived from his *Melanesian Pidgin English: Grammar, Texts Vocabulary* (Baltimore: Waverly Press, 1943). Beginning on page 543, Hymes's reader has an extensive bibliography of works dealing with pidgins and creoles, and a recent flurry of interest has resulted in some excellent new studies of West Indian creoles, including Robert B. LePage and David DeCamp, *Jamaican Creole* (London: Macmillan; 1960), Frederick G. Cassidy, *Jamaica Talk* (London: Macmillan, 1961) and Beryl Bailey *Jamaican Creole Syntax* (London: Cambridge University Press, 1966).

My example of Nissaya Burmese is derived from John Okell, "Nissaya Burmese," *Indo-Pacific Linguistic Studies* (*Lingua 15*) (Amsterdam: North Holland Publishing Company, 1965), and this article has been reproduced in slightly expanded form in the *Journal of the Burma Research Society*, 50 (1967), 95–123. The example of mutual adjustment of Marathi and Kannada derives from John J. Gumperz, "Communication in Multilingual Communities" in S. Tyler, ed., *Cognitive Anthropology* (New York: Holt, Rinehart and Winston, Inc., 1969)

Chapter 13

Linguistic diversification has been studied far less intensively than linguistic borrowing, and it is only rather recently that we have begun to get a solid grasp of some of the kinds of innovations that can draw dialects and languages apart. Here as elsewhere, the work of William Labov stands out, particularly his articles, "The Social motivation of sound change," *Word*, 19 (1963) 273–309, which describes the situation in Martha's Vineyard and "On the Mechanism of Linguistic Change" in C. W. Kreidler, ed., *Report of the Sixteenth Annual Round Table Meeting on Linguistic and Language Studies* (Washington, D.C.: Georgetown University Press, 1965). Acute observations on dynamics of change in India will be found in William Bright, "Social Dialect and Language History," *Current Anthropology*, 1 (1960), 424–425 and reprinted in Hymes's reader. David W. Maurer's wonderful description of the lingo of con men is found in his book *The Big Con* (New York: Bobbs-Merrill, 1940)

INDEX